T0307178

ARUNDHATI ROY ■ KANCHA ILAIAH
JOHN PILGER ■ YANIS VAROUFAKIS
DAVID IRVING ■ OLIVER STONE
UG KRISHNAMURTI

WITH A CAUSE

FAMOUS DISSENTERS
AND WHY THEY ARE
NOT BEING HEARD

T.T. RAM MOHAN

PORTFOLIO
PENGUIN

An imprint of Penguin Random House

PORTFOLIO

USA | Canada | UK | Ireland | Australia
New Zealand | India | South Africa | China

Portfolio is part of the Penguin Random House group of companies
whose addresses can be found at global.penguinrandomhouse.com

Published by Penguin Random House India Pvt. Ltd
7th Floor, Infinity Tower C, DLF Cyber City,
Gurgaon 122 002, Haryana, India

First published in Portfolio by Penguin Random House India 2020

10 9 8 7 6 5 4 3 2

ISBN 9780670089963

Typeset in Adobe Caslon Pro by Manipal Technologies Limited, Manipal
Printed at Replika Press Pvt. Ltd, India

www.penguin.co.in

To all those who have had the courage to express dissent when others chose to be silent

Contents

Preface

We don't like dissenting voices and we don't like to express dissent.

Authority, in particular, doesn't like to be questioned or challenged. And people don't like to challenge or question authority because they know there's a price to be paid for doing so.

We are exhorted by wise men and women to 'stand up for what is right' and 'speak truth to fear'. We are careful not to heed these exhortations. Our survival instincts tell us otherwise. It's far more rewarding to stay quiet, nod assent or, better still, practise unabashed sycophancy.

One of the fascinating stories from World War II is about Adolf Hitler's architect, Albert Speer. Speer was an accomplished professional, a devout Christian and father of six children. As minister of armaments and a member of Hitler's inner circle, Speer was party to the destruction wrought by the Third Reich. At the very least, he was aware of the deportation and killing of large numbers of Jews.

As the horrors of the Nazi regime came to light, many wondered how somebody like Speer could have been a mute witness to all that went on. Speer answers the question quite candidly in his memoir, *Inside the Third Reich*. He says that at the age of thirty-eight he was made a member of Hitler's government, one that held sway over much of Europe. That meant something. To have posed difficult questions would have meant losing the coveted prize.

We may profess to be shocked at Speer's conduct. However, if we reflect carefully, we will realize that the Speer syndrome is by no means uncommon. In all institutions and in all parts of the world, people understand that there is much to be gained by toeing the line and a great deal to be lost by speaking up.

Go to any official meeting almost anywhere. Watch the tone, actions and body language of the person sitting in the chair and those around him or her. You may see the occasional polite disagreement on relatively inconsequential matters. For the most part, however, you are apt to see deference, acquiescence, a general eagerness to please. 'I hear and obey' is the dominant note amongst subordinates. At many meetings, one may be pardoned for supposing that one was in the midst of audio-vocally challenged people.

In recent years, we have heard a great deal in India about intolerance and the supposed muffling of dissent on the part of the present government. Governments everywhere do try to stifle or manage dissent in varying degrees and in different ways. But the situation is not very different in other spheres of life, such as the corporate world, the bureaucracy, non-government organizations or even academia.

This is truly a sad state of affairs. Dissent is invaluable. We need dissent, whether in government or in the other institutions of society, in order to ensure accountability of those in authority. Dissent is also vital for generating ideas and solving problems. It is only through the clash of ideas that the best solutions emerge. Herd mentality or 'group think', as it is now called, is the surest recipe for mediocrity and underperformance. Institutions must be designed to protect and foster dissent.

Since dissent is all too rare, it's worth celebrating dissenters. In this book, I profile seven of them from different walks of life.

Three are Indian. Arundhati Roy is a novelist and activist. Kancha Ilaiah is an academic and intellectual who represents the cause of Dalits and Other Backward Classes. U.G. Krishnamurti (now no more) is best characterized as a demolisher of the spirituality industry.

As for the four who are non-Indian, Oliver Stone is an American film-maker. David Irving is a British historian of World War II. Yanis Varoufakis is a Greek economist and former finance minister of Greece. John Pilger, an Australian, is a journalist and maker of documentary films.

The personalities I have chosen are not necessarily the most famous or the most effective dissenters. The American linguist and intellectual, Noam Chomsky, would have easily qualified. So would the economist and Nobel Laureate Joseph Stiglitz. But these are celebrities whose ideas are quite well known. I have chosen to write about individuals whose dissenting ideas may not be known to many. Ideally, I would have liked to meet the individuals in person or at least interview them over the Net. Alas, I had no luck, except with Kancha Ilaiah.

I have not attempted to be comprehensive in my treatment of these personalities and, indeed, lay no claim to being familiar with all of their works. They are all so prolific that whole books could be written about them. Rather, I have focused on some of their works or themes just to capture the flavour of their dissent.

In what ways are these dissenters questioning the mainstream view? What challenges have they mounted to the establishment? How have they managed to shape public perceptions on important issues? These are the questions I have attempted to answer.

The impact the dissenters in this book have had is quite modest. Roy has been able to influence policy on large dams and the rehabilitation of displaced individuals. Stone has contributed to the anti-war sentiment in the US and to the conspiracy theories about the assassination of President Kennedy. Ilaiah has raised awareness of the inequities in the Hindu order but hasn't had much luck in stopping the Hindutva juggernaut. U.G. Krishnamurti has got people thinking seriously about spirituality and the pursuit of enlightenment. Varoufakis languishes on the margins of European politics. Irving is a virtual pariah amongst historians and in the mainstream media. Pilger's journalism thrives mostly on the Net.

The value of these dissenters is to be judged by positing the counterfactual: If it were not for the likes of them, how would the establishment have behaved? These individuals may not have been able to change the dominant narrative. But they have, at times, been able to apply the brakes on it. That is a valuable contribution.

With the possible exception of Irving, the dissenters in this book have been professionally and financially successful. This suggests that despite the hostility of the establishment, there is room in the market economy for dissent of high quality. Indeed, as I note later, it is the celebrity status of these dissenters that acts as a protective charm and keeps them from being trampled on. The moral in today's world seems to be that if you want to express serious dissent, make sure that you are rich and famous enough to be able to afford it.

T.T. Ram Mohan
10 February 2020

1

Arundhati Roy: India's Irrepressible Gadfly

In early 2014, Arundhati Roy wrote a lengthy introduction to one of B.R. Ambedkar's most powerful works, *Annihilation of Caste*, published by Navayana, a publishing house in New Delhi.[1] The introduction is not just about the book or even about Ambedkar. A large portion of it is devoted to Gandhi. The Gandhi that Roy portrays is not the champion of the oppressed that we know. He is a spokesman for the 'haves' in society, whether in South Africa or in India. Roy's essay takes Gandhi down a peg or two.

Much as Roy admires Ambedkar, she doesn't spare him either. She suggests his views on Adivasis are as patronizing as Gandhi's on Untouchables. She says Ambedkar saw Adivasis as backward, even savage. The Indian Constitution, of which Ambedkar was the author, allowed the Indian state to appropriate Adivasi homelands, reducing Adivasis to 'squatters on their own land'.

The book set off a storm. Rajmohan Gandhi, a historian and Gandhi's grandson, said the chief purpose of the book was neither an exploration of the thesis of *Annihilation* nor the Gandhi–Ambedkar relationship. Its 'true aim' was the demolition of

Gandhi.[2] Dalits criticized Roy for much the same reasons. Some even saw the introduction as an exercise in blatant self-promotion.[3]

Roy's introduction had, however, served the publisher's purpose. The controversy brought *Annihilation* a degree of attention it had not received before. The book was extensively reviewed and commented upon. Roy was invited to Columbia University to talk about it. There was a book launch in London. Roy was interviewed widely. The publisher's instinct that Roy's anti-establishment status and her rousing, polemical style would work wonders for Ambedkar's book had been proved right. Ambedkar's assault on Hinduism had finally got the audience it deserved.

* * *

Arundhati Roy is the quintessential gadfly. She is nothing if not controversial. She is forever taking on the establishment, siding with the underdog. The Indian government, the Indian judiciary, the United States, Israel, large corporates, the mainstream media, Mahatma Gandhi, Narendra Modi—all these and others have earned her scorn. Roy wants to set the whole world right.

When you make so many enemies, it's hard to survive. Roy's international stature has spared her the crippling costs that often go with denouncing the high and mighty. But for her celebrity status, she may well have been trampled over long back, perhaps languished in obscurity in an Indian jail.

Roy shot into prominence in 1997 when her novel, *The God of Small Things*, won the Booker Prize and went on to become a bestseller. Roy is said to have received an advance of half a million pounds. The book was translated into some forty languages and sold over 6 million copies.

Most writers would have capitalized on the spectacular success of a first work by churning out more fiction. Roy did not for a long, long time. Her second novel, *The Ministry of Utmost Happiness*, was released only in May 2017 and became an instant bestseller.

In the intervening two decades, Roy instead used her celebrity status and her skills as a writer to fight injustice and oppression in various forms. In the process, she has become a public intellectual and social activist. She has written articles, essays and books; given numerous interviews and speeches; taken part in demonstrations and courted arrest.

Roy has taken up all manner of causes. She has joined hands with Medha Patkar, another well-known social activist, in opposing the Sardar Sarovar Project (SSP) for setting up a dam on the river Narmada. She has been an advocate of Kashmiri separatism. She championed the case of Afzal Guru, a Kashmiri who was convicted and hanged for his involvement in the attack on India's Parliament in 2001.

Roy has shown solidarity with the revolt in the forest belts of the state of Chhattisgarh and elsewhere. She rejects the characterization of the insurgents as 'Maoists'. She sees the insurgency as a struggle of the poor against corporate exploitation, aided and abetted by a mendacious state. She has lashed out against American foreign policy, Israel's policy towards Palestinians, and the killing of civilians by the Sri Lankan government in its war against the Liberation Tigers of Tamil Eelam (LTTE). She has railed against Narendra Modi and the Hindu Right.

Roy's writings and comments have got her into trouble with India's courts. In March 2002, she spent a day in jail and had to pay a fine of ₹2000 after being convicted for contempt of India's Supreme Court.[4] The court held that some comments Roy had made in an affidavit she had filed in connection with the SSP amounted to lowering the dignity of the court. In December 2015, Roy had another brush with the courts. The Bombay High Court issued a contempt notice to Roy for remarks she had made in connection with a case the high court was dealing with.[5] In July 2017, the Supreme Court issued a stay on the proceedings.[6]

At times, Roy's positions, while contrarian, have seemed persuasive. Roy was critical of the anti-corruption campaign of another social activist, Anna Hazare. The campaign had received enormous publicity in the media and roused the Indian middle classes for a while. Roy was not impressed by Hazare. She faulted the campaign for focusing entirely on corruption in government while ignoring corruption in the private sector. Corruption, Roy argued, was merely the symptom of a deeper problem, namely, a deeply unequal society.

At other times, her positions have seemed eccentric. In November 2008, there were terrorist attacks in Mumbai. These are widely believed to have been orchestrated by the Pakistani establishment and drew universal condemnation. Roy angered many by arguing that these attacks should be viewed in the wider context of events such as the Partition of India, the killing of Muslims in the 2002 Gujarat riots and the Kashmir conflict. All the events that Roy mentions may have inflamed passions in Pakistan. But do they justify Pakistan-sponsored attacks on civilians in India?

If there's a common thread to these seemingly unrelated causes, it is opposition to the establishment. Roy's problem is not this or that policy, event or political party. Her problem is the existing order, whether in India or in the world at large. She sees the order as fundamentally iniquitous. She believes, as the Naxalites do, that the problems in the present order cannot be remedied from within the system. The system has to be overthrown. What is to take its place is not clear, though.

* * *

It's been quite a journey for Roy. She was born in Shillong in the state of Meghalaya to a Bengali Hindu father, Ranjit Roy, and a Malayali Syrian Christian mother, Mary. Mary happened to be a secretary at Metal Box, at the time a prominent British-promoted company based in Calcutta. She met her future husband through his brother (father of Prannoy Roy, the well-known media personality and founder of the TV channel, NDTV) who was also at Metal Box.

On her wedding night, Mary found out that her husband was an alcoholic. When Roy was two years old, her parents separated. (They never got divorced.) Her mother went with Roy and her brother to a cottage in Ooty that belonged to her mother's family. Two years later, the children moved with their mother to Kottayam in Kerala where her mother had been invited to start a school by the Rotary Club. On land given by the club, Mary opened her school, Corpus Christi, with seven students (including her two children). Within a year, she had added forty students. Today, it has come to be known in the town as an 'elitist' school.[7]

Mary became well known in Kerala when she filed a public interest litigation case challenging the Syrian Christian inheritance law under which a woman could inherit only one-fourth of her father's property or ₹5000, whichever was less. The Supreme Court ruled that women could claim equal inheritance with retrospective effect from 1956.[8] Roy seems to have inherited her mother's fierce independence and spirit of rebellion. She has said, 'Growing up in a little village in Kerala was a nightmare for me. All I wanted to do was escape.'[9]

And escape she did. Roy went to the Lawrence School at Lovedale in the hill station Ooty in Tamil Nadu. She then studied at the School of Planning and Architecture, Delhi. There she met an architect with whom she lived together in Delhi and Goa until their relationship broke up. She returned to Delhi to join the National Institute of Urban Affairs. In 1984 she met a film-maker, Pradip Krishen, who introduced her to the film industry. The years that followed were quite uneventful. She worked for television and films. A screenplay she wrote for a movie, directed by her husband, *In Which Annie Gives It those Ones* (1989), won the National Film Award for Best Screenplay.

Then, *The God of Small Things* happened. The novel won the Booker Prize for Fiction. It brought Roy instant fame and wealth. Thereafter, she plunged headlong into a life of political activism.

* * *

In May 1936, B.R. Ambedkar was invited to deliver the presidential address at a conference organized by the Jat-Pat Todak Mandal (Forum for the Break-up of Caste), a Hindu reformist organization in Lahore. When the Mandal received the text of Ambedkar's address, it found that there were parts that the Hindu community would find offensive. The Mandal advised Ambedkar to delete those parts. Ambedkar refused to oblige and the lecture was cancelled. Ambedkar then proceeded to print 1500 copies of the lecture at his own expense. It was titled *Annihilation of Caste*.

Like most of Ambedkar's writings, *Annihilation of Caste* was read avidly by Dalits but remained unknown to or unread by the upper castes. In 2014, S. Anand, who runs a publishing house, Navayana, decided to publish *Annihilation* with an introduction by Arundhati Roy. As we mentioned at the beginning, Roy's introduction brought Ambedkar's treatise a degree of attention it had not received earlier. It also brought Roy into the line of fire.

Annihilation is revolutionary in its intent. It argues that caste cannot be annihilated by abolishing untouchability or through inter-caste marriage or inter-caste dining, means that many Hindu reformers had urged over the years. Ambedkar contends that caste and all its inequities were embodied in the most venerated texts of the Hindus, such as the Vedas, the shastras and the puranas. Hinduism could be reinvigorated only by comprehensively rejecting these texts. Ambedkar was, in effect, asking Hindus to reject Hinduism as they had known it for centuries.

Ambedkar argued that this did not mean the destruction of Hindu religion. He drew a distinction between religion as a set of principles and religion as a set of rules. Hindu religion, as contained in the sacred texts, was 'nothing but a mass of sacrificial, social, political, and sanitary rules and regulations, all mixed up. What is called religion by the Hindus is nothing but a multitude of commands and prohibitions.' The abolition of caste was possible only if Hindus rejected the texts with their elaborate rules and replaced these with a standard book acceptable to all Hindus. Ambedkar also asked that priesthood not be hereditary. It should be made a government service open to all like the civil services. Hindus, in short, must reinvent Hinduism.

Roy's lengthy introduction does not say a great deal about *Annihilation* itself. It talks more about the evolution of the caste system and the predicament of the Untouchables in Hindu society. 'Untouchables' is one of two expressions Ambedkar preferred to use, the other being Depressed Classes. The expression 'Dalit' came into vogue much later. (I use the word 'Untouchables' in this essay only to be true to Ambedkar's usage. Roy uses the same expression.) Roy also pits Gandhi against Ambedkar in the battle against the caste system.

Roy sees Gandhi as a defender of the caste system. His campaign against untouchability, she argues, was intended to keep the Untouchables within the Hindu fold without dismantling the caste system itself. Roy dwells at length on how Gandhi frustrated Ambedkar's ceaseless efforts to get justice for the Untouchables. Then comes the unkindest cut of all: Gandhi's views on caste were consistent with his reactionary views on race while in Africa—on both matters, Gandhi was a spokesman for the privileged. I touch upon Gandhi's views on race during his stay in Africa a little later.

Roy's essay drew a fierce reaction from Rajmohan Gandhi, grandson of the Mahatma. Rajmohan contends that Roy's 'true aim' in the essay is the 'demolition' of Gandhi.[10] There is merit in this contention. Roy has herself confessed in one place that she wanted to 'move the Gandhi monument out of the way' so that Ambedkar could be better understood.[11] Let us leave aside the

matter of how much space Gandhi occupies in the essay and focus
on what Roy has to say.

Roy quotes Gandhi as saying in 1921:[12]

> I believe that if Hindu Society has been able to stand, it is
> because it is founded on the caste system . . . To destroy the caste
> system and adopt the Western European social system means
> that Hindus must give up the principle of hereditary occupation
> which is the soul of the caste system. Hereditary principle is an
> eternal principle. To change it is to create disorder. I have no
> use for a Brahmin if I cannot call him a Brahmin for my life. It
> will be chaos if every day a Brahmin is changed into a Shudra
> and a Shudra is to be changed into a Brahmin.

Again, in 1921, Gandhi wrote in his journal *Navjivan*:[13]

> Caste is another name for control. Caste puts a limit on
> enjoyment. Caste does not allow a person to transgress caste
> limits in pursuit of his enjoyment. That is the meaning of such
> caste restrictions as inter-dining and inter-marriage . . . These
> being my views I am opposed to all those who are out to destroy
> the Caste System.

Gandhi could not have been more explicit in his views on the
subject.

Roy says that many of Gandhi's early interventions in caste
conflicts showed that he was interested in abolishing untouchability
but not the caste system itself. In 1924, some of the backward
castes and Untouchables in Vaikom in Kerala agitated for the use
of public roads that skirted a famous temple (not for the use of the
temple itself, mind you). This was a peaceful protest that has come
to be known as the Vaikom Satyagraha.

The compromise that Gandhi negotiated was the realignment
of the roads so that they were no longer within polluting distance of

the temple. He then advised the agitators to call off the satyagraha, leaving many of his admirers deeply disenchanted.

In March 1927, Untouchables in Mahad attempted to use a water tank years after the municipality had said it had no objection to their doing so. They marched to the tank in a procession and drank water from it. This infuriated the upper castes. They attacked the Untouchables with clubs and sticks. In the spirit of satyagraha, Ambedkar advised the Untouchables not to hit back. The upper castes thereafter obtained a lower court injunction against the Untouchables using the tank.

Later in December, Ambedkar organized another conference of Untouchables at Mahad and reiterated their determination to use the tank. However, this time he kept his followers from marching to the tank, hoping that the upper judiciary would come to their rescue. The high court did lift the injunction but did not give a declaration in favour of the Untouchables.

To Ambedkar's consternation, Gandhi opposed the satyagraha. Gandhi said loftily that the Untouchables should fight for their rights 'by sweet persuasion and not by Satyagraha!'[14] Ambedkar wrote bitterly, 'Mr Gandhi however did not give his support to the satyagraha. Not only did he not give his support, he condemned it in strong terms.'[15]

Gandhi said many things about caste, and it is possible to pick and choose quotes to defend or malign him. Roy is emphatic that Gandhi 'never once denounced the caste system in clear uncertain terms'. Gandhi was against untouchability but he was not against the caste system.[16]

Roy also believes that the furthest Gandhi moved in terms of reforming the system was to suggest that it be replaced with the varna system from which caste originally sprang.[17] In the varna system, there were four occupations: priest, warrior, merchant and labourer. One's occupation was hereditary and individuals had to stick to what they were genetically suited for. Ambedkar was emphatic in his rejection of both caste and varna.

A clash between these two competing views on caste was inevitable. Ahead of the Round-table Conference called by the British government in 1931, Ambedkar petitioned the British government for separate electorates for the Untouchables. He argued that since Untouchables were spread all over the country, they would never be able to elect their own candidate in any constituency. Only a separate electorate could give them due representation. Gandhi opposed separate electorates for Untouchables although he was willing to grant these for Muslims and Sikhs.

Ambedkar had suggested that a separate electorate be limited to ten years. British Prime Minister Ramsay MacDonald granted the Untouchables a separate electorate for twenty years. Gandhi, then imprisoned in Yerwada Jail in Poona, announced a fast unto death in protest against the award. Roy writes trenchantly, 'This fast was completely against his own maxims of satyagraha. It was barefaced blackmail, nothing less manipulative than the threat of committing public suicide.'[18]

Ambedkar knew that if Gandhi died, the Untouchables would face the fury of the upper castes. He was forced to modify his position. Under the Poona Pact, he and Gandhi agreed that the Untouchables would have reserved seats. However, the reserved seats would be in general constituencies where everybody would vote, not just the Untouchables. As the upper castes outnumbered the Untouchables, this meant that it was the upper castes who would choose the Untouchables who would represent the reserved seats. Roy writes, '. . . an apparently generous form of enfranchisement has ensured the virtual disenfranchisement of the Dalit population.'She adds, 'The Poona Pact was meant to defuse or at least delay the political awakening of Untouchables.'[19]

Gandhi was also alarmed by Ambedkar's talk of renouncing Hinduism and embracing some other religion. (Ambedkar finally settled on Buddhism.)Gandhi's remarks to an American evangelist on Christian attempts at converting the Untouchables are revealing:[20]

> Would you, Dr Mott, preach the Gospel to a cow? Well, some of the untouchables are worse than cows in understanding. I mean they can no more distinguish between the relative merits of Islam and Hinduism and Christianity than a cow.

Gandhi's views on the caste system and his battles with Ambedkar may not be news to those with some familiarity with the history of the Indian Independence movement. But Gandhi's attitude towards the indigenous people of South Africa during his stay of two decades there certainly will. Roy seeks to connect Gandhi's position on caste with his views on race while in South Africa: in both matters, she contends, Gandhi stood for the privileged minority.

Roy's account of Gandhi's stay in South Africa is something of an eye-opener. This is not the Gandhi story that we grew up with, the story of his heroic struggles in the cause of the oppressed that earned him the title of 'Mahatma'. Roy argues that Gandhi's was a limited battle intended to benefit the better-off Indians in South Africa. In this battle, Gandhi initially tried his best to collaborate with the British Empire in the hope of winning concessions. He showed little interest in the ordinary Indian worker or the black population. Roy believes that Gandhi's views on the Blacks in South Africa were downright racist and that his 'views on race presaged his views on caste'.[21]

Gandhi went to South Africa to take up a case for a wealthy Indian merchant. A few months later, there occurred the famous incident in which Gandhi was thrown out of the first-class compartment of a train because it happened to be reserved for Whites. The story we have all been told is that this traumatic incident produced the great awakening in Gandhi about the racist nature of rule by the white man and led to his battles with the British Raj in South Africa and in India.

But that is not Roy's understanding of this incident. Her interpretation is explosive:[22]

> Gandhi was not offended by racial segregation. He was offended that 'passenger Indians'—Indian merchants who were predominantly Muslim but also privileged-caste Hindus—who had come to South Africa to do business, were being treated on a par with native Black Africans. Gandhi's argument was that passenger Indians came to Natal as British subjects and were entitled to equal treatment on the basis of Queen Victoria's 1858 proclamation, which asserted the equality of all imperial subjects.

In other words, Gandhi was offended by racism only insofar as it affected a privileged category of Indians. He wasn't troubled by the racism that the white rulers practised towards the vast majority of people in South Africa.

Gandhi soon became secretary of the Natal Indian Congress, funded by rich Indians and traders. One of its 'earliest political victories', Roy writes with grim sarcasm, was to find a 'solution' to the Durban Post Office problem. The post office had two entrances, one for Whites and another for Blacks. Gandhi petitioned the authorities to have a third entrance opened for Indians so that they did not have to use the same entrance as 'Kaffirs', a derogatory expression used to describe the native African population. In an open letter to the Natal Legislative Assembly written in December 1894, Gandhi complained that the 'Indian is being dragged down to the position of a raw Kaffir'.[23]

Gandhi sought not only to distinguish Indians from the native Africans but also to distinguish passenger Indians—merchants and professionals—from indentured Indian workers. The indentured workers were the ones who had been brought over the years to Africa to work on sugarcane farms and in mines and were subject to inhuman treatment. Gandhi's views on indentured workers will have many of his admirers squirming:[24]

Whether they are Hindus or Mahommedans, they are absolutely without any moral or religious instruction worthy of the name. They have not learned enough to educate themselves without any outside help. Placed thus, they are apt to yield to the slightest temptation to tell a lie. After some time, lying with them becomes a habit and a disease. They would lie without any reason, without any prospect of bettering themselves materially, indeed, without knowing what they are doing. They reach a stage in life when their moral faculties have completely collapsed owing to neglect.

Before you have recovered from the shock of quotes such as these, Roy goes on to narrate how Gandhi collaborated with the British Empire in the Boer War and the Zulu Rebellion, two important events that took place when he was in South Africa.

The Boer War was fought between the British and the Dutch settlers in South Africa. It was a brutal war in which thousands of Boers were massacred. Gandhi sided with the British. Along with other passenger Indians, he offered his services to the Ambulance Corps created by the British. According to Roy, Gandhi was hoping that by offering a helping hand to the British Empire, he could negotiate a better deal for passenger Indians. These hopes were swiftly scotched when the British instead arrived at an understanding with the Boers under which the latter would be given self-rule in colonies carved out for them. The native Blacks as well as the Indians were cut out of the deal.

Not to be deterred, Gandhi again offered his services to the British during the uprising by the native Zulus, who were fighting to protect their rights. Roy quotes Gandhi's justification for siding with the British:[25]

What is our duty during these calamitous times in the Colony? It is not for us to say whether the revolt of the Kaffirs [Zulus] is justified or not. We are in Natal by virtue of British Power. Our very existence depends on it. It is therefore our duty to render whatever help we can.

These acts of cooperation on Gandhi's part did not exactly melt the hearts of the British. The discrimination against passenger Indians continued. Gandhi resumed his struggles and ended up in jail with the 'Kaffirs'. He resented this and wrote to the jail authorities asking for separate wards for Indians.

Roy points out that it was only towards the end of his twenty-year stay that Gandhi joined hands with the workers, the coal miners and the plantation workers. The settlement that Gandhi finally signed with the government was seen by the Indian community as unsatisfactory. Roy quotes P.S. Aiyar, one of the leaders of the Indian community, as saying that Gandhi's 'ephemeral fame and popularity in India rest on no glorious achievement for his countrymen, but on a series of failures, which has resulted in causing endless misery, loss of wealth, and deprivation of existing rights'.[26] This is not the triumphant ending to Gandhi's stay in South Africa that we have read about in school textbooks.

The facts that Roy states are not in dispute. Two South African authors of Indian origin, Ashwin Desai and Goolam Vahed, have written a book on Gandhi's stay in South Africa. They corroborate Roy's contention that Gandhi sought to identify himself with the ruling white class on behalf of the passenger Indians to the exclusion of poorer Indians and Blacks. The authors write:[27]

> His political strategies carved out an exclusivist Indian political identity that relied on him taking up Indian issues in ways that cut off Indians from Africans, while his attitude towards Africans paralleled those of whites in the early years . . . Also excluded from Gandhi's radar for most of his South African years were the many Indians who laboured under conditions of semi-slavery as white sugar barons and mining magnates

squeezed the maximum out of their employees' five years of indenture.

Rajmohan Gandhi admits that the Mahatma had his prejudices during his stay in South Africa. He mounts a feeble defence:

> Gandhi's stance regarding South Africa's blacks was influenced by the circumstances and prejudices and also the equations of his time. Since blacks lay at the lowest rung of South Africa's political and social ladder, Gandhi's fight for Indian equality with whites necessarily, if also regrettably, called for separating Indians from blacks.[28]

In other words, prejudice towards Blacks was all too common in Gandhi's time, so we should not fault Gandhi on this score.

How serious was Gandhi in addressing the limitations on individual growth imposed by the caste system? Rajmohan Gandhi contends that the Mahatma was a pragmatist who sought to undermine caste by attacking untouchability. Tackling caste head-on would unite the orthodox elements amongst Hindus and make his task more difficult. There were two struggles going on at the time: the struggle for freedom and the struggle for reform of the Hindu social system. Focusing too much on reform of the Hindu social system would have meant antagonizing a large number of upper-caste Hindus. That could well have undermined the struggle for freedom.

But was Gandhi sincere even in attacking untouchability? Roy has her doubts. She has a devastating quote from an account of one of Gandhi's well-publicized visits to a *bhangi* (sweeper) colony:[29]

> . . . half the residents were moved out before his visit and the shacks of the residents torn down and neat little huts constructed in their place. The entrances and windows of the huts were screened with matting, and during the length

of Gandhi's visit, were kept sprinkled with water to provide
a cooling effect. The local temple was white-washed and new
brick paths were laid.

Gandhi's position on the caste system will remain a matter of
controversy. Roy's contribution is to bring to our attention a
narrative that is not to be found in the mainstream account. This is
even more true of Gandhi's struggles in South Africa. Roy awakens
us to the fact that there is an unsettling aspect to these struggles,
one that doesn't quite accord with the popular perception. We are
given so much to hero-worship, we don't want to hear anything
negative about our heroes. We need Roy the dissenter to rouse us
out of our slumber.

* * *

Roy has lent her full support to the cause of self-determination of
the people of Kashmir, the demand for *azadi*. Kashmir is a deeply
emotive issue in India. Any talk of an independent Kashmir or
Kashmir joining Pakistan revives hurtful memories of the Partition
of India in 1947 and the creation of Pakistan.

Jammu and Kashmir was among the princely states at the
time of Partition, that is, states ruled by princes owing allegiance
to the British Raj. These states were given the choice of joining
either India or Pakistan. Kashmir had a Muslim majority and was
contiguous to Pakistan. However, it had a Hindu ruler, Maharaja
Hari Singh.

Singh received overtures from the newly formed Pakistan
but was reluctant to accede to it. He couldn't quite make up his
mind about acceding to India either. In September 1947, Pakistan
sought to force the issue by sending armed Pathan tribesmen
into the Kashmir Valley. The tribesmen were expected to foment
an insurgency against the maharaja and force the accession of
Kashmir to Pakistan.

Singh turned to India for help. India insisted that Singh first agree to accede to India. Singh agreed and signed the Instrument of Accession with India. While accepting the accession, the then governor-general of India, Lord Mountbatten, made it clear that, once the state had been cleared of invaders, the question of accession would be decided by reference to the people of Jammu and Kashmir. Indian troops landed thereafter in Srinagar and commenced the job of clearing the invaders. At some point, Pakistani troops got involved in the conflict and this became the first of four conflicts between India and Pakistan.

India subsequently referred the matter to the United Nations. A UN-mandated ceasefire came into effect only in January 1949. The UN required both India and Pakistan to withdraw their troops, after which a plebiscite would be held to determine whether the people of Kashmir wanted to join India or Pakistan. At that point, India had one part of Kashmir, and Pakistan had another, called 'Azad' Kashmir. The situation has remained unchanged since then. The plebiscite has not happened.

India has sought to integrate its part of Kashmir in many ways. First, it ensured that Maharaja Hari Singh handed over power to Sheikh Abdullah, the leader of the National Conference party that enjoyed popular support. Article 370 of the Indian Constitution granted special status to Jammu and Kashmir. (In the tumultuous developments of August 2019, the Indian Parliament approved changes to the provisions of the Constitution whereby the special status accorded to Jammu and Kashmir was nullified.) There have been periodical elections in Jammu and Kashmir that were intended to give the Kashmiris a representative government. However, many of these elections are widely perceived as having been rigged. This has led to disenchantment and alienation among Kashmiris over the years.

Starting in 1990, the Kashmir Valley has seen repeated bouts of insurgency interspersed with spells of relative calm. In the initial years, these were seen to be largely the work of militants trained and armed by Pakistan. However, thanks partly to international pressure, Pakistan's support for militancy may have waned somewhat. Many believe that since 2008, unrest in Kashmir has been largely home-grown, whatever covert support it might be getting from Pakistan. Others contend that Pakistan remains the driving force behind militancy in Kashmir.

Roy waded into the Kashmir issue consequent to the popular uprising of recent years. In 2008, the Jammu and Kashmir government decided to transfer 100 acres of land to a trust that runs the famous Amarnath temple located in the Valley. The land was meant to house pilgrims visiting the temple. The Valley erupted in protest. Kashmir's Muslims saw the move as a sinister attempt to allocate property to those outside Kashmir, bypassing the provisions of the Indian Constitution. (Under the constitutional changes of August 2019, referred to above, the ban on those from outside Kashmir buying property in the state no longer obtains.)

Roy visited the Valley to chronicle the protests. She noted that the number of pilgrims visiting Amarnath had risen from 20,000 in 1989 to 500,000 in 2008. This 'dramatic increase in numbers', Roy wrote, 'was seen as an aggressive political statement by an increasingly Hindu-fundamentalist Indian State . . . It triggered an apprehension that it was the beginning of an elaborate plan to build Israeli-style settlements, and change the demography of the Valley.'[30]

Thousands of people took to the streets, pelting stones at the security forces. The technique used resembled that of Palestinian protests against Israeli occupation in the West Bank. Roy made no bones about where her sympathies lay:

> Not surprisingly, the voice that the Government of India has tried so hard to silence in Kashmir has massed into a deafening roar. Hundreds of thousands of unarmed people have come out to reclaim their cities, their streets and mohallas. They have simply overwhelmed the heavily armed security forces by their sheer numbers, and with a remarkable display of raw courage.

Raised in a playground of army camps, checkposts and bunkers, with screams from torture chambers for a soundtrack, the young generation has suddenly discovered the power of mass protest, and above all, the dignity of being able to straighten their shoulders and speak for themselves, represent themselves.

Roy scoffed at the notion that the periods of calm that Kashmir had witnessed since 1989 ever meant that the Kashmiris were reconciled to their status in the Indian Union:

To anybody who cared to ask, or, more importantly, to listen, it was always clear that even in their darkest moments, people in Kashmir had kept the fires burning and that it was not peace they yearned for, but freedom too.

The protests stretched out until 2010 when the Central government came out with a package of measures to defuse the tension. The protests seemed to subside thereafter. In October 2010, Roy stirred up controversy when she said that Kashmir was not an integral part of India.[31] There was talk of arresting her under charges of sedition. The move was not pursued.

In July 2016, the security forces cornered and killed Burhan Wani, a young militant who had captured the imagination of Kashmir's youth. Wani was said to have been driven into militancy by the heavy-handed behaviour of security forces. As a teenager, he had felt humiliated by security personnel barging into his home. His brother had been shot in a police encounter even though he was not a militant. It's a story with which many young Kashmiris can readily empathize.

Wani's killing triggered a wave of protests of a magnitude not seen before. The Valley remained closed for months on end and the protests continued well into the middle of 2017. Roy again spoke of azadi for Kashmiris:

The people of Kashmir have made it clear once again, as they have done year upon year, decade upon decade, grave upon grave, that what they want is azadi . . . We have to have an honest conversation. However diverse the views may be, however opposed to one another—the subject of that conversation has to be azadi: What exactly does azadi mean to Kashmiris? Why can't it be discussed? Since when have maps been sacrosanct?[32]

Roy's anguish over the killings in Kashmir is widely shared in India. Many will applaud her courage in speaking up about the abuse perpetrated by the security forces. But her belief that independence is a pat solution for a problem that has festered for seven decades seems hopelessly naive.

An independent Kashmir bordered by several interested parties—India, Pakistan, China, Afghanistan, Iran and Russia—does not seem a viable project at all. There is every prospect that nations in the vicinity will attempt to fish in troubled waters. Moreover, there are reports that the gentler Sufi traditions of Kashmir have been overshadowed in recent years by more militant forms of Islam. This presents problems not just for India but for the rest of the world. Another failed, radical Islamic state is not a prospect the West relishes at all. This, perhaps, explains why international support for the Kashmiri cause has dwindled over the years.

Self-determination is a lofty ideal. However, it is inevitable that, in any nation, the right to self-determination of a group of people will be weighed against the larger national interest. What happens in Kashmir, a border state, has security implications for India. It also has implications for communal harmony in the rest of the country. We must accept that there are limits to self-determination in today's world. Can we contemplate with equanimity the application of the right to self-determination in other parts of the country? For that matter, can the principle be applied to the original Indians of the US or the Aboriginals of Australia?

Human rights activists such as Roy make an important contribution by highlighting the excesses of the Indian state and the sufferings of ordinary people in Kashmir. It is in India's interest to ensure that the actions of the security forces do not lead to ever-increasing alienation amongst Kashmiris. Roy's dissent on Kashmir deserves our attention. However, Roy must be careful not to presume that she has the answers to difficult issues.

* * *

Nehru famously hailed big dams as the 'temples of modern India'.[33] India was desperate for an improvement in living standards. Dams held out the promise of power, irrigation, drinking water and flood control. India feverishly embarked on constructing dams, including large dams. In 1947, there were fewer than 300 dams in India. By 2000, the number had increased to 4000. India ranks third in dam building, after the US and China. Big dams have been a subject of huge controversy. We are still not sure whether the costs of big dams, including the social and ecological costs, outweigh their presumed benefits. In India, controversy exploded over the Narmada Valley Project, which envisaged the creation of several dams across the Narmada river and its tributaries.[34]

One of the dams in this project was the Sardar Sarovar Project (SSP) planned on the western extremity of the Narmada river near Gujarat. The project was conceived in late 1979. The SSP became the subject of a long and bitter agitation. The agitation was spearheaded by the Narmada BachaoAndolan (NBA), a movement led by the social activist, Medha Patkar. The protests began in the late 1980s and havecontinued for two decades.

In 1994, the NBA filed a petition challenging the construction of the dam in the Supreme Court. The court granted a stay on the construction of the project. In September 2000, however, the court allowed work on the project to proceed subject to various conditions. Roy, by then a celebrity, plunged into the protest movement with gusto sometime in 1999. She travelled to the Narmada valley and joined the protesters. She became a prominent figure in the NBA's demonstrations and campaigned vigorously on behalf of those facing displacement on account of the project.

In May 1999, Roy wrote an article in *Outlook* magazine that described some of the battles that NBA had fought. It sought to rouse the conscience of the Indian elite against the SSP. The article is vintage Roy: hard-hitting, evocative, passionately on the side of the poor, virulently anti-establishment.

Roy wrote:[35]

> Big Dams started well, but have ended badly . . . All over the world there is a movement growing against Big Dams. The fact that they do more harm than good is no longer just conjecture. Big Dams are obsolete. They're uncool. They're undemocratic.

In the quote above, Roy makes a number of assertions as though these are unassailable truths. You would think that the debate on big dams was settled—big dams are no longer cool. That is certainly not true. Large dams do have substantial potential benefits. But we still don't know how best to realize these.

Indian agriculture has long been at the mercy of the monsoon. If the monsoon fails, agricultural output suffers. The irrigation provided by big dams helps maintain output in the face of the vagaries of the monsoon. Dams are, of course, not the only way to provide irrigation. Groundwater management, that is, conservation and efficient use of water present below the earth's surface, is another important source of irrigation. Nevertheless, dams retain their importance in boosting agricultural productivity.

Big dams do entail social and environmental costs. Dams have a 'catchment' area, which is the portion of the dam where water is stored and a 'command' area which is the area fed by the waters of the dam through irrigation canals. While those living in the 'command' area stand to gain, those in the 'catchment' area tend to lose their homes and livelihoods as the areas they live in get submerged.

Most dam projects have failed to address one important issue: the rehabilitation of those displaced. Another issue is the damage to the ecology of the region—the destruction of forests, flora and fauna. A sensible approach would be to make a comprehensive assessment of costs and benefits before a big dam project is undertaken and judge whether the benefits exceed the costs. A few years after a dam is completed, we need to evaluate the actual outcomes, how costs and benefits compare with those estimated earlier. This would tell us whether the dam was a worthwhile investment—and what lessons are to be learnt from the experience.

This sort of systematic assessment of outcomes seldom happens, not just in India but in most parts of the world. Many big dams seem to involve a leap of faith. Roy is right to express indignation about lack of careful evaluation of dams and the disregard for the plight of those displaced by dams:[36]

> . . . the government has not commissioned a post-project evaluation of a single one of its 3,600 dams to gauge whether or not it has achieved what it set out to achieve, whether or not the (always phenomenal) costs were justified, or even what the costs actually were . . . the Government of India does not have a figure for the number of people that have been displaced by dams or sacrificed in other ways at the altars of 'National Progress'. Isn't this astounding?

The failure to properly evaluate dam projects has been documented in a report published in November 2000 by the World Commission on Dams, a panel of independent experts set up under the patronage of Nelson Mandela.[37] The report, however, is careful not to condemn big dams per se. Instead, it outlines a framework that countries need to adopt in undertaking big dam projects. The message seems to be that large dams can be worthwhile provided certain conditions are met.

This is a reasonable line to take, given what we know of large dams. But that is not Roy's position. Roy sees dams as a big racket, simply a way for dishonest politicians, bureaucrats and contractors to make money. Roy does not stop there. She goes so far as to call them 'weapons of mass destruction'. This highlights an aspect of her writings that her critics have pounced upon: a tendency towards hyperbole or hysterical denunciation:[38]

> The International Dam Industry is worth $20 billion a year. If you follow the trails of big dams the world over, wherever you go—China, Japan, Malaysia, Thailand, Brazil, Guatemala— you'll rub up against the same story, encounter the same actors: the Iron Triangle (dam-jargon for the nexus between politicians, bureaucrats and dam construction companies), the racketeers who call themselves International Environmental Consultants (who are usually directly employed by or subsidiaries of dam-builders), and, more often than not, the friendly, neighbourhood World Bank.
>
> . . . Big Dams are to a Nation's 'Development' what Nuclear Bombs are to its Military Arsenal. They're both weapons of mass destruction. They're both weapons Governments use to control their own people. Both Twentieth Century emblems that mark a point in time when human intelligence has outstripped its own instinct for survival. They're both malignant indications of civilisation turning upon itself. They represent the severing of the link, not just the link—the understanding—between human beings and the planet they live on. They scramble the intelligence that connects eggs to hens, milk to cows, food to forests, water to rivers, air to life and the earth to human existence.

Roy is getting carried away. Yes, one would expect corruption in dam projects as in almost any government-funded project. But that does not detract from the potential benefits of large dams. Corruption in dam projects cannot be a reason for viewing dams as manifestations of an evil state.

Roy's article drew a scathing response from the late B.G. Verghese, the highly respected journalist.[39] Verghese makes the elementary point that while dams displace people, so does deprivation. With dams, displaced people at least have a hope of being rehabilitated. Those displaced by deprivation are simply damned.

Roy had written in her essay that those displaced had been callously 'dumped in rows of corrugated tin sheds which are furnaces in summer and fridges in winter'. Verghese points out that they had been provided temporary accommodation at 'their own request to enable displaced persons (DPs) to cultivate allocated lands at the new site even before they are statutorily bound to move from their old site!'

Roy made a number of other assertions in her essay: the promise of drinking water was a mirage; large tracts of forest would be destroyed; hilsa fish and freshwater prawn would be destroyed by the project, leaving thousands of fishermen without work.[40]

Verghese meticulously demolishes many of these claims. The SSP did include elaborate plans for the provision of drinking water (some of which have since materialized). The forests that were being lost were degraded forests and would be replaced by compensatory afforestation. There was no question of large destruction of fish as most of the breeding happened in the upstream areas—whatever loss occurred downstream would be more than offset by addition to fisheries at the reservoir.

It's also evident that Roy lacks an adequate appreciation of economic issues. She writes, 'According to the World Bank Annual Report, last year (1998), after the arithmetic, India paid the Bank $478 million more than it received. Over the last five years ('93 to'98) India paid the Bank $1.475 billion more than it received. The relationship between us is exactly like the relationship between a landless labourer steeped in debt and the local Bania—it is an affectionate relationship, the poor man loves his Bania because he's always there when he's needed.'

The analogy with the Bania is incorrect. India's borrowings from the World Bank have decreased over the years. The loan-servicing obligations of the earlier years would, however, remain. As a result, India would be a net lender to the Bank. This does not mean the Bank has a vice-like grip over India. On the contrary, it would mean that India has got out of the clutches of the World Bank—unlike the poor man in his relationship with the Bania. Roy has little use for these nuances.

Historian Ramachandra Guha, with whom Roy has had sharp exchanges over the years, seemed to capture the limitations of Roy's essay on dams very well when he wrote:

> Altogether, this was an essay written with passion but without care. In her stream-of-consciousness style, the arguments were served up in a jumble of images and exclamations with the odd number thrown in. The most serious objections to the dam, on grounds of social justice, ecological prudence and economic efficiency, were lost in the presentation. What struck one most forcibly was her atavistic hatred of science and a romantic celebration of adivasi lifestyles.[41]

The point is not who was right—Roy or Verghese—about the SSP at the time the project was undertaken. It is that the case against dams is not as clear-cut as Roy makes it out to be. It is indeed true that displaced persons have been badly treated in dam projects in India. We have had a problem not just in respect of land acquired for public projects. The state has historically shown scant regard for the rights of those displaced even where it acquired land for private projects.

However, there has been a marked improvement in recent years. India now has in place much better provisions for treatment of those displaced by large projects. Various constituencies—the media, social activists, the judiciary, international organizations, and the affected people themselves—have compelled the state to adopt a more humanitarian approach. In 2013, Parliament passed the Right to Fair Compensation and Transparency in Land Acquisition, Rehabilitation and Resettlement Act, 2013. The Act addresses issues of compensation, rehabilitation and resettlement in ways that were perceived to be far more equitable than in the past. Compensation promised to the displaced has improved substantially.

However, implementation of the new policy on the ground remains unsatisfactory. We need agencies that ensure effective implementation of the policies on resettlement and rehabilitation. Civil society groups and activists such as Roy have an important role to play in monitoring the implementation of the new policies.

Where does this leave us in respect of the debate on large dams and the SSP? The scholarly answer to the question is quite different from Roy's outright rejection. A committee headed by Mihir Shah, a former member of India's erstwhile Planning Commission (since changed to NITI Aayog) and an expert on water resources, has submitted a report on planning for water in the decades ahead.[42]

The report makes an important point. The problem with large dams is not the social and environmental costs that Roy and others so loudly protest against. It is that the water stored in these dams simply does not reach the farmer in adequate quantities—or what is termed 'last mile connectivity'.

This happens because the canals needed to carry the water stored to farmlands are not created. We have dams but we do not have irrigation. The report quotes the chief minister of Maharashtra lamenting that the state has 40 per cent of the country's large dams but 82 per cent of the area in the state remains rainfed! The irrigation potential created by large dams is 113 million hectares; the utilization is 89 million hectares—a gap of 24 million hectares. 'By focusing our efforts on bridging this gap we could add millions of hectares to irrigation at half the cost involved in irrigating through a new dam,' the report says.[43]

In other words, the issue today is not the social and environmental costs of large dams—these can be contained through proper policies and planning. The issue is that dams don't automatically translate into improved irrigation. As a result, the benefits of dams don't justify the costs. The answer, the report argues, is the use of Participatory Irrigation Management (PIM) which has been successful in many countries in the world. Under PIM, farmers are actively involved in the management of tertiary canals through Water Users Associations. With PIM, water stored in dams finds its way into farmlands through a complex system that involves the main system, secondary canals and tertiary canals. Irrigation happens, and the intended benefits of dams are realized.

The experience worldwide is that PIM leads to greater efficiency in water use, more equity and better management of irrigation systems. It is the best way to address the issue of 'last mile connectivity' in dams. Now, this is very different from condemning large dams wholesale. We certainly need ways to address the social and environmental costs such dams impose. More importantly, however, we need to make dams more effective by adopting a decentralized approach to the management of irrigation systems.

As for the SSP, it is still work in progress. According to a journalist, it was intended to provide irrigation to 1.8 million hectares of land; only 0.45 million hectares have been covered thus far.[44]Very little irrigation has reached Kutch and Saurashtra. The management of the command area has been unsatisfactory and the lofty principle of creating Water Users Associations has not been adequately translated into reality.

Many believe that the rehabilitation of the displaced falls well short of what was required. However, the situation may be improving. A recent survey of oustees in the project points to several positive outcomes.[45] The survey compared oustees or resettled persons with their former neighbours in semi-evacuated villages. The figures for landownership for self-cultivation for the two categories were 83 per cent and 65 per cent respectively; for tenant cultivation 3 per cent and 2 per cent; for landless or marginal farmers working as agricultural labourers 4 per cent and 23 per cent; for cell phone ownership 88 per cent and 59 per cent; and for tractor ownership 7 per cent and 2 per cent. Some oustees had found new vocations.

The survey also found that displacement had not damaged tribal customs and practices as activists had feared. Of the oustees surveyed, 60 per cent said their religious practices had not been affected; 56 per cent said their traditional customs and rituals had remained unaffected; 58 per cent said their social status had remained unchanged. Interestingly, 55 per cent of those surveyed said they would rather return to the land they once occupied. However, of those under forty years, 56 per cent opposed return. The younger generation seems quite willing to abandon traditional habitats for higher standards of living. Two groups in the forest were asked whether they would like to quit the forest and be resettled. In one group, 52 per cent were willing; in the other, 31 per cent.

It is important not to jump to conclusions from one survey. The fact that oustees are better off than those still living in forests may not mean much, given that the indicators for the latter are so poor. However, the results of the survey hold out hope. They suggest that we can make a success of resettlement if we have the will to do so. It is important that we talk to those likely to be affected, give them choices and involve them in decision-making.

It does appear that the SSP has done a reasonably good job of rehabilitation, but this is not true of Madhya Pradesh and

Maharashtra. Displaced persons continue to approach the courts for relief. As recently as February 2017, the Supreme Court handed down a judgment ordering compensation of ₹60 lakh per family for 2 hectares of land for each of 681 families displaced in Madhya Pradesh. The court observed that the compensation had been increased by almost four times the amount offered earlier and yet the NBA wanted to stall the project.[46]

The outcomes in the SSP itself owe a great deal to the determined efforts of the NBA movement and the contributions of celebrities such as Roy. Thanks to them, the Indian system has come round to more humane treatment of those adversely affected by large dam projects. We need the likes of them to stand up for the rights of the dispossessed. We need them to ensure that the voices of the displaced are heard in such debates and that their rights are recognized and enforced. However, we cannot look to the Roys of the world to pronounce judgement on the merits of large dams. Sound judgement on technical issues such as the effectiveness of dams can come only through rigorous research into the issues involved.

* * *

Displacement through dams is only one of many forms of displacement that the poor face. In Odisha, Chhattisgarh, Andhra Pradesh and other places, India's tribals have faced displacement because of massive mining projects, national parks and sanctuaries. Development has come at the cost of India's tribals.

Ramachandra Guha writes, '. . . the tribals of peninsular India are the unacknowledged victims of six decades of democratic development. In this period they have continued to be exploited and dispossessed by the wider economy and polity.' Guha says the number of tribals displaced could be as high as 20 million.[47]In the initial years, they were displaced by large government projects. In more recent years, they have been displaced as the government has signed away lands inhabited by them to private companies for mining projects.

Several official reports from the 1950s to the 1980s have documented the suffering inflicted on the tribals by state policies. These have made little difference on the ground. Unlike Dalits and Muslims, tribals have been unable to form an effective political constituency with an influence on decisions at the national level. They have been grossly unrepresented in important government posts.

Guha believes that one reason for this is that the tribals are concentrated in a few areas but form only a small proportion of the population in most places (say, 6–12 per cent). Unlike the Dalits, they do not live in mixed villages with other castes and communities and hence do not constitute an important vote bank. Most importantly, they have not thrown up a leader such as Ambedkar who could articulate their cause vigorously.

The tribals have been trampled upon by brutal state policies but lack political mobilization. This has opened up space for militancy. The tribal areas have become home to armed groups and the cult of the gun. The armed groups are commonly known as Naxalites, after the Naxalbari district of West Bengal where the insurrection against the Indian state began in the late 1960s under the auspices of the Communist Party of India (Marxist–Leninist).

The Naxalites claim to represent the cause of the tribals. The 'Red corridor' stretches across the eastern, southern and central parts of India, covering the states of Andhra Pradesh, Bihar, Chhattisgarh, Jharkhand, Madhya Pradesh, Maharashtra, Odisha, Telangana, Uttar Pradesh and West Bengal. Across the entire corridor, the Naxalites have been at war with the Indian state for several decades now.

Ramachandra Guha writes:

The increasing presence of Naxalites in areas dominated by adivasis has a geographical reason—namely, that the hills and forests of central India are well suited to the methods of roaming guerrilla warfare. But it also has a historical reason—namely, that the adivasis have gained least and lost most from 60 years of political independence.

Arundhati Roy decided she would visit the Naxalites and ascertain the conditions on the ground for herself. She spent several days in the jungles of Dantewada, a district in Chhattisgarh where the Naxalites have a significant presence. In March 2010, Roy penned a lengthy account of her sojourn in the forests in the company of the Naxalites.[48] The Naxalites were aware of her sympathy with their cause and arranged the visit.

Roy gives a colourful account of her sojourn. She travels from Raipur to Dantewada, a ten-hour journey. She's met outside a temple by a small boy, Mangtu, and taken towards a bus stand. There, two men are waiting on motorbikes. She gets on to one of them. There is a three-hour ride that ends on an empty road with forest on either side.

Roy and Mangtu get off and head into the forest. They reach a shallow stream. On the other side of the banks is an older boy. A long walk over hills and down rocky paths finally brings them to a village. Roy enters a house which she finds 'beautiful'. She's greeted with cries of '*Lal Salaam, Kaamraid*' (Red Salute, Comrade). Roy spends the night at the house and commences her journey early the next morning. There's more walking; more villages are crossed. She has lunch at one of them.

At one place along the way, she meets about twenty young boys and girls, all armed with guns. This is the village-level militia, the lowest rung in the Maoists' military hierarchy. Roy is impressed with them. 'They are full of fun and curiosity. The girls are easy and confident with the boys.'[49] After some more walking, they arrive at a glade where they are going to spend the night. 'It's the most beautiful room I have slept in, in a long time. My private suite in a thousand-star hotel. I'm surrounded by these strange, beautiful children with their curious arsenal.'[50]

Finally, a group arrives to take Roy to the main camp. After a few hours' walk, Roy arrives to a rousing welcome. There she meets more comrades, including several women. During her stay, Roy learns of the struggles the Naxalites have waged on behalf of the tribals over the years. The first one was to get the tribals a better price for tendu leaf (which is used to make bidis). Then, they negotiated with Ballarpur Paper Mills to get a price for the bamboo the tribals sold to the company. The worst oppressors were the Forest Department officials who raided the villages periodically to prevent the tribals from using the land. They were only enforcing the law. According to the law, forest land belonged to the state and the tribals were engaged in an unlawful activity.

In 1986, the Forest Department announced a national park in Bijapur, which meant the eviction of sixty villages. After half the villages had been emptied, the Naxalites stepped in and prevented the construction of the park. They also ensured that no more villages were disturbed. After assuming control of a 60,000-sq.-metre stretch of forest, the Naxalites set up an elaborate administrative structure to run the area under their control with representatives from groups of villages.

The Naxalites' growing influence threatened the big landlords in the area. The tribals were no longer as deferential to them as they had been in the past. They started taking their problems to the Naxalites. With the help of the police, the big landlords sought to assert their authority by killing people and molesting women. The Naxalites struck back, killing some of the landlords.

One of the big landlords, Mahendra Karma, who had joined the Congress party, formed a militia called Salwa Judum to take on the Naxalites. The Salwa Judum focused on moving villagers into designated camps. The security forces could then assume that those outside the camps were Naxalites and target them more effectively. The Salwa Judum appointed special police officers (SPOs), mostly unemployed youth, on a monthly salary of ₹1500 to carry out these operations. The Naxalites attacked these camps, killing policemen and SPOs. Many villagers then went back to their homes. It is accepted that the brutality of the SPOs matches that of the Naxalites. The Supreme Court ordered that Salwa Judum be dismantled.

Roy writes, 'Here in the forests of Dantewada, a battle rages for the soul of India.' She sees the Naxalites as backing the villagers who are pitted against the Indian state:[51]

> The antagonists in the forest are disparate and unequal in almost every way. On one side is a massive paramilitary force armed with the money, the firepower, the media, and the hubris of an emerging Superpower. On the other, ordinary villagers armed with traditional weapons, backed by a superbly organised, hugely motivated Maoist guerrilla fighting force with an extraordinary and violent history of armed rebellion.

Roy is being more than a little disingenuous. It is not as if the villagers and Naxalites are solidly together. Other observers have noted that the villagers feel as oppressed by the Naxalites as by the state. Ramachandra Guha visited Dantewada along with five other members of a citizens' group and interacted with various groups, including Adivasis and Naxalites. He reported:[52]

> We met adivasis who had been persecuted by the Naxalites, and other adivasis who had been tormented by the Salwa Judum vigilantes. The situation of the community was poignantly captured by one tribal, who said: 'Ek taraf Naxaliyon, doosri taraf Salwa Judum, aur hum beech mein, pisgaye' (placed between the Maoists and the vigilantes, we adivasis are being squeezed from both sides).

Roy overlooks an important point in the ongoing war in the forests. Whatever the Naxalites' concern for the tribals, their long-term goal is the overthrow of the Indian state and the creation of a new order. There is no way that the Naxalites will succeed in this objective. The Indian state, with the army and paramilitary forces at its disposal, is fully capable of dealing with the Naxalites if they dare to venture out of the forests.

At best, the Naxalites can hold on to the limited areas under their control in the forests. But the Naxalites seem unwilling to give up their long-term goal and participate in the democratic process. This condemns the entire area under Naxalite occupation to a protracted war of attrition. The principal sufferers will be the tribals themselves. By conflating the interests of the tribals and the Naxalites, Roy obscures this reality.

What is to be done about the Naxalite problem? One important element surely has to be to undermine whatever support they enjoy amongst the tribals by ensuring that the interests of the tribals are taken care of. Roy seems to suggest that the supposedly idyllic lives of the tribals should not be disturbed at all. She recalls a visit to a tribal area in Odisha:[53]

> There was forest there once. And children like these. Now the land is like a raw, red wound. Red dust fills your nostrils and lungs. The water is red, the air is red, the people are red, their lungs and hair are red. All day and all night trucks rumble through their villages, bumper to bumper, thousands and thousands of trucks, taking ore to Paradip port from where it will go to China. There it will turn into cars and smoke and sudden cities that spring up overnight. Into a 'growth rate' that leaves economists breathless. Into weapons to make war.

Can we accept the proposition that forest dwellers remain forest dwellers forever? Can forest land that contains valuable ores not be touched at all? Most reasonable people would accept that much of what we understand as development involves claiming land, including forest land, for industrial projects. But this must be subject to safeguards that address the concerns of those living in the forests.

Roy writes:[54]

> The (Indian) Constitution ratified colonial policy and made the State custodian of tribal homelands. Overnight, it turned the entire tribal population into squatters on their own land. It denied them their traditional rights to forest produce, it criminalised a whole way of life. In exchange for the right to vote, it snatched away their right to livelihood and dignity . . .

All this is undoubtedly true. But there has been at least a belated attempt at redress. The Scheduled Tribes and Other Traditional Forest Dwellers (Recognition of Forest Rights) Act 2006, more simply called the Indian Forest Rights Act, attempted to give a measure of protection to the tribals. It superseded the Indian Forest Act, 1927, which had declared forests as state property. Under the earlier Act, a single official could declare an area a 'forest' and settle the rights of the people there. The Indian Forest Rights Act 2006 sought to remedy this failing by granting forest dwellers legal rights. These include: the right to hold and live in the forest land, rights of use and rights to protect and conserve forest resources including wildlife. Until the Act came into force, theserights had belonged entirely to the Forest Department. The Act lays down a procedure for identifying those eligible for such rights. Among other things, the procedure involves the participation of the gram panchayat, the village-level representative body.

This is the right way to go. In 2013, the government of Manmohan Singh sought to dilute the provisions of the 2006 Act. It decided that infrastructure projects would not require the consent of gram panchayats even while the other provisions of the Act would apply.[55] Activists promptly denounced the dilution and said it was an attempt to appease corporate interests. However, the government's move highlights the genuine conflict between the need for growth and development and the interests of particular groups. How to strike a balance in a given case is not easy to decide.

Political parties, civil groups, the media and the judiciary all have a role to play in mediating such conflicts. The answer is not to leave it to armed groups, such as Naxalites, to decide on behalf of the tribals. Roy is right to highlight the plight of the tribals and the suffering inflicted on them in the past. But she falls short of offering constructive solutions.

Development, the use of forest land for mining, cannot leave the tribals unaffected. As in the case of dams, we need to ensure that development happens with the consent and participation of the tribals and that their interests are secured. This is the direction in which the Indian state has been moving in recent years, however belatedly. Romanticizing the role of the Naxalites will not do much for the cause of the tribals.

* * *

Roy stands outside Antilla, the twenty-seven-storey mansion of industrialist Mukesh Ambani on Altamount Road, and rues the unfairness of the capitalist system. A few industrialists, such as Ambani, Tata, Jindal, Mittal, Ruia and others, own billions, while a large proportion of the population lives on less than ₹20 a day.

How did these industrial houses acquire their wealth? Roy writes:[56]

India's new megacorporations, Tatas, Jindals, Essar, Reliance, Sterlite, are those that have managed to muscle their way to the head of the spigot that is spewing money extracted from deep inside the earth. The industrial houses have grown big by grabbing mining, telecom and other licenses and land allocated by the state for industrial projects.

Roy's account is a trifle too facile. It's true that liberalization did not entirely end the old system of patronage. But many of the industrial houses were big even before the sale of licences for mining and telecom during the tenure of the Manmohan Singh government. Again, she is right in saying that public land has been given away cheaply to industrial houses. But land by itself does not contribute to the wealth of an enterprise. It is the profits generated by business that account for most of the market value of enterprises. Roy's diatribe against industrial houses has little use for such elementary facts.

Roy places Infosys Ltd, an information technology company, in the same category as the industrial houses. This is patently incorrect. The promoters of Infosys are wealthy but they are self-made professionals, not the inheritors of an industrial house. If anything, Infosys shows how middle-class professionals can vault into the top league. There have been other such success stories in India's post-liberalization era. New entrepreneurs have elbowed aside some of the older industrial houses.

These stories repudiate Roy's view that the capitalist system operates exclusively to the advantage of the entrenched and the powerful.

There is a problem with Roy's critique of capitalism and, indeed, with her writings on matters of public policy: the absence of a rigorous analytical framework and a tendency to take liberties with facts. Roy contends in her writings that we don't need experts to explain things to us. Ordinary people can understand very well issues of public policy. Well, yes, they can—provided they take the trouble to acquire the basic tools of analysis.

When land is acquired for private projects, it need not amount to looting. It is looting if we do not have proper mechanisms for consent and compensation for the acquired land. Again, where projects displace large numbers of people, we need compensation and resettlement. In the past, the

Indian state, as we have seen, has been badly wanting on these counts. However, there has certainly been an attempt at reform in recent years.

The system has provided correctives in other cases as well. Several telecom licences, said to have been given away cheaply and without a proper process, were cancelled on the orders of the Supreme Court. So was the allocation of coal blocks to favoured businessmen. The sale of telecom licences as well as coal blocks has since become more transparent and rule-bound. These illustrate an elementary truth about capitalism. It is prone to abuse everywhere but the market system also has the potential to correct gross abuses.

Roy is horrified at the prospect of the creation of the Delhi–Mumbai Industrial Corridor (DMIC), which aims to create infrastructure for industrial zones along a 1500-km-long corridor. The DMIC is not intended as an assault on the poor. It is intended to boost industrial output and create jobs and incomes. India will not be the first country to go down this route. If anything, it is a latecomer to such projects.

Lacking a proper framework, Roy can only see the seamy side of capitalism. To her, the entire capitalist system is one vast conspiracy against the poor. In India, it is a conspiracy in which the industrialists enlist the support of the police and the armed forces in order to put down insurrections by those affected by large projects. The media, bought by advertisements, is very much part of this conspiracy. So are foundations and philanthropic trusts, promoted by businesses. Literature, films and think tanks in India are liberally funded by business houses and are intended to keep 'the world safe for capitalism'.[57] In this, Tata, Ambani and others are only following in the footsteps of Rockefeller, Carnegie, Ford, Bill Gates and others in the US. There is truth in all this but it is not the whole truth. Some of the biggest names in Indian businesses are no longer around, whatever clout they may have enjoyed in their heyday. New names have arisen in their place.

Consequent to the economic reforms of 1991, we have had several first-generation entrepreneurs.

Roy sees microfinance as part of this gigantic conspiracy. It is intended to drive the poor into debt—and suicide. 'Microfinance companies in India are responsible for hundreds of suicides—two hundred people in Andhra Pradesh in 2010 alone.'[58] Now, there have been some excesses in lending by microfinance institutions in India, notably in the state of Andhra Pradesh. But the point about microfinance is that it has shown that lending to the poor is profitable because the poor are capable of using credit wisely enough to be able to service their debt.

Microfinance is no longer the monopoly of microfinance institutions. Banks, which once shied away from microfinance because of the risks and the costs of delivery, now see it as a huge opportunity. Microfinance provided by banks holds out the prospect of getting the poor out of the clutches of moneylenders and their usurious rates. In short, microfinance has turned out to be a very useful tool in the attempt to augment the incomes of the poor. Roy's narrative ignores these healthy developments in microfinance.

Roy is equally scathing in her comments on globalization:[59]

> India—the world's biggest democracy—is currently at the forefront of the corporate globalisation project. Its 'market' of one billion people is being prised open by the WTO . . . As the disparity between the rich and the poor grows, the fight to corner resources is intensifying. To push through their 'sweetheart deals', to corporatize the crops we grow, the water we drink, the air we breathe, and the dreams we dream, corporate globalisation needs an international confederation of loyal, corrupt, authoritarian governments in poorer countries to push through unpopular reforms and quell the mutinies. Corporate Globalization—or shall we call it by its name?— Imperialism—needs a press that pretends to be free. It needs courts that pretend to dispense justice.

Again, globalization is not a conspiracy against the poor. The integration of China and India into the world economy has helped raise incomes in the two countries and has contributed to reduced inequality across nations, whatever the increase in inequality within nations. The world has benefited from free trade in goods and services and the free movement of labour.

But globalization, like any other economic project, needs to be properly managed. There is a backlash against globalization today in the US and Europe because there are aspects that have not been managed well. For instance, the free movement of labour is seen as culturally threatening in some countries. In the US, globalization (along with other factors such as technological change) has resulted in huge losses of jobs in manufacturing without the losers being compensated. How to manage the disruptive effects of globalization, and how to take care of the losers are important policy challenges. But hardly any economist would make a case for autarchy. Lashing out wildly against globalization is not terribly sensible.

Roy writes:[60]

A world run by a handful of greedy bankers and CEOs who nobody elected can't possibly last. Soviet-style communism failed, not because it was intrinsically evil, but because it was flawed. It allowed too few people to usurp too much power. Twenty-first-century market capitalism, American-style, will fail for the same reasons. Both are edifices constructed by human intelligence, undone by human nature.

Well, capitalism has its excesses. There is concern among many about the growing inequalities in the developed world since the 1980s. But the capitalist system has, over the last 250 years, made possible a stupendous improvement in living standards. From almost the dawn of civilization until the mid-eighteenth century, the average income per capita was almost stagnant. It has risen continuously thereafter, thanks to the capitalist system. Any critique of capitalism that does not acknowledge these basic facts is seriously flawed. Alas, what Roy offers is not a critique but a rant.

* * *

Roy's assault on the establishment is all-encompassing. She has questioned the hanging of Afzal Guru, a Kashmiri convicted for his role in an attack on India's Parliament in December 2001; condemned the Congress for its role in the Sikh riots of 1984; castigated Prime Minister Narendra Modi for the communal riots that happened in Gujarat during his tenure as chief minister; lashed out against American imperialism; railed against Israel's policies towards the Palestinians; criticized the government of Sri Lanka for human rights abuses during its confrontation with the LTTE; spoken out against the surge in Hindu nationalism in recent years.

It's hard not to admire the energy she brings to her causes. Roy has the capacity to burrow through mounds of literature on any subject, be it irrigation or power generation. She may not always be able to persuade but she certainly challenges you to think through your own position. Take her essay on the hanging of Afzal Guru, for example.[61]Roy raises doubts about Guru's culpability in the attack on the Indian Parliament. Her account is bound to leave the reader unsettled; you are left wondering whether the case was not cooked up by the law-enforcement agencies.She could be wrong about Guru. But it's hard to dispute her basic contention: wherever we look, what we have today is a brutal and iniquitous system that pits the elite against large numbers of ordinary people.

When you ask what is to be done, Roy leaves you groping for an answer. Roy would like the existing structures to be razed but she does not tell us what should take their place. If governments, political parties, corporates, the judiciary and the media are all fatally flawed, where do we begin in terms of setting things right? Parliamentary democracy and capitalism have their shortcomings but what alternatives do we have? How do we progress other than by bringing about incremental change, demanding greater accountability? Roy has all the right questions; she provides no answers.

What Roy is clear about is that she is a compulsive dissenter. 'The only way to keep power on a tight leash is to oppose it, never to seek to own it or have it. Opposition is permanent.' She adds, 'There are people who have comfortable relationships with power and people with natural antagonism to power. I think it's easy to guess where I am in that.'[62]

Taking on the establishment the way Roy has done is not easy anywhere in the world, certainly not in India. A lesser person would probably be in jail on some frivolous charge or the other. Or she could get bumped off, as has happened to several dissenters such as the rationalists Narendra Dabholkar and M.M. Kalburgi or the journalist, Gauri Lankesh. Roy's international stature is, perhaps, what keeps a vengeful state or corporate and other interests from harming her.

But she is well aware of the tenuous nature of the protection her fame gives her. She told an interviewer, '. . . it's become really frightening. There are people who say, "She should be shot. She should be jailed." I've had rocks thrown at my house . . . If I'm supposed to speak somewhere, these gangs of storm troopers gather, shouting, "Arundhati Roy, she's a traitor, she's a friend of Pakistan"—all just stupid stuff.'[63]

She is equally aware that when you are so completely at odds with the establishment, it is vital to have sources of sustenance. Roy finds sustenance within herself and in her friendships. She told a writer from the *Guardian*, '. . . It's a game of survival, and if you allow yourself to become unhappy, you will lose everything . . . I think it's important to patrol the borders of your happiness, to understand your sources of joy and to protect them, and to know that, so often, it's only when that happiness has gone that you know what it was. But you can be cooking or listening to music and think, I don't need anything else to happen or anyone else to be any other way in order to be happy.'[64]

She calls her friends 'extraordinary people' who have learnt to deal with her fame and money and who have kept the 'democratic nature of our relationships'. The *Guardian* interviewer writes, 'Happiness for her, she says, might be going to the market and choosing glass beads after weeks of late nights drafting an affidavit, or just lying on the floor all day with friends under a ceiling fan in the Delhi summer. Even gossiping with friends about relationships as the police move in to break up a demonstration at a dam site.'[65]

It's not easy to be Arundhati Roy. It takes extraordinary courage to have lived the life she has lived—whether it was leaving home at sixteen to study in Delhi; living in a tin shack while pursuing her studies; marrying somebody several years her senior and then separating; standing up for the underdog in Indian society and elsewhere; railing against top politicians and businessmen.

It would have been simple enough for Roy to use her stardom to find a cosy niche for herself in the establishment. She could have become a member of the Sahitya Akademi committee, India's national academy intended for the promotion of literature in Indian languages, won state honours, become a nominated member of Parliament, or obtained government land for a cultural organization she wanted to set up. She could easily have become a member of Delhi's Lutyens elite, attending lavish parties and rubbing shoulders with ministers, bureaucrats and other members of the establishment.

Roy has eschewed these safe sanctuaries in favour of the dangerous life of a dissenter. She may be incorrect in her reading of the causes she has chosen to take up—Kashmir, dams, Naxalism, economic liberalization, globalization, etc. She may not have the answers to the problems of our times. At times, her criticism may seem to border on nihilism. But we need her to pose the questions.

We need her to speak up for the oppressed, to challenge and shake up the establishment.

Not many of us can speak up as freely as she does because we have jobs to protect and we lack the means to withstand any onslaught that any serious challenge to the system would bring. If Roy is willing to use her celebrity status to hit at the establishment, more power to her. In a world of conformists and cowards, Roy's courage inspires and kindles hope. Roy sums up her philosophical outlook aptly: 'Whether you're fearful or fearless, what happens will happen. It's idiotic to be fearless, but it's not worth living in fear.'[66]

2

Oliver Stone: The Moviemaker as Iconoclast

Over four days in June 2017, a television programme created waves in the US and elsewhere. Showtime, the American TV channel, featured interviews of Russian President Vladimir Putin with the acclaimed film-maker Oliver Stone. The interviews were titled *Putin*. In the US and in other parts of the Western world, all hell broke loose. Stone was roundly denounced by the media.

The *New York Times* carried a commentary titled, 'How Putin Seduced Oliver Stone—and Trump'.[1] The author noted, 'Mr. Stone appears to have the same sort of breathless admiration for Mr. Putin as Mr. Trump does.' The *New Republic* carried a commentary titled, 'Natural Born Buddies', an allusion to one of Oliver Stone's famous movies, *Natural Born Killers*.[2] The *Daily Beast* website termed the interviews 'Oliver Stone's Wildly Irresponsible Love Letter to Vladimir Putin'.[3]

The commentators faulted the interviews on several counts. Stone had been too uncritical in his questioning. He had not challenged Putin's claims on important matters such as the war in Ukraine or alleged Russian interference with America's presidential elections in 2016. His portrait was far too flattering to a dictator.

Yet, somebody in a non-Western country, say, India, who watches the interviews or reads them in book form (as I did),[4] is likely to form a more favourable impression of the interviews. Stone does a good job of interviewing Putin—his tone is affable but he doesn't shy away from asking difficult questions. The Russian leader comes across as a reasonable and extremely competent head of state with a firm grasp of the important issues that the world faces today.

So what were Western commentators complaining about? Well, their problem was that somebody who has been demonized for so long had been shown to be human and fair-minded. They just couldn't take it. Stone had committed blasphemy. Putin anticipates the adverse reaction to the interviews. He tells Stone towards the end, '. . . You are going to suffer for what you are doing.' Stone replies, 'I know, but it's worth it, to try to bring some more peace and consciousness to the world.'[5]

* * *

Putin is eminently worth watching (or reading)—as much for what it tells you about Putin as it does about Stone himself.

The Russian leader rose from humble beginnings to become the most powerful man in Russia for the past two decades. His parents had lived through the horrors of World War II. His grandfather had fought in World War I. After studying law at Leningrad (now St Petersburg) University, Putin joined the KGB, then the Soviet Union's spy agency. He worked for ten years at Leningrad and Moscow. Then he was sent to Dresden in East Germany. The Soviet Union was going through perestroika, the restructuring of the Soviet political and economic system initiated by President Mikhail Gorbachev. For all the upheaval this was causing, Putin sensed a 'spirit of innovation' in Russian society.[6]

Putin tells Stone that Gorbachev was right in sensing the need for major changes in the system. But Gorbachev never quite understood what changes were required nor the implications of the changes he had set in motion. Perestroika was badly managed, and it eventually led to the collapse of the Soviet Union.

Gorbachev was succeeded by Boris Yeltsin. Putin went to Moscow to work for Yeltsin's administration. He rose to become director of the FSB, the successor to the KGB. Putin says that he's often portrayed as someone who regrets the disintegration of the Soviet Union. He insists there is cause for regret: the break-up of the Soviet Union and the creation of new states meant that 25 million Russians found themselves in a country other than Russia. Putin calls it 'one of the greatest catastrophes of the 20th century'.[7]

Putin became first deputy prime minister, then prime minister in Yeltsin's government. He accepted the post of PM with some reluctance. If Yeltsin sacked him, he would no longer have bodyguards. He asked himself, 'Where do I hide my children?'[8] Moreover, Yeltsin had indicated that he wanted Putin to run for President. Putin wasn't sure he wanted to be responsible for the lives of millions of his fellow men.

When Yeltsin resigned abruptly on 31 December 1999, Putin was named Acting President. Three months later, Putin was elected President of Russia. He has since been the most powerful person in Russia, whether as President or as prime minister. As President, Putin put an end to the looting that had been going on in the name of privatization: state property had been handed out at throwaway prices to a few oligarchs. He improved the pension system, cut the poverty rate by two-thirds and raised per capita income in Russia from 2700 roubles in 2000 to 29,000 roubles in 2012.[9] We begin to understand why Putin's popularity among the people of Russia is so high. He brought Russia back from the brink and restored some of its pride in itself.

Putin outlines how the Cold War has been resurrected, eventually leading to the worst phase in US–Russia relations in decades. Gorbachev took the bold step of bringing back Russian troops from Eastern Europe. He was trying to signal the West that he wanted every nation to determine its own destiny. The US was in no mood to reciprocate this gesture. Its response was to send troops illegally into Panama a few months later. Then, in 1991, it sent 500,000 troops to Iraq, following Iraqi President Saddam Hussein's invasion of Kuwait.

Russia provided logistical support to the US when it went after al-Qaeda in Afghanistan. That did not prevent the US from supporting Islamic extremists, including elements of al-Qaeda, in Chechnya and elsewhere. The US, Putin says, 'was using those terrorists in order to destabilize the internal political situation in Russia. And frankly speaking, we were much disappointed.'[10]

When the historic reunification of Germany took place in 1990, Gorbachev was assured that NATO, then an alliance between the US and the countries of Western Europe, would not be extended beyond the eastern border of then East Germany. Putin says Gorbachev made the mistake of not getting the assurance on paper. Since then, there have been two waves of NATO expansion towards the borders of Russia. NATO, which was a product of the Cold War between two systems, has now become an instrument of the foreign policy of the US. It will do whatever the US wants it to. Putin remarks caustically, 'It [the US] has no allies within—it has only vassals.'[11]

During the term of the second George Bush, the US withdrew unilaterally from the Anti-Ballistic Missile (ABM) Treaty, under which the US and the Soviet Union had agreed to limit the number of systems to be used in defending against nuclear weapons delivered by ballistic missiles. The objective of the ABM Treaty was to limit the race between the US and the Soviet Union in producing missiles. Bush contended that a missile shield was needed in order to deal with the threat of Iran! Putin points out that America's withdrawal from the ABM Treaty threatens Russia in two ways. First, it has allowed the US to place ABMs in Eastern Europe on Russia's borders. Second, the launching pads for these missiles can be quickly transformed for launching offensive weapons.

During the discussion on the ABM Treaty, Russia warned that it would be compelled to increase its offensive capabilities if the treaty were scrapped. The Americans seemed to shrug off the warning. And yet when Russia started renovating its nuclear arsenals as promised, the Americans got jittery. Putin's point is clear: Russia has repeatedly reached out to the West and acted in good faith only to be rebuffed by shows of Western belligerence.

In the course of the interview, Putin lets drop a fascinating piece of information. After the US had developed an atomic bomb, the Soviet Union was able to develop one quickly, partly thanks to information it had received from some of the very same scientists who had helped develop the atomic bomb in the US. Putin says the scientists parted with the information in order to 'restore the nuclear balance in the world'.[12] This is something that has long been suspected and talked about but it's interesting to have it confirmed by Putin, no less.

Stone questions Putin at length about Russia's actions in Ukraine. These actions have been widely condemned in the West. Ukraine had long been contemplating joining the European Union (EU). Ukraine was a member of the Free Trade Area (FTA) of the Commonwealth of Independent States comprising Russia and nine other former states of the Soviet Union.

Russia made it clear to Ukraine that if it joined the EU, it stood to lose the preferences it enjoyed in the FTA. The President of Ukraine decided to postpone its accession to the EU. The EU and the US responded by mounting a coup d'état and installing their choice as President. The new regime signalled that it would limit the use of the Russian language in Ukraine.

The move alarmed regions with a preponderant Russian population. One of these was Crimea, where, in a referendum, the population voted overwhelmingly in favour of joining Russia. Russia then proceeded to annex Crimea. The annexation was condemned in the West as an invasion of a sovereign country. In the case of the Republic of Kosovo, the US and other Western countries had taken a different stance. Kosovo had declared independence from Serbia in February 2008 based on a mere resolution passed by Kosovo's Parliament. At the time, the West had argued that Kosovo had the right to self-determination. However, it was not willing to concede the same right to the people of Crimea.

Ukraine also launched a fierce onslaught on the Russian-dominated region of Donbass, again provoking Russian intervention. Putin argues that the new regime had repeatedly violated the Minsk agreements arrived at by Ukraine, Russia and the separatists in Ukraine. A tenuous peace has been holding there since. Ukraine has been a big loser in many ways. Its trade with the EU fell by 23 per cent after the EU reduced its tariff on Ukrainian goods to zero. With Russia, trade fell by 50 per cent. Ukraine, which had been an industrialized country, has since seen complete deindustrialization.

Syria has turned out to be another area of confrontation between Russia and the West. Russia is in Syria at the request of the regime there. The US and its allies, Putin points out, are in Syria without the authorization of the UN Security Council. (The US has since announced the withdrawal of its troops from Syria.) Putin shared with the G20 leaders photos of thousands of ISIS trucks heading towards the Turkish border. ISIS was using Turkey to sell oil and fund itself. The US and its allies were happy to look the other way.

Critics say that Stone did not question Putin closely enough about the fact that he runs a dictatorial state. This is not true. Stone does bring up the nature of the Russian political system. Putin tells him that Russia was a monarchy for a thousand years; then came communism and Stalin. Only in the 1990s was a fundamental change set in motion.

Putin makes it clear that it is unrealistic to expect Russia to reproduce the democratic structures of the US and Western

Europe in a jiffy. 'Society, just as every living organism, has to develop stage-by-stage, gradually.'[13] Russia, he points out, has four political parties compared to the two parties the US has. Russia has hundreds of TV and radio stations that the government does not control.

Stone asks Putin, 'What is the US policy? What is its strategy in the world as a whole?' Putin replies tongue-in-cheek, 'Certainly, I am going to reply to this question very candidly, in great detail—but only once I retire.'[14] Stone answers his own question without mincing words, '. . . many learned people think the US strategy right now is to destroy the Russian economy, bring it to its feet, back to 1990s levels, and change the leadership of Russia—make a new ally out of Russia for the United States to basically dominate Russia as they once did.'[15] The United States would not work with Russia in addressing common threats because '. . . the United States needs enemies'.[16]

Stone is surprised that the US should be attempting such a strategy, knowing that Russian nuclear capability had improved enormously in Putin's time. Stone mentions Russian Intercontinental Ballistic Missiles (ICBMs) that could hit New York in just twenty-four minutes. Putin suggests that some in the US believe that the level of science and technology in the US is currently so high that they could make a breakthrough in arms technology that no one could catch up with.[17]

Putin makes it clear that it is futile for the US to attempt a regime change in Russia in the hope of having a more subservient country. '. . . the most important thing about Russia is the Russian people, and its self-consciousness. The inner state of the Russian people, the inability of the Russian people to exist without sovereignty . . .'[18] Stone agrees that Russia would never give up its sovereignty as it did not give it up during World War II.

Stone brings up one of the hottest issues in American politics today: Russia's alleged interference in the US elections in 2016.

One of the serious charges against Russia is that hackers from the Russian state accessed materials of the Democrats and leaked these, causing great embarrassment to presidential candidate Hilary Clinton and others and thereby benefiting Trump. Putin says that Russia certainly liked the fact that, as a candidate for the post of President, Trump was willing to restore American–Russian relations. However, Russia was not involved in hacking the election in any way. The information uncovered by the hackers has not been disputed. '. . . unrecognised hackers . . . brought to light the problems that existed, but they didn't tell any lies, they were not trying to deceive or fool anyone . . . So hackers are not the ones to blame [for the outcome of the elections].'[19]

Putin sees the whole story of Russia hacking the election as an attempt to 'undermine the legitimacy of President Trump . . . they are trying to create conditions that preclude us from normalizing our relations with the US.'[20] Putin also makes the point that in both 2000 and 2012, it was the US that had tried to interfere in elections in Russia.

It's a fascinating exchange. The broad narrative that emerges is hard to dispute. After the collapse of the Soviet Union, the US came to believe that it could impose its will on the world, what Stone calls 'the pursuit of world domination'.[21] Russia, resurgent under Putin, has challenged this notion in a robust way, most notably in Syria. The American establishment doesn't like this one bit. Hence the vitriolic reaction to *Putin*.

Stone's critics have said that he was too obsequious, that he did not challenge Putin adequately. Stone has said that his intention was to get Western audiences to understand Putin's views on a range of matters.[22] Stone succeeds admirably. We not only get the other side of the story; we get a good picture of one of the world's most formidable leaders.

The *Guardian* critic refutes the suggestion that Stone let Putin off lightly:[23]

With the Putin Interviews, Stone has done a great service to democracy. If the first two episodes are won, in boxing terms, by the interviewee, fair referees would call the third a draw and the fourth, if not a knockout, a victory for Stone in terms of undefended punches.

* * *

It was just like Oliver Stone to have done a film on Putin at a time when Putin was, perhaps, the most loathed person in the Western establishment. Stone has never shied away from controversy. During his career as director, producer and screenwriter, he has made movies that targeted the establishment and made it uncomfortable.

His trilogy of films on the Vietnam War raised doubts about the role of the US in the war and brought home the terrible effect it had on ordinary soldiers. *Wall Street* mocked the greed and contempt for law and regulation in America's premier financial centre. *JFK*, a film on John F. Kennedy, hinted at a conspiracy behind the assassination of Kennedy, one that involved important players in government. *Nixon* and *W.* (about the younger George Bush) were unflattering portraits of two American presidents.

Stone has produced three sympathetic documentaries of the Cuban leader Fidel Castro. His documentaries on South America shine a light on the harm done by American intervention in the region. Stone's tour de force was *The Untold History of the United States*, a ten-part documentary that also came out as a book. (It was done in collaboration with an American historian.) The book portrays the US as an aggressive imperialist power through most of its history. In his long career as a film-maker, Stone hasn't worried about the consequences that go with taking unpopular positions. As one writer has said, '[Stone] lacks what you might call the deliberation gene, whatever prevents us from saying things that will get us in trouble, lose us friendships, even jobs.'[24]

Oliver Stone is somebody you would not fail to notice in a crowd. Tall, well built, with a large face, bushy eyebrows and the rugged look of somebody who has spent time in the jungles, Stone has a presence. His has been a life of adventure tinged with a little wildness. He has dropped out of college, served in Vietnam, worked as a menial on a ship, been jailed for possessing marijuana, married thrice (his oldest child has converted to Islam and changed his name to Ali), and held forth on a range of social and political issues. He once spoke of Jewish domination of the media and foreign policy—and then apologized.

Stone was the child of an American father and French mother. His parents had met when Stone's father was serving in France as a member of the Allied forces during World War II. His father was a stockbroker and a Republican who 'instilled in his son an almost-paralyzing fear of Russia's global military and economic ascendancy'.[25] The senior Stone was a failed writer, his desk strewn with unpublished poems and plays. He communicated his passion for writing to his son. The precocious junior would write plays while holidaying with the family in France. Stone has said that his father and mother both had a wild side to them, which he seems to have inherited. They were unfaithful to each other—and didn't trouble to hide the fact. His father used call girls and even procured one for his son.

Stone grew up in the affluent Upper East Side of Manhattan. He attended school in Manhattan and then, for four years, went to a boarding school in Pottstown, Pennsylvania. He went on to Yale University. His parents had been drifting apart. Yet, when Stone learnt that his parents were divorcing, it came as a shock.

Unable to focus on his studies and then only nineteen, Stone dropped out of Yale. He went to a school in Saigon to teach English to Vietnamese kids. That was a time when the first American troops had begun to arrive in Vietnam. There followed a job as a 'wiper' on an American merchant ship. (It's a job in a ship's engine room that mostly involves cleaning.) His travels took him from Asia back to Oregon in the US and then to Mexico. Stone returned to Yale and again had a problem focusing on his studies. He started penning a novel, *A Child's Night Dream* (which was published thirty years later in 1997) before dropping out a second time from his university.

In April 1967, Stone enlisted in the US Army and joined combat duty in Vietnam. He was wounded twice in action and was awarded the Bronze Star for heroism and the Purple Heart for his service. It was, as he said later, a grim struggle for survival and a struggle to preserve his own humanity in the midst of the brutality of war.

In professional terms, Vietnam was a turning point for Stone. He gave up his ambition to become a novelist and turned towards film-making. The author of a book devoted to Stone's films writes:[26]

> If the sudden shock of his parents' divorce had caused the inner turmoil that sparked his militant non-conformism, Vietnam was a second turning point, spurring the transition from books to film. Unable to write in the sweltering jungle heat, Stone had turned to photography. This was a symptom of a wider change of perspective. 'I was a novelist . . . gave up the idea because the nature of warfare was very uncerebral,' said Stone, 'It's about sensuality, the six inches in front of your face. That translated me into movies.' He had moved from introverted intellectual writing to the immediate, the visceral, the visual.

Stone returned from Vietnam in late 1968 only to be almost immediately arrested on charges of smuggling marijuana from Mexico. The charges were dismissed but Stone has never denied his long use of drugs—he has even called them 'God's gift'.[27] He eventually enrolled in a film course at New York University (NYU), taking advantage of the GI Bill, a law originally intended to provide benefits to World War II veterans. NYU had some great names on the faculty, including the well-known director Martin Scorsese. They taught Stone about the work of legendary directors such as Orson Welles and Jean-Luc Godard. Stone produced a ten-minute film as part of the coursework. Titled *Last Year in Viet Nam*, it was to foreshadow his later work on the subject.

Once out of the university, Stone found himself at a loose end. He kept himself going by taking up menial jobs: copy boy, messenger, sales representative, cab driver, production assistant. He was supported by a girl who worked at the Moroccan mission to the UN and whom he had met while at NYU. They were married in 1971. Stone produced several screen scripts in the years that followed. He got his first break in 1974 when, along with a Canadian production company, he made a low-budget horror film, *Seizure*. The film was made on a budget of $150,000.

Then, in 1978, came *Midnight Express*, a film based on the real-life story of an American college student who had been jailed in Turkey for trying to smuggle drugs out of the country. The film portrayed the terrible conditions in Turkish jails. Stone's stay in a prison in San Diego (although only for two weeks) after his return from Vietnam had given him a taste of life in jail. *Midnight Express* showed the prisoners as the good guys and the prison wardens as corrupt and brutal. The film had a racist side to it: all Turkish characters were portrayed as dirty and vicious while the Whites came out in shining colours. It was widely criticized on this account. However, it was a commercial success and received five Academy Award nominations. Stone won his first Academy Award for Best Adapted Screenplay. He also received the Golden Globe Award bestowed by the Hollywood Foreign Press Association.[28]

* * *

In 1986, Stone wrote and directed *Platoon*, a film that sealed his reputation as a director. The vast majority of war movies have a straightforward narrative: there are good guys on one side and bad guys on the other. The good guys display heroism and win. Having experienced war at first-hand, Stone knew better. *Platoon* focuses on the brutality of war itself and how it brings out the worst in people. There's no heroism and glory in the film. Good, evil and the confused middle ground between the two are all to be found in it. Stone is careful not to take any position on America's role in Vietnam.

Platoon is about a young man, Chris Taylor, who enlists for service in Vietnam in the belief that it isn't just poor people who should be doing the fighting on their country's behalf. His comrades in the platoon include Sergeant Barnes, a skilled fighter devoid of humanity, and Elias, a dope-taking soldier who has kept his decency. There are frequent clashes between the two. There are also career soldiers for whom the war has no particular meaning. Their only objective is to survive and to get released at the earliest.

There is a memorable scene based on the infamous My Lai massacre in which scores of innocent Vietnamese were gunned down by American soldiers. The platoon sets out to investigate a village that might be harbouring Vietnamese militants. On their way, the soldiers find one of their colleagues hanged.

Blinded by rage, they burst into the village, shouting and throwing questions. The terrified villagers, who don't understand the language, are unable to respond. Chris comes close to killing one of them. Barnes guns down the wife of a villager and threatens to shoot his daughter as well. Elias throws himself on Barnes and a fight erupts between the two. Chris has to intervene to prevent some members of the platoon from molesting a child. Order is restored among the warring members of the platoon with great difficulty. This is a slice, not just of the Vietnam War, but of war in general. In the grim struggle for survival and as they see their comrades tortured and killed, soldiers stop viewing the enemy as human. They cease to distinguish between soldiers and civilians.

Soon, the platoon is ambushed. In the fight that breaks out, Barnes seizes a chance to shoot Elias in the chest. As the men lift off in a rescue helicopter, they see Elias stumbling towards the 'copter only to be gunned down by his pursuers. Later, Chris attacks and nearly gets killed by Barnes. Towards the end, the platoon is given the task of guarding the battalion headquarters. Several members of the platoon are killed in an attack on the headquarters. Chris is badly wounded and he stumbles over a prostrate Barnes. Chris kills Barnes and is soon flown out. War blurs the distinction between one's own side and the enemy.

America's involvement in Vietnam is peripheral to *Platoon*. It's the hopelessness and despair of war that registers, not the great defence of democracy against communism that the war in Vietnam was touted to be. Stone is questioning the conventional narrative of war as a triumph of good over evil. He wants society to think deeply about war.

The movie left audiences divided, drawing both cheers and jeers, and it ignited a debate on the Vietnam War itself. It was a huge box office success, raking in $140 million on a budget of $6 million.[29] It won ten Oscar nominations and picked up four, including Best Director. It is hailed as one of the best war movies ever made.

* * *

Stone didn't rest on his laurels. In 1985, he directed *Wall Street*, a film about a corporate raider, Gordon Gekko (played by Michael Douglas), who doesn't suffer from an excess of scruple. He will manipulate share prices and indulge in insider trading in order to make a fast buck. Gekko entices into his games a junior broker, Bud Fox (Charlie Sheen), eager to make it big. Bud passes on insider information and helps rig share prices by buying and selling shares on Gekko's behalf.

Bud's moment of truth happens when he tries to get Gekko to invest in Bluestar, an airline company in which Bud's father is a union representative. The idea is to revive the company by getting concessions from the unions in the form of wage cuts and an increase in working hours. Bud learns to his dismay that Gekko has no interest in reviving the company. He wants to sell the assets of Bluestar at the earliest opportunity and make a killing for himself. Bud decides to teach Gekko a lesson. He approaches another investor, Larry Wildman, who had earlier lost out to Gekko on another deal. Wildman is willing to revive the company.

Bud sets out to inflate the share prices of Bluestar by spreading takeover rumours. Gekko keeps buying. The union representatives then tell Gekko that their offer of concessions is off. Gekko then tries to sell the shares but Bud has already arranged for his contacts to sell. The share price drops steeply and Wildman then picks up Gekko's shares at a throwaway price. Bud returns to his office. Moments later the Securities and Exchange Commission (SEC), which has been on to his games, arrives with a warrant for his arrest. Gekko confronts Bud in Central Park and holds forth on all that he has done for Bud. The conversation is recorded. Gekko is implicated and will likely get his comeuppance even while Bud will have to do his time in jail.

Stone has indicated that *Wall Street* was not intended as a condemnation of financial markets nor is it anti-capitalism. He has said, 'There was no conscious political motivation to do *Wall Street* . . . It was disguised biography.'[30] Stone was trying to put into the movie some of what he had known about brokers and Wall Street from his father. (The film is dedicated to Stone's father.)

And yet it is not as if *Wall Street* has no political undertone to it. The broad message is that, while the pursuit of self-interest has its uses, Wall Street's brand of unbridled greed can undermine the larger good. One notices that the people in the film are all very young. A new generation has come to Wall Street. Stone seems to suggest that the values of this generation are very different from the older lot. Brokers in his father's time cared for clients. Not so the present lot.

At any rate, critics viewed the film as a critique of American capitalism just as they had seen *Platoon* as a commentary on America's intervention in Vietnam. Stone became identified with the Left. He was now suspect in the eyes of the establishment. Stone was to later observe bitterly, '. . . the response [to *Wall Street*] was devastating. I knew I could never be a good guy with these people because *Platoon* was too commercially successful and *Wall Street* . . . they kind of sliced it up, you know.'[31]

Stone became more explicit about his view of Wall Street after the financial crisis of 2007. He remarked, 'The concept of a bank just existing to roll over profits for itself, and taking bank deposits and leveraging like this—it was against the law in the old days . . . The banks used to work for companies. And somewhere along the line they said, "It's more important that we make money for Goldman than that we make money for our customers."'[32]

In September 2011, Occupy Wall Street, a mass protest against the excesses of capitalism, erupted. Stone lent his support to the movement. He wasn't being apolitical about Wall Street any more. Occupy Wall Street captured attention worldwide but petered out in a short while.

* * *

In December 1991, Stone released one of his most controversial films to date, *JFK*, about the assassination of President John F. Kennedy. Kennedy was shot while going in an open motorcade in Dallas, Texas. The official version is that a lone assassin, Lee Harvey Oswald, was responsible. Oswald himself was shot two days later by Jack Ruby while appearing in court. The authorities claimed that Ruby too was acting on his own. No motives were ascribed to either killing.

There was widespread public scepticism about the official story. In response, the US government constituted a commission, headed by Chief Justice Earl Warren, to probe the assassination.

The Warren Commission produced a twenty-six-volume report on the assassination which upheld the official version.[33] However, a wide body of work has questioned this conclusion, and the controversy over the assassination has never quite died down.

In response to continued scepticism amongst the public, more investigations and reports followed. The most prominent was the House Select Committee on Assassinations in 1977–78. The committee supported the basic Warren Commission conclusion that Oswald was the assassin but added that there was an unidentified person who had fired a shot that had missed.

Stone's *JFK* draws on vast literature on the subject to raise serious doubts about the official version. The film centres on Jim Garrison, New Orleans District Attorney, who opens an investigation into the assassination after the official version is put out. (Garrison wrote a book, *On the Trail of the Assassins*, which is one of the important sources for Stone's film.)[34] The investigation is dropped after the Warren Commission is set up.

Three years later, after the Warren Commission report comes out, Garrison is shocked at the shoddiness of the commission's investigations and decides to reopen the case. The film highlights Oswald's bizarre background. Oswald was no ordinary worker in a book depository. He had been a US Marine. After obtaining a discharge, he travelled to Russia and obtained Russian citizenship. He married a Russian and returned to the US with help from the State Department. Oswald's background sets you thinking. Many believed that Oswald was a CIA agent; otherwise he would not have been able to move in and out of Russia so easily. Adding to the mystery is Oswald's connections with groups that were for as well as against Cuban President Fidel Castro.

There are plenty of other mysteries around the assassination. How could one bullet have caused seven wounds in two individuals (JFK and Texas Governor John Connally)? How could Oswald have shot so accurately being positioned where he was? Why would a lone gunman, Oswald, want to kill President Kennedy? The film dwells on these and other mysteries. Stone doesn't stop there. He goes on to suggest that that the assassination was the work of actors in government who deeply resented some of Kennedy's plans after the Cuban missile crisis: cutting defence expenditure, a retreat from Vietnam, a rapprochement with the Soviet Union. Many have ridiculed the thesis. They say that Kennedy had no such plans, so it makes no sense to say that these provided a motive for vested interests to bump him off.

Garrison brought charges against a businessman, Clay Shaw, who he believed was a key figure in the conspiracy. The charges were rejected by a jury. In the film, Garrison makes an impassioned plea for the truth to be exposed and asks for the release of all JFK files. So great was the impact of the film and the widespread belief in a conspiracy to assassinate Kennedy that, a year after *JFK* was released in 1991, the US Congress decided in 1992 that all official files at the National Archives related to the assassination would be released in the year 2017. In October 2017, the files were released. They did not reveal anything that detracted from the findings of the Warren Commission. The CIA paper in the files disclaimed any association with Oswald.

Was Stone, therefore, completely wrong in his portrayal of a conspiracy? Perhaps not. There is evidence that the CIA and FBI were well aware that Oswald posed a threat to Kennedy but did not act on the knowledge. There may not have been a cover-up on who assassinated Kennedy but there is evidence of a cover-up of the failure of the CIA and the FBI to take preventive steps.[35]

JFK is best seen as presenting a different side altogether to the assassination story. It gets you thinking hard about the official version. Stone has said, 'I do not think of myself as a cinematic historian now or ever and, to the best of my knowledge, have not made that claim. I'm presenting what I call the countermyth to the myth of the Warren Commission report because, honestly, I don't have all the facts.'[36]

JFK did more than reinforce the perception of Stone as somebody who was virulently anti-establishment. It created an enduring impression of Stone as some sort of crackpot conspiracy theorist out to discredit the United States. The reaction to *JFK* is a reminder of the limits to which dissent is tolerated even in seemingly liberal societies. There are some questions that cannot be asked, some possibilities that cannot even be hinted at.

* * *

In spite of being singed by the criticism of *JFK*, Stone went on to produce more films on political personalities. In 1995, he produced *Nixon*, a biographical drama about the controversial and disgraced President. Those who expected Stone to do a hatchet job on Nixon must have been disappointed. The film attempted to understand Nixon and his motivations rather than to condemn him outright. *Nixon* received a far better reception from critics than *JFK*. Some wrote that, after watching the film, they felt a certain empathy for Nixon.[37]

The film was unsparing in its portrayal of Nixon's failings. It brought out clearly the Watergate affair in which the Democratic Party's headquarters were burgled with Nixon's knowledge. The episode eventually led to Nixon's resignation as President. The movie hinted at a connection between the attempts to assassinate Cuban leader Fidel Castro, which commenced when Nixon was vice president under Eisenhower, and the assassination of Kennedy. It highlighted Nixon's insecurity, his paranoia, and his disregard for the terrible consequences of the bombing of Cambodia during the Vietnam War. In one scene, he hints at using the nuclear weapon against North Vietnam; his cabinet colleagues are shaken.

The Vietnam War triggered nationwide protests. College students were among the active protesters. The film shows Nixon meeting a group of students with a statue of Lincoln in the background. One student tells him that he hasn't fulfilled his promise to stop the Vietnam War because the system would not let him do so. Hustled away from the meeting by his aides, he suggests that there is truth in what the student says.

The film gives credit to Nixon for his successes: the integration of China into the international mainstream; the successful completion of talks with the Soviet Union to limit nuclear weapons; his ultimately ending the war in Vietnam. It also portrayed Nixon as human. It showed that Nixon had had a difficult childhood and had to overcome great odds in rising to become President. There are many flashbacks to Nixon's growing-up years. His father had a modest job first and then was a small farmer. He lost his two brothers to tuberculosis. The scenes of one of his brothers coughing and throwing up before passing away are poignant. Nixon always felt that the East Coast elite never quite accepted him, and that was the reason he was hounded out of office.

Nixon's wife, Pat, is a huge support to him. She is one of the very few people for whom Nixon has something close to love. (He calls her 'buddy'.) However, there are moments when even Pat finds her patience severely tested. The Watergate affair is one of them. Even as the involvement of the White House in the Watergate affair is clearly established, Nixon has difficulty coming to terms with the fact that he would have to quit as President. Pat tells him that she can understand why people hate him so.

The film suggests that Nixon was a man who was unable to handle the enormous power conferred on him and ultimately charted his own destruction. Stone's judgement on Nixon is kinder than that of most people:

> I think it [the film] speaks to a sort of national consensus: This is a man, this man suffered, he did wrong and he did right, and we must weigh a life in the balance of that. We must look at the whole. Clinton said more or less the same thing at the funeral,

you know: You must judge the life as a whole, he said, not just
one Watergate incident. He was right. A life like Nixon's is
filled with shame and filled with glory.[38]

There are references in the film to the 'Beast', the military-
industrial complex that largely governs America. In one place,
Nixon is heard saying on tape, '. . . Whoever killed Kennedy came
from this thing we created, the Beast.'[39] Stone thinks of the Beast
as an aspect of the US establishment or the US government that is
fundamentally untameable. Stone remarks:[40]

> I do feel after that point [the killing of Kennedy], and especially
> after Watergate, we're doomed. There's no coming back from
> wars, aggression, the Beast. Reagan fed the Beast. Carter tried
> temporarily to soothe the Beast, but it didn't work, we're back
> at it. Obama's the same. Nothing changes.
>
> The Beast is only getting bigger, and worse. It's on the
> Russian border, the Chinese periphery, drones everywhere,
> basically trying to dominate the world, control the resources,
> own the resources of the world, of Eurasia.

In 2008, Stone directed *W.*, a film on President George Bush
junior. Stone and Bush had been at Yale at the same time but
their paths did not cross until many years later, after Bush became
President.

W. was sympathetic to Bush as *Nixon* had been to its subject. It
showed how Bush had gone from being an alcoholic and a trouble-
prone young man to becoming the President of the United States.

Bush junior had to struggle hard to get out of the shadow of
his father, a World War II hero, successful businessman and US
President. In one scene in the film, a drunk Bush drives his car on
to his parents' lawn and challenges his father to a fist fight. Another
scene shows Bush suffering humiliation at an initiation ceremony
at Yale. He impresses his fellow students by remembering their

names and nicknames. Bush was forever getting into scrapes and getting bailed out by his father. On one occasion, he was arrested and held in a lock-up. The film shows his father phoning the police station in order to get him out.

Thereafter came a startling transformation. Bush gave up alcohol, found God and became governor of Texas in 1994. In 2000, he became President. Stone has said in an interview, 'He had tremendous personal problems, and I have to give him enormous credit—he did overcome them, through willpower. Whether he solved them is another issue, but he overcame certain states of mind.'[41]

The low point of Bush's term was undoubtedly the invasion of Iraq on the false pretext that Saddam Hussein was harbouring 'weapons of mass destruction'. This was a story cooked up by the war-hungry coterie around Bush: Vice President Dick Cheney, Defence Secretary Donald Rumsfeld and political adviser Karl Rove.

Although extensive searches by UN inspectors had turned up no such weapons, the US administration fed a pliant media false stories about the threat posed by Saddam. The film begins with a chilling scene that shows Bush presiding over a war cabinet. The motivations behind the invasion of Iraq become clear from the conversation around the table: gaining control over an oil-rich country and sending out a message to others in the region that it doesn't pay to defy the US. After the invasion, Bush is shown confronting the awkward reality that there were no weapons of mass destruction in Iraq.

Stone was criticized by some for having treated Bush with kid gloves. There was no mention in the film of the Bush government's failure to act on intelligence warnings about 9/11 or the rigging that went into Bush's hugely controversial electoral win in the presidential elections of 2000. There is little of the anger and outrage over wrongdoing that we see in Stone's other films. Stone explained:[42]

I went through this hatred that so many of the American people are going through now, but fortunately I got over it. I had all this anger for this loss for our country, a serious eight-year loss, and now I just want to say you've got to laugh, a little bit, about this whole thing. It gets so painful that humour is the only antidote. If you didn't, you'd go bonkers. You'd become a raging lunatic on a blogosphere, writing anti-Bush screeds.

In the 2000s, Stone remained as prolific as ever. He produced three documentaries on Fidel Castro, a documentary on Israel–Palestine relations and one on the rise of leftist governments in Latin America, including Venezuela's Hugo Chavez. They served to reinforce Stone's image as a left-wing sympathizer.

* * *

It is said of Lord Byron that he woke up one day and found himself famous. Much the same could be said of Edward Snowden. Until June 2013, the world had not heard of Snowden. Today, when you type 'Edward' in Google search, the first prompt that shows up is 'Edward Snowden'.

Snowden was an employee at Booz Allen Hamilton, the well-known consulting firm that happened to be a contractor for America's National Security Agency (NSA), the super-secret snooping arm of American intelligence. In May 2013, Snowden flew to Hong Kong. A month later, he shared thousands of classified NSA documents with three journalists. Stories based on the material appeared in the *Guardian* and the *Washington Post* and, later, in other papers. The stories revealed that the US had carried out massive surveillance on thousands of ordinary citizens worldwide, including American citizens. Widespread condemnation of the US government followed. Snowden became a household name.

The US government charged Snowden under the Espionage Act and for theft of government property. From Hong Kong, Snowden flew to Moscow. According to some accounts, he had intended to head for Ecuador from Moscow. However, the American authorities revoked Snowden's passport when he was on his way to Russia (or, according to some, even before he left Hong Kong) so that he was stranded in Moscow. After over a month in the transit section of Moscow's airport, Snowden was granted asylum in Russia for one year. At the end of that period, he received a three-year residency permit allowing him to travel freely within Russia and to go abroad for up to three months.

Not one to miss out on a great opportunity, in 2016 Stone produced *Snowden*, a 'dramatisation of actual events'.[43] The characterization is important. *Snowden*, as we shall see a little later, is not entirely a factual account—parts of it are meant for dramatic effect. It was made against great odds—no American studio was willing to fund it. Stone had Snowden's help in writing the script. Snowden himself appears briefly towards the end of the film.

The film starts with a scene at the Mira, the hotel in Hong Kong where Snowden met the three journalists who first broke the story. Snowden's career is shown in flashback. He enlists with US Special Forces in 2004. During training, Snowden breaks his legs and is given a discharge. The doctor tells him that there are 'other ways to serve your country'.

Snowden then applies for a job at the CIA. He is selected and sent for training at a facility in 2006. There, he runs into an old hand, played by Nicholas Cage. Cage gives Snowden an early indication that all is not well with the place. Cage has been sidelined over the years for having expressed concerns over surveillance to his superiors. He mentions how a project that he had started for targeting known enemies of the state had been handed over to an outside contractor for $4 billion.

Snowden joins other trainees for his first test. The boss tells them that the average time clocked is five hours. Snowden finishes the assignment in thirty-eight minutes. The boss understands that this is unusual talent. (The real-life Snowden was acknowledged everywhere as a computer genius.)

In the meantime, Snowden meets up with a girl he got to know online, Lindsay Mills. Mills is an acrobat and pole dancer. She is uneasy about the fact that Snowden does not tell her exactly what work he is doing. When Snowden is posted to Geneva, Mills goes with him.

In Geneva, Snowden has an experience that jolts him. At a party, he is told about one of the guests, a Pakistani banker, who would have information valuable to the CIA. He is to be set up. A colleague shows how it could be done. The CIA has information on the banker's family. His daughter is dating a Turkish national who is in the US with his mother without proper papers.

The Turk is arrested. This creates turmoil in the banker's family. In his emotionally disturbed state, the banker is lured to a strip joint. An undercover CIA agent gets him drunk and then gets him charged for drunk driving. The part about the banker being set up is true. Bringing his daughter into the dramatization is intended to show the dirty tricks the CIA is known to play. Snowden is disgusted by the incident and resigns from the CIA.

Snowden then joins the National Security Agency (NSA) and is posted to Japan. (One may well wonder how Snowden thought the NSA would be very different in character from the CIA.) There he learns that the US is in the habit of planting malware in the computers of even those countries that it counts as allies. In the event that Japan or any other ally turns against the US, the country can be shut down. In one telling video interaction with his boss, Snowden realizes that he and his girlfriend, Mills, are under surveillance—his boss knows exactly what his girlfriend is up to.

The stresses of the job have led to a break-up in the relationship between Snowden and Mills. Snowden leaves his job and goes back to Maryland to be reunited with Mills. Snowden's boss then offers him an assignment in Hawaii that involves dealing with

Chinese cyberwarfare. (In real life, Snowden joined Dell which was a contractor for the CIA and other government agencies.)

In Hawaii, Snowden is horrified to learn about the uses to which surveillance is put; for instance, in drone warfare. Individuals are tracked and blown up, often with innocent bystanders getting killed. Thousands are being tracked so that the information obtained on them can be used someday if required. Snowden realizes that he cannot be part of what is going on. He must tell the world what the US government is up to. He downloads vital data on a small device and smuggles the device out of his office in Hawaii. The rest is history.

Snowden is sufficiently true to real life to be taken seriously by viewers. Stone makes no bones about which side he is on. To him, Snowden is a hero who has stood up for his principles and for the higher values enshrined in the US Constitution. He is a kid who wanted to serve his country, first in the army and then in the CIA. It hurt his conscience to see what was going on. That's why he did what he did—tell the world what the agencies were up to. He's a whistle-blower who did the right thing by his country.

There are those who disagree. They say that Snowden downloaded and released not just data relating to US surveillance of American citizens but also sensitive information about NSA targets in countries such as China and Russia. Some in the intelligence community have said that the NSA's operations directed at adversaries were compromised as a result of Snowden's leaks. Not all his actions were in the interest of the American people.

How far can or should governments go in snooping on their own citizens or others? Some argue that snooping is justified only where there is a threat perception and where surveillance is approved by due process. Others will shrug and say that it doesn't matter. If the security agencies snoop on individuals, they needn't worry as long as they are not engaged in any activity that threatens US national security.

Widespread surveillance, however, cannot be dismissed lightly. Data on individuals can be abused by those who have access to it. It can be used by the state to silence dissent, to get people to toe the line. 'National security' is an expression that anonymous bureaucrats can invoke for furthering their own interests or those of their political masters.

Snowden highlights the lack of accountability of intelligence agencies and the broader defence establishment. As Stone puts it, 'There's no end to cyber-warfare. No one knows who is doing what to whom, under whose command. When the next war begins, no one's going to know who started it. It's frightening, what's going on in our lifetime.'[44] The movie was not a great success at the box office. It received mixed reviews.[45] I found the movie educative but not particularly absorbing.

* * *

The twentieth century saw the US emerge as the pre-eminent global power. It had the Soviet Union for a rival for about five decades after World War II. The collapse of the Soviet Union in 1991 left the US as the world's sole superpower.

Most Americans, as well as others in the Western world, think this is an unmitigated good. They see American dominance as a force for good. They believe that, thanks mainly to America's underwriting the global order, the period since World War II has turned out to be an era of prosperity and relative peace. They view America as a beacon of freedom and free enterprise, values that it seeks to spread to the rest of the world.

Many American intellectuals don't quite see America the same way. The novelist Gore Vidal saw the US as a nation in which an elite ruled by violence and deceit over its own people as well as over the rest of the world. Noam Chomsky, the linguist and professor at MIT, has chronicled the brutality that the US has practised in various parts of the world in pursuing its own interests. Paul Craig

Roberts, an academic and journalist who has also worked for the US government, regards American governments in recent decades as criminal.

Oliver Stone formally joined the ranks of the sceptics in 2012 when he collaborated with historian Peter Kuznick to produce a ten-part series on Showtime called *The Untold Story of the United States*. The film has a 750-page companion volume. The story begins with World War I and ends with President Barack Obama's first term. The book shows that, on important issues such as foreign policy, it doesn't matter whether the President of the US is a Democrat or a Republican: there is a certain continuity in policies pursued by presidents who came after World War II. The book captures Stone's view of the US and his active dissent in a way that no other single work of his does, so it's worth dwelling on it at some length.

The authors make clear their stance in their introduction. They write:[46]

> The United States' run as global hegemon—the most powerful and dominant nation the world has ever seen—has been marked by proud achievements and terrible disappointments. It is the latter—the darker side of U.S. history—that we explore in the following pages.

The root of the problem, Stone and Kuznick contend, is the belief in American 'exceptionalism', the view that America is the 'most powerful and most righteous empire the world has ever seen'.[47] Imperialism, the quest for resources and domination, is coded into the American DNA. It has always been justified by high-sounding motives: advancing freedom, spreading progress and civilization, etc.

Unlike other imperial powers, the US has not thought it necessary to occupy or colonize other nations (except in a few cases where its economic interests were threatened). It prefers to dominate and prise open markets rather than exercise control over populations and territory. In recent decades, the US has tended to operate through military bases. In 2002, the US had some form of military presence in 132 of the UN's 190 member nations and anywhere from 700-1000 bases all over the world.

America's conservatives deny that the country has had imperial ambitions. Alas, America's actions over a long period contradict this cosy belief. America's empire-building efforts began as early as the nineteenth century. The United States purchased Louisiana from France in 1803. This was followed by the acquisitions of Puerto Rico, the Philippines, Guam, Hawaii and Alaska. The regime change and 'nation-building efforts' in more recent years in Somalia, Haiti, Bosnia, Kosovo and Afghanistan, the authors say, are merely an extension of the same imperialist impulse.

The acquisition of the Philippines is a telling example of the methods the US has used to pursue its interests. The US wrested the Philippines from Spain in 1898 after a three-month naval war in which the Spanish fleet was destroyed. The Filipinos, who had long been rebelling against Spanish rule, had been foolish enough to think that the US would help them gain independence.

Filipino resistance to American occupation was put down with an iron hand. Following one ambush of American troops, the American general ordered all towns within a 12-mile radius destroyed and all their inhabitants killed. The US wanted to control the Philippines as it was seen as a door to the great Chinese market for which the European powers were also contenders.

The US then turned its attention to Cuba. American troops were stationed in Cuba consequent to the Spanish-American War that started in 1898. The Platt Amendment of March 1901 gave the US the right to intervene in Cuban affairs. The US made it clear to Cuba that its troops would not leave until the amendment was incorporated into the Cuban Constitution. Cuba duly obliged. In South America, the US fostered the independence of Panama from Colombia in order to be able to build the Panama Canal that would connect the Caribbean with the Pacific Ocean. The US received the same right to intervene in Panama that it had extracted from Cuba.

American military might was used to protect its investments in South America. In the period 1900–25, the US sent its troops into Honduras, Cuba, Nicaragua, the Dominican Republic, Haiti, Panama, Mexico and Guatemala. The troops often stayed for long spells of time. A US Army general later wrote of his experiences:[48]

> I served in all commissioned ranks from Second Lieutenant to Major-General. And during that period, I spent most of my time being a high class muscle-man for Big Business, for Wall Street and for the Bankers. In short, I was a racketeer, a gangster for capitalism.

* * *

The Western world doesn't like to be reminded of this but the Soviet Union was a key constituent of the Allied forces that helped thwart and defeat Hitler in World War II. Without the enormous sacrifice of lives made by the Soviet Union, the defeat of Germany may not have happened. The bonhomie between the Soviet Union and the Western nations led by the US did not last for long. Soon after the War ended, a Cold War developed between the US and the Soviet Union. It has continued to this day except for a small break during the years when Mikhail Gorbachev and Boris Yeltsin were at the helm of affairs in the Soviet Union/Russia. (The Cold War is now between the US and Russia.)

Stone and Kuznick's account of the emergence of the Cold War is fascinating. They say it has its origins in the mistrust created by America's attitude towards the Soviet Union during World War II. The US was a reluctant entrant into the War. It required a lot of persuasion from the British prime minister,

Winston Churchill, and the Soviet leader, Josef Stalin, to get the US on the Allied side.

America's President at the time, Franklin Roosevelt, saw the dangers posed by Hitler. However, he was greatly hampered by opposition in the US. Most Americans did not want to have anything to do with a war being fought amongst Europeans. Since Roosevelt could not directly help the war effort without approval from the US Congress, he initially devised the Lend-Lease programme under which the US would lend weapons and equipment to Britain in return for long leases on some of the British territories. It required the Japanese attack on Pearl Harbour in December 1941 for America to formally enter the War.

America's support to the Soviet Union's war effort was small and painfully slow in coming; so was Britain's. Stalin suspected that the West was, perhaps, happy to see communist Soviet Union being laid waste by Hitler. Two other developments contributed to Stalin's suspicion of the motives of the Soviet Union's Western partners. Stalin wanted his partners to recognize the areas the Soviet Union had annexed prior to the German invasion of the Soviet Union in June 1941. These included the Baltic states of Lithuania, Latvia and Estonia, eastern Poland, and parts of Romania. He also wanted them to quickly open a second front against the Germans by invading France in early 1942. Stalin's Allied partners took their own time in obliging Stalin on either count.

Roosevelt was reluctant to make territorial concessions to Stalin despite Churchill pressing him to do so in the interest of the war effort. He was willing to accede to the second request, namely, opening a second front against the Germans. However, this was not a priority for Britain. Churchill convinced Roosevelt to instead mount an invasion of oil-rich North Africa where Britain had important interests. The second front was delayed until June 1944—one and a half years later than promised—and the Soviets were left pretty much to their own devices. Stalin felt badly let down by the West.

The Soviet Union was able to fend off Hitler's aggression on its own. In February 1943, Hitler's forces were defeated and captured in the titanic battle of Stalingrad that had raged for over six months. The battle is seen as a turning point in World War II and as paving the way for Hitler's ultimate defeat.

Roosevelt, Churchill and Stalin met for the first time in Teheran in November 1943. Roosevelt, now keenly aware that the Soviet Union had the upper hand in the war with Germany, finally acceded to Stalin's territorial claims in Eastern Europe. He also promised to open the long-delayed second front against the Germans in spring 1944. In return, Stalin agreed to enter the war against Japan after Germany had been defeated.

The story should have turned out differently thereafter but it didn't. America again turned hostile towards the Soviet Union following the death of Roosevelt. Harry Truman, then vice president, became the President of the United States. Henry Wallace had been vice president in Roosevelt's earlier term. Stone and Kuznick contend that Truman was thrust as vice president on a reluctant Roosevelt by the party bosses who did not relish Wallace's humanistic views.

The account of how the well-meaning Wallace was thwarted by powerful interests in the Democratic Party is revealing. Wallace had made no secret of his anti-imperialist views, including his preference for emancipating the subjects of Britain's colonial empire. He favoured cooperation with the Soviet Union in ensuring world peace. He was hugely popular in Latin America. The Democratic Party bosses manipulated the party convention to ensure that Wallace didn't get a second term as vice president— Truman got the job instead. The authors are convinced that if only Wallace had become President, the course of post-War history would have been very different.

Truman, the authors contend, allowed himself to be guided by the hawks in the administration. Germany had surrendered on 7 May 1945. The US and its allies were left to confront the

Japanese who were fighting on resolutely. By the time Truman
met Stalin at Potsdam in July 1945, the US had tested a nuclear
bomb. Truman felt he could do without the Soviet Union's help
in concluding the war with Japan. So he didn't think it necessary
to honour Roosevelt's commitment to help the Soviets with post-
War reconstruction or to make any territorial concessions to
Stalin. America also believed that the use of a nuclear bomb would
convey to the Soviet Union that the US was in a position to dictate
terms in the post-War world. Relations between the US and the
Soviet Union took a turn from which there would be no return.
Thus, America's testing of a nuclear bomb and its decision to use
it against the Japanese had everything to do with the politics of the
emerging Cold War.

* * *

George Wallace, who remained as a member of Truman's
cabinet after he stepped down as vice president, tried his best
to persuade Truman to adopt a conciliatory position towards the
Soviet Union. He wanted Truman to help the Soviet Union out
with a loan similar to the one offered to Britain. He continued
to root for a different vision for America, one in which all
forms of imperialism were condemned and the US and the
Soviet Union competed peacefully to win acceptance for their
respective economic models. Truman was in no mood to listen.
He fired Wallace from his cabinet and steered the US towards
confrontation with the Soviet Union.

General Eisenhower, who succeeded Truman, continued
in the same vein. He had been favourably disposed towards the
Soviet Union before he became President. After assuming office,
he changed tack. This has happened with many other American
presidents since. It's almost as if the American establishment, which
some call the Deep State, would not allow any US President to be
friendly towards the Soviet Union (or today's Russia). Witness the

fierce response to even a mild attempt on the part of President Trump to reset relations with Russia.

Hostilities had erupted between North and South Korea. Eisenhower threatened the use of tactical nuclear weapons against North Korea and atomic weapons against China. Soon after, an armistice was signed between North Korea, China and the US. The authors argue that this unfortunately encouraged Eisenhower and later presidents, including Nixon, to believe that nuclear blackmail would work.

Eisenhower went on to argue that there was no distinction between conventional weapons and atomic weapons: all weapons, he felt, would in due course become conventional.[49] He also proceeded to transfer an increasing proportion of nuclear weapons from civilian to military control. The authors write:[50]

> Whereas Truman, after Hiroshima and Nagasaki, had viewed atomic bombs as weapons that would be used only in the most desperate circumstances, Eisenhower made them the foundation of the US defense strategy.

Perhaps the most extraordinary part of Eisenhower's tenure as President was his farewell address. In the address, he warned of the increasingly powerful and threatening 'military-industrial complex', an expression that has since been frequently used to describe the hold of military and commercial interests over America's domestic and foreign policies.[51] It was almost as if, after having kowtowed to these interests during his tenure, Eisenhower wanted to make amends by alerting his nation to their existence as he demitted office.

Under John F. Kennedy, who succeeded Eisenhower, the Cold War intensified. The threat of nuclear war was very real. Americans started building their own private nuclear shelters. Many declared that they would shoot neighbours who tried to break into their own shelters!—such was the level of paranoia.

American officials openly talked about a surprise first attack on the Soviet Union as an option.

The Soviet Union was justifiably alarmed. It possessed just ten ICBMs compared to the 2000 the US had; 300 nuclear warheads against the US's 5000. It gambled on placing missiles in Cuba, a communist state, in order to deter an American attack. The US threatened to invade Cuba unless the missiles were removed. For nearly two weeks, the world teetered on the edge of a nuclear holocaust. Soviet President Nikita Khrushchev finally yielded to the American demand to remove missiles from Cuba. In exchange, the US gave a public commitment not to invade Cuba. Secretly, it also agreed to dismantle missiles it had deployed in Turkey against the Soviet Union.

Stone and Kuznick describe a chilling episode in the crisis. A Soviet submarine carrying nuclear weapons came under attack from American depth charges. The captain of the submarine believed that a nuclear war had, perhaps, commenced and was ready to launch nuclear weapons at the US. He was dissuaded by a colleague. The officer who kept his cool was later acclaimed a hero. Thanks to him, the world had averted a nuclear catastrophe.

Much of this is known. There are things that are less known— these are elements of the 'untold history'—because the mainstream narrative chooses not to highlight them. For instance, following the Cuban crisis, Khrushchev made several bold proposals for making the world a safer place: a non-aggression treaty between NATO and the Warsaw Pact countries; a treaty for the cessation of all nuclear weapons testing; formal acceptance of two Germanys based on the existing borders; and so on. Kennedy's response was tepid and subject to conditions. The Cold War did not abate.

The authors portray Kennedy as a reluctant entrant into Vietnam, one of the most controversial interventions in the post-War history of the United States. Kennedy repeatedly told the American people that he could not afford to surrender Vietnam to communism. Stone and Kuznick would have us believe that, privately, Kennedy was telling confidants that he was taking this position merely to ensure re-election in 1964. His intention was to get out of Vietnam at the earliest. The authors go so far as to suggest that Kennedy's assassination may have been the result of his having made many enemies in the military and intelligence establishment. Other commentators are not inclined to be as kind to Kennedy: they would prefer to judge Kennedy by his actions, rather than by his supposed intentions. They hold Kennedy squarely responsible for America's disastrous intervention in Vietnam.

* * *

The downslide into greater interventionism continued under JFK's successor, Lyndon Johnson. The authors detail the escalation of America's involvement in Vietnam under Johnson. The generals wanted a massive use of naval and air power. Johnson opted for a gradual escalation. He felt this reduced the risk of Chinese intervention and the possibility of World War III. As the US got dragged deeper into the quagmire in Vietnam, Johnson's standing with the American people declined. He thought it prudent not to seek a second term.

After Johnson came Richard Nixon and the curious partnership between Nixon and his foreign policy aide, Henry Kissinger. Nixon and Kissinger were contemptuous of each other in private but that did not prevent them from using each other:[52]

> Kissinger disparaged Nixon as 'that madman', 'our drunken friend' and 'the meatball mind', while fawning all over him in his presence. Nixon referred to Kissinger as his 'Jew boy' and called him 'psychopathic'.

Even while commencing peace talks with North Vietnam, Nixon continued the policy of trying to bomb North Vietnam into submission. He ordered the secret bombing of Cambodia which provided sanctuaries to North Vietnamese forces and Viet Cong guerrillas. The bombing was of an altogether different intensity from that in the time of Johnson. Nixon and Kissinger even tried to use the nuclear threat to pressure the Soviet Union and Vietnam.

As the war raged on, Americans seemed to have become inured to the suffering they were responsible for. In 1969, the My Lai massacre in which over 500 civilians had been massacred by American forces came to light. Yet, in a poll carried out after the massacre, 65 per cent of Americans said they weren't bothered by the massacre.

Finally, in January 1973, the US signed the Paris Peace Accords under which US troops departed. The war dragged on for two more years until April 1975 when North Vietnamese forces seized Saigon. Nixon was eventually engulfed by the Watergate scandal to which we have referred earlier while talking about Stone's film on the President. Nixon resigned in August 1974. Vice President Gerald Ford succeeded him but could not win the presidency.

Next came Jimmy Carter. He is somewhat derisively regarded as an outstanding ex-President, a man who has championed numerous worthy causes after stepping down as President. (He was awarded the Nobel Peace Prize in 2002.) As President, however, Carter was a disappointment. He seemed helpless in the face of the Deep State, the strong military and other interests that seem to drive America's policies.

Jimmy Carter came to power on a promise of cutting defence spending. During his election campaign, he had denounced America's nuclear hypocrisy in asking other nations to forgo nuclear weapons while keeping a huge stockpile of such weapons itself. He wanted the US to set an example by eliminating its nuclear arsenal. He declared that the lesson from Vietnam was that the US should never again get its military involved in the affairs of another nation unless there was a direct threat to the US.

Once Carter was ensconced in office, his actions belied his lofty words. The SALT-II (Strategic Arms Limitation Talks) treaty that he negotiated with the Soviet Union in 1979 allowed both sides to continue their build-up but at a reduced rate than before, a far cry from the elimination of nuclear weapons Carter had promised. In response to the Soviet Union's invasion of Afghanistan in 1979, Carter stepped up arms spending and issued a directive that sanctioned the fighting of limited nuclear wars that the US could win. He went on to support research on the neutron bomb, authorize deployment of nuclear-armed missiles to Europe and double the number of warheads aimed at the Soviet Union. He didn't sound like a prospective winner of the Nobel Peace Prize at all.

The authors ask, 'How did that happen? Were the same forces at work during the Carter years that had undermined the administrations of other Democratic presidents, including Wilson, Truman, Johnson, Bill Clinton, and Barack Obama?'[53]

Then came Ronald Reagan. Stone and Kuznick note that this was a President who found it difficult to differentiate between reality and fantasy. They cite an instance to drive home their point:[54]

In a late 1983 Oval Office meeting, he [Reagan] told Israeli Prime Minister Yitzhak Shamir that as a photographer during the Second World War he had filmed the Allies liberating the Nazi death camps and had been so moved by the suffering he witnessed that he had decided to keep a copy of the film in case he ever encountered a Holocaust skeptic. . . . Hearing the story, Washington Post reporter Lou Cannon noted that Reagan had never left the United States during or immediately after the war. The story was entirely fanciful.

Reagan went on to authorize an enormous military build-up on the plea that the US was vulnerable to a Soviet attack and 'in greater danger today than we were the day after Pearl Harbour!'[55]

Reagan and Soviet President Mikhail Gorbachev met at Reykjavik in Iceland in October 1986. Gorbachev came up with bold proposals to curb the arms race, including steep cuts in the arsenals of both nations. He was especially keen that Reagan roll back Star Wars (or Strategic Defence Initiative), an ambitious US plan to build a shield against incoming missiles. Gorbachev argued that Star Wars would compel the Soviets to steeply increase the number of missiles at their disposal. The meeting failed to produce any agreements.

Following the Soviet invasion of Afghanistan, the CIA in Reagan's time engaged in its largest covert operation until that date, funnelling billions of dollars to Islamic insurgents fighting the Soviet regime in Kabul. In this operation, the US worked closely with Saudi Arabia and Pakistan. Although Gorbachev had made it clear that he wanted to pull out Soviet troops as early as possible, the US was determined to tie down Soviet troops for as long as possible as a way of bleeding the Soviet Union economically. Out of the insurgency in Afghanistan was born Osama bin Laden and the presence of large numbers of Islamic extremists in Pakistan, a problem that was to sap Pakistan's energies in the years to come and pose a threat to the Western world itself. The US chose to ignore warnings that Islamic extremism might one day turn on them.

George H. Bush succeeded Reagan at a time when Gorbachev was ushering in sweeping changes in both the Soviet Union and Eastern Europe. The Berlin Wall between the two Germanys came crashing down. Gorbachev supported the reunification of Germany on the understanding that NATO forces would not expand eastwards. NATO has relentlessly expanded eastwards right up to the doorstep of Russia. The US maintains that there was no commitment on its part not to expand NATO eastwards.

Bush authorized the invasion of Panama in order to depose General Manuel Noriega, a one-time American favourite, without securing congressional law. He thus chose to violate both international law and US law. The action went unchallenged in the US Congress.

Bush then turned his attention to Iraq, which the US had actively aided in its war with Iran. Following Iraq's annexation of its neighbour Kuwait, Bush decided to go to war with Iraq. Hussein, whom the US had supported for years, became an arch-villain: he was now portrayed as a latter-day Hitler. Stories of atrocities perpetrated by Hussein's forces in Kuwait were planted in the media.

The UN Security Council authorized the use of 'all necessary means' to force Iraq out of Kuwait. Stone and Kuznick document how valuable votes in the Security Council were bought by the US through generous offers of financial assistance. America's military might swiftly accomplished Iraq's ouster from Kuwait—at a terrible human cost to Iraq. With the disintegration of the Soviet Union, the US emerged as the global hegemon. Bush was the first President to make the point that the US would perform that role with or without UN sanction.

Bush's 91 per cent approval rating at the end of the Gulf War proved deceptive. He was defeated in the presidential elections of 1992 by Democratic candidate Bill Clinton. Clinton's efforts at reform suffered a setback when the Republicans gained control of both branches of Congress in 1994. Clinton moved to the Right as a result. He ended an aid programme for poor families which had been in place since the Great Depression, supported the war on drugs and enacted tough legislation on crime, measures one would associate with conservatives.

Despite the fact that there was no threat from a greatly weakened Russia, Clinton continued the tradition of stepping up defence spending. He spent heavily on missile defence even though experts warned that it would send out wrong signals about the US wanting a first-strike capability in nuclear weapons.

Tough sanctions on Iraq continued despite reports that half a million children had died there as a result. Somebody asked

Clinton's secretary of state, Madeleine Albright, whether the price was worth it. She replied, 'I think this is a very hard choice but the price—the price is worth it.'[56] On another occasion, she declared, 'If we have to use force, it is because we are America; we are the indispensable nation.'[57] Clinton's reign underlines a point we made earlier: America's basic postures do not change whatever the complexion of the government.

In 2000, George W. Bush won the presidential election defeating Democratic candidate Al Gore. It was a controversial election marred by serious charges of rigging on the part of the Bush team. Bush's tenure was marked by two wars, one against Afghanistan and another against Iraq. Both were in response to the 11 September 2001 destruction of the World Trade Centre in New York and the attack on the Pentagon.

Bush and Vice President Dick Cheney seized the opportunity to implement the neo-conservative agenda of imposing America's will on the world in the name of fighting the 'war on terror'. The agenda included overthrowing regimes the US did not approve of. One of the means to be used in the 'war on terror' was setting up detention facilities outside the US where torture would be employed. The CIA was authorized to seize suspected terrorists anywhere in the world and transfer them to these torture chambers.

From day one of the Bush administration, it was clear to everybody in it that removing Saddam Hussein from power was a top priority. The only question was finding a way to do it. Iraq was repeatedly linked to the 9/11 attack even though there was not a shred of evidence in support of any link. When that did not work, the Bush administration conjured up the bogey of 'weapons of mass destruction' that Hussein possessed.

Ignoring opposition in the UN Security Council as well as massive anti-war protests worldwide, Bush launched an attack on Iraq. The war was not just about securing oil supplies for the US: at this point, America was far less dependent on oil imports than in the past. It was about the US controlling access to the oil sitting in the Middle East. It was about sending a message to regimes in Iran, North Korea, Syria and other places that those who did not toe the US line would meet a similar fate.

When Bush's successor, Barack Obama, assumed office, there were high hopes of a meaningful change in the way the US was run. He was to disappoint in a big way. The child of a black father and a white Kansan mother, and a graduate of Columbia University, Obama seemed to represent much that was progressive in the American political culture. During his election campaign, he spoke about defending civil liberties, rejecting unilateralism and opposition to the Iraq War. As with his predecessors, his record turned out to be very different from his campaign promises. The authors write:[58]

> Yet, rather than repudiating the policies of Bush and his predecessors, Obama has perpetuated them. Rather than diminishing the influence of Wall Street and the major corporations in US life, Obama has given them latitude to continue most of their predatory practices.

Obama shied away from tough legislation to rein in bankers. He compromised heavily on his health reform programme as he didn't want to fight the health insurance and pharmaceutical businesses that had contributed heavily to his campaign. He extended the Bush tax cuts for the wealthiest Americans while slashing social programmes for the vulnerable. These decisions were not surprising: Obama had turned down public campaign financing and relied instead on Wall Street firms, defence contractors and pharmaceutical companies to fund his campaign. Economist Paul Krugman wondered, 'Who is this bland, timid guy who doesn't seem to stand for anything in particular?'[59]

Obama backtracked on his commitment to transparency in government. The Obama administration classified more information and responded more slowly to Freedom of Information

Act requests than its predecessor. It prosecuted more whistle-blowers than all previous administrations.

Obama promised on his second day in office to bar the use of torture, close the CIA's interrogation centres in various parts of the world and shut down the military prison at Guantanamo Bay within one year. He failed to deliver on many of these promises. For instance, the detention centre at Guantanamo Bay that holds numerous alleged terrorists without charges or trial, continued to operate during his tenure. Nor did Obama pursue prosecution of Bush-era torture and other abuses, instead invoking the 'state secrets privilege' more often than any President to halt lawsuits involving torture and illegal wiretapping. Over the years, the expansion of state powers for surveillance, search and arbitrary detention had expanded hugely—for instance, surveillance without warrants and monitoring of citizens without court orders and the power of indefinite detention. Obama chose not to use some of these powers but he did not curtail them either, leaving ample room for his successors to abuse them.

In the story told by Stone and Kuznick, there's a common theme that runs through successive presidencies. It's the attempt on the part of the US to impose its writ on the rest of the world without the slightest concern for other nations and peoples. That attempt was restrained until the collapse of the Soviet Union. Since the US emerged as the sole superpower, it has been far less inhibited in its actions. And the motivation for intervention is not altruism but the ruthless pursuit of America's interests.

* * *

Stone and Kuznick received mixed reviews for their untold story. Some said that they had not uncovered anything new. Their story had been told before, only it wasn't the dominant narrative among American historians. The authors were accused of distorting or misrepresenting facts. The book was seen as an exercise in America-bashing.[60]

Even if these criticisms are valid, it doesn't take away from the overall narrative. It's a view of America that Americans as well as non-Americans don't get to see at all. That's because the mainstream media and public schools choose to hide it completely. The book and the documentary reinforced the general perception of Stone as a leftist and America-baiter.

That is not an accurate description of the man. Stone is a critic of America's interventionist policies and its propensity to wage wars abroad. But he is not against the free market or the capitalist system per se (although *Untold History* does highlight problems such as widening inequalities). He cannot be as he has prospered and become famous by making use of the very possibilities that the capitalist system offers

Stone has paid a price for his dissent. Big studios have shied away from some of his projects. He has been sidelined by some in the mainstream media. Stone remarks bitterly, 'The editorial page of the *New York Times* has refused to print any column or letter of rebuttal I have written since 1991, thereby allowing me to be easily misunderstood and set up as a straw man with a conspiratorial mind-set.'[61]

But these are relatively minor costs for the sort of criticism Stone has mounted of the American establishment. They pale in comparison with the commercial success and fame he has had. The establishment may shun him but the public at large does not. Like Arundhati Roy, he has the resources and the public standing to be able to fight for his cause. Those in power may revile him, they may try to marginalize him but they cannot muzzle him. Much as his critics may despise his views, they cannot question his patriotism. He's a decorated soldier who volunteered to risk his life for his country, unlike many in power who found ways to dodge the draft during the Vietnam War.

In the evening of his life, Stone continues to stand up to the American establishment. Through his public appearances, interviews and tweets, he keeps up a relentless barrage of criticism of America's policies. He champions all manner of causes. In March 2018, Stone criticized the decision of the Ecuador government to cut off Internet access to WikiLeaks founder Julian Assange who had been granted asylum at the country's embassy in London.

Stone has spoken up for the independence of the province of Catalonia in Spain and lambasted Germany for detaining Catalonia's President on behalf of the Government of Spain. Visiting Iran for the first time for a film festival in April 2018, he compared Trump with the biblical demonic figure, Beelzebub, and slammed US policies in the Middle East. It's no small irony that Stone's son works for Russia Today, a private channel that Western commentators tend to see as a front for Putin and the Russian state. This is not something Stone may have intended. But you can be pretty sure that he would be grinning hugely at the discomfiture it must cause the American establishment.

3

Kancha Ilaiah: Challenger of the Hindu Order

Hindutva is very much in vogue today. There is an assertion of the Hindu identity. In his book *A Million Mutinies Now*, V.S. Naipaul viewed this assertion in positive terms. After having been subjugated and ruled over for centuries, Hindus were finally discovering themselves in post-Independence India. With economic advancement, they had come to recognize their potential. This newly developed self-belief could help Hindus make something of their nation.

To Kancha Ilaiah, an intellectual and a Dalit activist, talk of a Hindu identity is baffling. It is news to him that he—and millions of others who are supposedly part of the Hindu fold—should be called a Hindu at all. In a book that mounts a frontal challenge to the Hindu order, *Why I Am Not a Hindu*, he wrote:[1]

> . . . What do we, the lower Sudras and ati-Sudras (whom I also called Dalitbahujans), have to do with Hinduism or Hindutva itself? I, indeed not only I, but all of us, the Dalitbahujans of India, have never heard the word 'Hindu'—not as a word, nor

as the name of a culture, nor as the name of a religion in our early childhood days.

Ilaiah is one of the foremost intellectuals of the Sudra caste, traditionally regarded as the lowest of four castes in the Hindu religion. He is a familiar figure on television. He appears frequently on issues related to Dalits: violence against them, affirmative action, Ambedkar, Gandhi. He also appears in discussions on Indian politics, especially where these relate to Hindutva and the activities of the Sangh Parivar. In his now familiar, high-pitched voice, he makes his points forcefully. He uses strong words to characterize those whose politics he loathes—'fascist', for instance.

Ilaiah champions the cause of the lower Sudra castes (there is hierarchy even within the Sudra caste) and the Dalits, formerly called the Untouchables, who were regarded as beyond the pale of the caste system. Dalit is an expression that Ambedkar used towards the end of his career to refer to Scheduled Castes. It means 'suppressed and exploited people'. Kanshi Ram, founder of the Bahujan Samaj Party (BSP), now led by Mayawati, used the expression Bahujan, which means 'majority', to refer to Scheduled Castes, Scheduled Tribes and Other Backward Classes (OBCs), all categories that exist in the Indian Constitution.

Kanshi Ram preferred not to refer to Dalits alone as he did not want to separate them from the other two categories who shared their plight. Ilaiah groups the Scheduled Castes and OBCs together in the expression 'Dalitbahujan' to connote the majority that is suppressed and exploited by the upper castes who constitute a minority. (He grants that Scheduled Tribes may also be included in the expression.)[2] Ilaiah believes that the Dalitbahujans have nothing in common with the other Hindu castes. They cannot be called Hindu at all. He finds the very idea of a homogeneous Hindu order, implied by Hindutva, revolting.

Ilaiah has been called a modern-day Ambedkar. He echoes the rage of Ambedkar against an order that has kept millions in backwardness for centuries. Like Ambedkar, he has strong academic credentials and an appetite for digging out unpleasant facts obscured by the mainstream narrative on Hinduism.

Ilaiah, who has taken to calling himself Kancha Ilaiah Shepherd to affirm his origins, was born in a small village in Warangal district in what is today the state of Telangana. His family belonged to the Kurumaa sheep-grazing caste. His father, he told me, was 'an innocent man' who was mostly away from home grazing the herd. The dominant figure in the family was his mother who also happened to be the head of the community of about twenty-five shepherd families, each with about a hundred sheep and goats.

Having a woman as head was something of a necessity. The men were away most of the time. A head was required for settlement of disputes that arose within the shepherd community or between the community and others. Besides, the sheep were an important source of income through the manure they produced when they rested at night on agricultural land. The owners of the land were willing to pay significant amounts of money for the herd to spend the night on their land. The leader of the shepherd community would negotiate the sums with the landlords.

An individual of the same caste had migrated from another village and had become the police 'patel' or head in the village. He coveted the leadership of the community and was looking for an opportunity to grab it from Ilaiah's mother. He colluded with another leader of the shepherd community to dislodge Ilaiah's mother.

It was common during festive occasions for people to get drunk and get into minor fights. On one such occasion, a fight erupted between Ilaiah's mother's team and the police patel's team of about fifteen persons. Ilaiah's mother rushed to intercede. The police patel and his team, who were on the spot, beat her up badly and she sustained serious internal injuries.

A quack administered some medicine. It resulted in tetanus. Ilaiah's mother passed away. Ilaiah was in the ninth standard at school at the time. Ilaiah regards his mother as an inspiration for his own rebellion.

Ilaiah was part of the first generation in Dalitbahujan history to go to school. His school was housed in a thatched hut and had one teacher. There were seven students in his class. Ilaiah studied up to the fifth class. Thereafter, he moved to a school 8 km from his village. A local landlord rented him a small room and Ilaiah cooked for himself. For high school, he moved to the taluka town of Narsampet where he studied up to the eleventh class, followed by one year of pre-university studies. He topped his school in the eleventh class. He did his BA in English literature in this college. He then moved to Osmania University, Hyderabad, where he did his master's in political science, MPhil and doctorate.

Ilaiah became acutely aware of caste while at school. Everything about the upper-caste children was different, although they had all been born in the same village. Their food habits, the stories they were familiar with, their religious practices and symbols (including the sacred thread they wore) were all alien to Ilaiah and to his companions from the lower castes. The gods and goddesses that Ilaiah encountered—Brahma, Vishnu, Shiva—were all unknown to him. The gods and goddesses that he was familiar with found no mention in the textbooks.

The Brahmin teachers resented having to teach Sudra children. They saw the Sudra children as coming from families that did lowly farm work. The heroes of the upper-caste children, the names that Ilaiah encountered in textbooks, belonged to a different world. This early experience at school led to his overwhelming conviction that Dalitbahujan culture and the culture of the upper castes were poles apart.[3]

Entering university, Ilaiah found his teachers silent on caste discrimination, however radical their views on other matters. Like the teachers he had encountered at school, they did not approve of lower-caste people in their classrooms. They considered them undeserving. They felt that the lower-caste people would only cause standards in higher education to fall. Of course, they wanted better wages and living conditions for the lower castes. But this should happen in their own villages and within the agrarian economy.[4]

Ilaiah's doctoral thesis was on the political thought of the Buddha. It was published later as a book. We will come to it shortly. He served as professor in the political science department of the university for many years. He then became director of the Centre for Social Exclusion and Inclusive Policy at Maulana Azad National Urdu University in Hyderabad. He has since retired from the position and is now actively engaged with various social organizations.

* * *

Why I Am Not a Hindu came out in 1995, a few years after the implementation of the report of the Mandal Commission on reservations in government institutions for OBCs. Reservations for OBCs were followed by the Ram Janmabhoomi (birthplace of Lord Rama) movement, started by BJP leader L.K. Advani. The movement sought to build a temple at a site in Ayodhya where a mosque was located. Following a judgement of the Supreme Court in November 2019, this objective has finally been met.

The Ram Janmabhoomi movement was widely seen as an attempt to keep the Hindu community from being splintered in the wake of the divisions created by caste and reservations. The idea was to forge a composite Hindu identity by invoking a deity, Lord Rama, whose appeal cut across caste divides.

Ilaiah believes that this is an effort that is doomed to fail. Dalitbahujans cannot be regarded as Hindu at all:[5]

I was not born a Hindu for the simple reason that my parents did not know that they were Hindus. This does not mean that I was born as a Muslim, a Christian, a Buddhist, a Sikh or a Parsee. My illiterate parents, who lived in a remote South Indian village, did not know that they belonged to any religion at all. People belong to a religion only when they know they are part of the people who worship that God, when they go to those temples and take part in the rituals and festivals of that religion. My parents had only one identity and that was their caste: they were Kurumaas.

Ilaiah's point is not just that the Dalitbahujans are *different* from the upper castes. He asserts that what Dalitbahujans have to offer by way of culture is vastly *superior*—more humanitarian, more egalitarian, more capable of liberating the energies of the people of India. He believes that the superiority that upper castes have traditionally claimed for themselves is a myth. The Hindutva project is thus seriously flawed. Hindutva aims at the Hinduization of India. What is required instead is the Bahujanization of Hindus. Ilaiah's thesis is breathtaking in its audacity. He spells it out at length.

A fundamental difference between Dalitbahujans and the upper castes is the orientation towards manual labour and production in Dalitbahujan culture. From childhood itself, boys and girls are trained in tasks related to production. Boys in Ilaiah's community were trained in sheep-rearing, the treatment of diseases of animals, the shearing of wool. Girls were trained not just in a range of household chores but in farm work such as the sowing of seed and weeding. Women have their own contribution to make to the production of goods and they can often step in for men in many tasks.

Familiarity with nature is a key aspect of the early training of Dalitbahujans. Children learn the names of trees, birds, insects, animals and the instruments used in producing wool, blankets, toddy. In contrast, Ilaiah notes, upper-caste children are taught to shun manual labour and to focus on book learning and the recitation of slokas and mantras.

In upper-caste families, age and sex determine the relationships. Children must obey elders and girls must obey boys. Relations within the Dalitbahujan family are more egalitarian. There is patriarchy in Dalitbahujan families but it is not as pronounced as in the upper castes (Ilaiah uses 'Hindu' synonymously with upper caste; I prefer to use the latter expression to avoid confusion).

Amongst Dalitbahujans, when the father abuses the mother, the mother can retort. She is not expected to keep quiet as in upper-caste families. Cooking is a big part of the mother's life amongst upper castes and the wife is expected to produce enough variety to satisfy the husband. When a Dalitbahujan woman has an extramarital relationship, the whole community gets to know about it and it is discussed. Child marriage was common in lower castes (as in upper castes). However, when the husband died, the widow was not expected to have her head shaved and be clad in white.

Divorce is more easily obtained amongst Dalitbahujans as are second husbands. Divorce is celebrated with food and drink as much as marriage. Sati, the practice of the widow jumping into the husband's funeral pyre, is unknown to Dalitbahujans. The ideal woman in the upper castes does not smoke or drink, no matter that her husband is a chain-smoker and drunkard. Among Dalitbahujans, smoking and drinking are common amongst women.

The ideal man in the upper castes is one who is knowledgeable about the scriptures, and the courageous man is one who kills his enemies, as in the Ramayana and Mahabharata. For Dalitbahujans, the knowledgeable man is somebody who is conversant with a range of productive tasks: sheep-breeding, agriculture, rope-making. The courageous man is somebody who can fight tigers, lions, snakes, swim in the rivers, dive deep into the forests.

Even if we allow for some exaggeration in the narrative, much of the above must come as a revelation to the reader. What has been presented as the dominant culture of Indian society is flawed;

what has been suppressed from the world is of a quality that most educated Indians would not be aware of.

* * *

Ilaiah writes about upper-caste gods and goddesses and those of Dalitbahujans. His interpretations of upper-caste gods and goddesses are fascinating.[6] He sees them as enemies and oppressors of Dalitbahujans. Like the nineteenth-century Sudra reformer, Jyotirao Phule, Ilaiah believes Brahmins were part of the Aryans who invaded India and conquered the indigenous people. This conquest involved violence and killing on a large scale. The violence is reflected in narratives about Hindu gods and goddesses.

Parashurama, one of the avatars of Vishnu, is portrayed in the scriptures as a violent person. Indra is regarded by upper castes as a hero because he was the original Aryan leader who killed hundreds of thousands of Dalitbahujans. (In his book, Ilaiah does not provide any basis for these assertions. When I asked him about it, he said he should have provided the necessary references.)

The first god of Hindus, Brahma, was the one who worked out the strategy for the conquest of the Dalitbahujans. Brahmins conceived the theory that Brahma created the Brahmins from his mouth, the Kshatriyas from his arms, the Vaishyas from his thighs and Sudras from his feet. This was the basis for the four varnas or social classes that legitimized inequality in the Hindu system. Brahma's wife, Saraswati, is the goddess of knowledge but there are no writings ascribed to her—the source of wisdom in the Vedas is Brahma himself. Ilaiah asks mockingly, 'How is it that the source of education is herself an illiterate woman?'[7]

The second god is Vishnu, who is portrayed as blue-skinned (and not fair-skinned like the Brahmins). Ilaiah conjectures that the Brahmins did this to project an association between themselves and Kshatriyas at a time when the Kshatriyas were in revolt against the Brahmins. It was a clever strategy to keep the Kshatriyas on their side.

Vishnu's wife, Lakshmi, is the goddess of wealth. Her role is to ensure wealth for the upper castes and to deny the same to Dalitbahujans. 'If she comes to know that a Dalitbahujan man or woman has acquired wealth or is revolting against the caste system, she is required to bring it to the notice of Vishnu who will go and exterminate such persons.'[8] Ilaiah quotes Phule as saying that while Lakshmi is the source of wealth, Brahmin women themselves were denied the right to property. Women are an oppressed gender amongst upper-caste Hindus; at the same time, goddesses are given an important role. This again was a clever way to co-opt upper-caste women into oppressing the other, namely, the Dalitbahujan.

The third god in the Hindu Trinity is Shiva. He is dark-skinned and tribal. His wife is Parvati, who plays a supporting role as the other two goddesses do. Ilaiah asks why the Brahmins thought it necessary to construct these two gods when Brahma, Vishnu, Saraswati and Lakshmi sufficed to control the minds of the Kshatriyas, Vaishyas and Dalitbahujans. He suggests that the motivation may have been to control the tribals, who would have found it difficult to identify with Brahma and Vishnu. Creating a god in the likeness of a tribal was intended to get the tribals to accept the authority of the Brahmins.

As Dalitbahujan revolts continued, the Brahmins conjured up more gods and goddesses through avatars (or incarnations) in order to keep things under control. Ilaiah provides a critique of three of these: Vamana, Krishna and Rama.

The story of Vamana is well known. A certain asura king, Bali, was ruling much of the world. Indra and other gods felt threatened and approached Vishnu, who then appeared on earth in the avatar of a dwarf, Vamana. Bali was known for his generosity. Vamana approached him and asked for three paces of land as a gift. Bali readily agreed. Vamana then grew into a giant of cosmic proportions. With one foot, he covered the heavens. With another, he covered the earth. He asked where he should place his third foot. Bali offered his head which Vamana proceeded to crush.

The story is typically presented as one of the triumphs of good over evil. Ilaiah has a different view altogether. He says the story is really about a Dalitbahujan king, Bali, who worked to create a casteless society. The Brahmins were upset and they projected a dwarf Brahmin boy as an incarnation of Vishnu. Vamana then proceeded to deceive Bali along the lines mentioned above.

In Ilaiah's account, the deception happened by Vamana going to the top of a building and pointing a foot towards the sky and saying that the entire sky was covered. Vamana then pointed another foot towards the earth and said the entire earth was covered. Bali's protests that these claims were lies were shouted down by the Brahmins. Vamana then descended from the building and asked for a place for the third foot. Bali offered his head which Vamana crushed with iron-studded footwear. Ilaiah writes, 'Thus, the Dalitbahujan kingdom was conquered by Hindu treachery and the most humanitarian Baliraja was murdered.' Phule was of the same view.[9]

If this reconstruction of a story often told with great relish among Hindus does not jolt you enough, you need to hear what Ilaiah has to say about Krishna, another famous avatar and greatly beloved of traditional Hindus. Krishna is said to have been born a Kshatriya but brought up by a Yadava family. (Yadava is a Sudra caste.) In the Mahabharata, Krishna was the strategist for the five Pandavas who were ranged against the more numerous Kauravas. Krishna is also the author of the Bhagavad Gita. How did a Yadava come to write a book at a time when Sudras had no right to literacy? And how is it that a Yadava author makes no mention of his community at all in his work?

Ilaiah provides answers. The Mahabharata was set in what is today Uttar Pradesh and Bihar. This region saw frequent revolts from the dominant Yadava community. The revolts were brutally suppressed. At the same time, the Brahmins saw the need to win the consent of the Yadavas.

They thought up the character of Krishna, a Kshatriya raised in a Yadava family. Krishna never identifies himself with the Yadava culture in which he grew up. He plays the role of a Kshatriya defending Brahminical dharma. Thus, he may have had several Yadava women (notably Radha) as lovers but all his eight wives were Kshatriya.

In the war between the five Pandavas (a metaphor for the Brahmin, Kshatriya and Vaishya minority) and the hundred Kauravas (a metaphor for the Dalitbahujan majority), Krishna throws his weight behind the former. For him, the ends justify the means. All manner of violence and treachery is employed to defeat the Kauravas. Krishna exhorts Arjuna to kill his opponents who had challenged the Brahminical dharma. The message is clear. It is the upper castes who must prevail—and the Kshatriyas as the warrior caste must not hesitate to use violence to put down the lower castes.

Thus, in Ilaiah's telling, a popular Hindu story, one that involves the god Krishna and the victory of dharma or righteousness, is reduced entirely to casteist terms. It becomes a story that is intended to reinforce the existing Hindu order. Ilaiah's suggestion that the Gita was intended to build a consent system for the dominance of the upper castes is not an original one. It was first propounded by Ambedkar. Ambedkar argued that the Gita is just '*Manusmriti* [the laws of Manu, one of the creators of the caste system] in a nutshell'.[10] Ilaiah makes the point that Gandhi too used the Gita during the freedom struggle to reinforce the consent system in favour of the upper castes.

Then, we have the Ramayana. Rama is an avatar of Vishnu, and Sita is an avatar of Lakshmi. Ilaiah asks why the Ramayana came to be written at all. He proceeds to give an answer. The Brahmins had established complete sway over the north after subduing the challenges from Dalitbahujans as well as Jainism and

Buddhism. In the south, however, Dalitbahujans ruled over several kingdoms. The principal villains in the Ramayana—Ravana, Tataki, Shambuka and Vali—were all Dalitbahujan rulers. The Brahmins decided to extend their hegemony to the south with Rama as their instrument.

The story of the Ramayana is basically the story of how the Dalitbahujan kingdoms of the south were brought under the control of the Brahmins. Like the Mahabharata, the Ramayana was intended to manipulate popular consciousness in favour of a particular caste dispensation.

After Ravana had been vanquished, Brahmins migrated from the north to the south. Brahminism came to be imposed on southern society. However, there were periodic revolts against it. Anti-Brahmin movements sprang up frequently. There were also several local cultural traditions that were antithetical to Brahminism. As a result, the Brahminical tradition remained on the surface in the south. The dominance of the Dravida parties is a manifestation of the fact that Brahmin dominance is not as well-entrenched in the south as in the north. It required the establishment of the BSP in the north to bring about the sort of awareness amongst Dalitbahujans that had happened much earlier in the south.

The whole point about the Hindu scriptures, gods and goddesses, in Ilaiah's view, is to produce consent for an iniquitous and illiberal order. It is to preserve the dominance of the upper castes. He writes, 'Hinduism has a socioeconomic and cultural design that manipulates the consciousness of the Dalitbahujans systematically. It has created several institutions to sustain the hegemony of the brahminical forces.'[11]

After taking down the traditional Hindu gods and goddesses, Ilaiah proceeds to acquaint us with a few Dalitbahujan gods and goddesses (most of whom members of the upper castes would not even have heard of). There are several striking facts about them. First, the gods are 'culturally rooted in production, protection and procreation'.[12] People pray to them for meeting their everyday needs—getting a good crop, curing the sick, ensuring supply of water, ensuring their safety, etc. There are no other-worldly reasons for praying to them. The god Pochamma is the discoverer of herbal medicine. Beerapa is a sheep breeder. Yanada is a steel technologist. And so on.

Second, the gods are accessible to all, irrespective of caste or even religion. Third, war and violence is not part of the religious philosophy unlike in the case of upper-caste gods and goddesses. Fourth, people can commune directly with the gods—no intermediation by the priest is required. Fifth, religion among Dalitbahujans is not male-centric with women being accorded a secondary role.

The culture and worldview of Dalitbahujans, Ilaiah insists, is thus superior in many ways to that of the upper castes. And yet it has never received an airing. What is projected as the worldview of the Hindus is that of the upper castes alone. Ilaiah's verdict is damning. 'For centuries, even when Dalitbahujans tried to unite all castes, the Brahmins, the Baniyas and the Kshatriyas opposed the effort. Even today, no Brahmin adopts the names of our Goddesses/Gods; even today, they do not understand that the Dalitbahujans have a much more humane and egalitarian tradition and culture than the Hindu tradition and culture.'[13]

* * *

Ilaiah's account of the differences between Dalitbahujans and upper castes and the means used by the latter to dominate the former is a compelling one. But the story is not as straightforward as it seems, as Ilaiah himself acknowledges. If the lower castes are so different, if they have been so thoroughly oppressed, one would have expected them to forge a united front in order to resist oppression by the upper castes. This hasn't quite happened.

The higher castes among the Sudras—or the 'neo-Kshatriyas', as Ilaiah calls them—have been moving closer to the upper castes.

They are getting co-opted into the Hindu order. (The neo-Kshatriyas go by last names such as Reddy, Rao, Patel and Singh.) The neo-Kshatriyas adopt first names borrowed from the upper castes. They tend towards vegetarianism. Their women are taught to be docile. They distance themselves from work in the fields. In many ways, they try to imitate the mores of the upper castes.

Ilaiah does not hide his disapproval of this development. 'The alliance of Brahmin-Baniya and neo-Kshatriya is being projected as a sort of modernity of India. This Hinduized modernity is historically a negative development. It is an antithesis of Dalitbahujan assertion.'[14] He ascribes the 'negative development' to the eagerness of the upper layer of Sudras to gain power and prestige by collecting crumbs from the upper castes, so to speak.

He believes, however, that 'Sanskritization', the process of imitating the ways of the upper castes, will bring the neo-Kshatriyas neither acceptability nor genuine power. They can never become priests in Hindu temples, for instance. They 'will have to operate within the ideological and philosophical domains of caste and Brahminism'.[15] Well, thus far, they seem quite happy to do so.

There are other complications in the caste narrative. In many parts of the country, the OBCs are seen as the worst oppressors of the Dalits. OBCs gaining political power has made little difference to the vast majority at the bottom of the caste pyramid. OBC parties have aligned themselves with the BJP or the Congress and against Dalit parties such as the BSP. Clearly, cracks have shown up among the Dalitbahujans whom Ilaiah sees as a homogeneous construct.

This gives rise to several questions. If the Dalitbahujans are not Hindus at all, as Ilaiah claims, why would the better off among the Dalitbahujans make common cause with the upper castes? How is the enormous cultural divide between the two getting bridged? Could it be that the operative factor is not caste, as Ilaiah claims, but class, as the Marxists have always contended? Is Ilaiah oversimplifying matters by ascribing all ills to caste alone? Is the problem mostly economic and not sociocultural in character? There are Dalit thinkers (such as Anand Teltumbde) who tend to hold this view.

Apart from ignoring the role of class, Ilaiah tends at times to take a romanticized view of Dalitbahujan culture. He talks at length about how egalitarian the Dalitbahujan consciousness is. There is nothing 'private' or 'personal' in this consciousness, he says. 'The individual is always part of the larger collective and the collective functions in an open way.'[16] Whatever is procured is shared equally, irrespective of the greater effort some individuals might have put in. 'Pleasure, pain and social events are all shared.'[17]

Among Dalitbahujans, the notion of private property is not very strong. This is in stark contrast to the upper-caste craving for property and the accumulation of it. Why would Dalitbahujans think very differently about property? Ilaiah suggests that they do so because of the confidence they have in their ability to labour. They do not feel the need to accumulate today because they can labour tomorrow to meet their needs.

All this may be true, but it may have more to do with income levels and the capacity to save rather than with any superior cultural attitude about property. At low levels of income, most of what is earned is consumed, leaving little scope for saving and accumulation. This is not so at higher levels of income.

The Dalitbahujan does not save because his income level is low—it's not because he does not feel the need to save. It follows that as the income levels of the Dalitbahujans rise, they will not be reluctant to imitate the saving and accumulation that Ilaiah derides in the upper castes.

Indeed, in recent years, we have seen a rise in Dalit businessmen and there is even a Dalit Chamber of Commerce. It is unthinkable that Dalits would be in business without having the propensity to accumulate. Similarly, the sharing and caring that Ilaiah associates with Dalitbahujans is very much to be found amongst even upper-caste families that live in, say, the chawls of Mumbai. These chawls function pretty much as a commune. Again, the key determinant of behaviour is income level or class, not caste.

The relative absence of notions of private property and the tendency towards a communal existence have long been facets of pastoral or agricultural peoples who live on the fringes of subsistence. With economic advancement and urbanization, these characteristics tend to erode. Communities tend to fragment. Ilaiah's contention that certain traits among Dalitbahujans are the result of a superior consciousness may thus not be terribly accurate.

Ilaiah is on firmer ground when he talks of the Dalitbahujans' intimate knowledge of nature and a range of production-oriented tasks. He makes the striking point that even while engaged in labour, the Dalitbahujan is constantly generating ideas that make labour a pleasure. 'If labour is not pleasure, if Dalitbahujan minds do not derive pleasure out of that labouring process, given the low levels of consumption on which they subsist, Dalitbahujan bodies would have died much earlier than they do.'[18]

Ilaiah gives a clarion call for the 'Dalitization' of civil society. 'Dalitization' will require assuming political power, an area in which Dalitbahujans have tasted success. But more needs to be done. He suggests that Dalitbahujans co-opt upper-caste women into their agenda as the latter are themselves oppressed. Hindu temples must be captured, their wealth seized and the temples converted into centres of public education where the Dalitbahujans begin to 'reschool' the upper castes. This will involve pushing Brahmin-Banias into productive work (by which Ilaiah implies manual work) and by 'completely diverting their attention from the temple, the office, power-seeking, and so on'.[19] The last proposal is eerily reminiscent of Mao's Cultural Revolution or even the experiments attempted by the Pol Pot regime in what was then Cambodia (now Kampuchea).

Ilaiah is, however, keen that the revolution that he urges be bloodless. He says that 'Dalitization must be handled very skilfully' lest it should be discredited by the hue and cry the upper castes will raise in international circles. He asks that an army of Dalit intellectuals be created who will examine what has happened in the past thoroughly and lay out a detailed roadmap for restructuring political and economic relations in Indian society. He concludes, 'It is through loving ourselves and taking pride in our culture that we can live a better life in future.'[20]

Ilaiah's account, as we have seen, is not without exaggeration and oversimplification. Nevertheless, it's hard not to be stirred by *Why I Am Not a Hindu*. It challenges every comfortable notion that most of us have grown up with. It compels us to take a hard look at the oppressive and inegalitarian order that has long obtained in India. It awakens us to the culture, attitudes and inherent strengths of the excluded majority in the country. It leaves us in little doubt that a massive churning in Indian society is both necessary and inevitable in the years ahead.

* * *

Why I Am Not a Hindu is a searing critique of Hindu society. In *Post-Hindu India*, which came out in 2009, a little over a decade after the earlier book, Ilaiah ups the ante, so to speak.[21] As the provocative title suggests, he takes the demise of the Hindu upper-caste order as a given. He shows how that might come about and what is to come thereafter.

The book got Ilaiah into serious trouble when some of its chapters were translated into Telugu and published as separate booklets. One chapter characterized Vaishyas or Banias, the trading castes, as 'social smugglers'. It caused a furore in Andhra Pradesh. A mob attacked Ilaiah's car. A member of the Telugu Desam Party said that Ilaiah should be hanged for his views.[22] In Warangal district, protesting Vaishya members threw chappals at Ilaiah. The writer had to seek shelter in a nearby police station.[23] Thereafter, Ilaiah announced that he was placing himself under 'house arrest' and would venture out only after informing the Osmania police station.

A lawyer from the Vaishya community moved a public interest litigation in the Supreme Court seeking a ban on the book on the grounds that it hurt the sentiments of certain communities. A two-judge bench of the Supreme Court dismissed the petition. In a judgment that would have gladdened the hearts of advocates of free speech, the court observed:[24]

> Suffice it to say that when an author writes a book, it is his or her right of expression. We do not think that it would be appropriate under Article 32 of the Constitution of India that this court should ban the book. Any request for banning a book of the present nature has to be strictly scrutinised because every author or writer has a fundamental right to speak out ideas freely and express thoughts adequately. Curtailment of an individual writer/author's right to freedom of speech and expression should never be lightly viewed.

Post-Hindu India is not as analytical and rigorous as *Why I Am Not a Hindu*. The controlled rage of the latter seems to have given way to an emotional outburst in the former. It's almost as if the frustrations of the intervening decade have got to Ilaiah. He's impatient for change, even a revolution. In some parts of the book, it seemed to me that Ilaiah was lashing out wildly.

I exchanged some correspondence with Ilaiah by email and had a lengthy chat with him over the phone. I told him I was going over to Hyderabad and would like to meet. Ilaiah readily agreed.

The omens for our meeting were not good. I called Ilaiah after reaching Hyderabad and asked to meet him the next day. He said he was in hospital looking after his brother, who was in the ICU. 'Let us try to contact each other tomorrow,' he said somewhat uncertainly.

The next morning, Ilaiah called to say that I should meet him at the hospital. He gave me the room number and time. I arrived at the hospital at the appointed time and went up to the room he had mentioned. A lady opened the door and said, 'Professor not here.' She then said something in Telugu. I was lost.

I called Ilaiah and told him that I had arrived. Ilaiah said there had been a change of plan. His brother's wife had decided to stay at the hospital and he was at his brother's flat (where he had been living for many years). He suggested we meet at the flat which was close to the hospital. 'Just give the phone to the driver, I will give him directions,' Ilaiah said.

I went back to my taxi only to find the driver missing. I couldn't reach him on my mobile phone. I called Ilaiah and told him. We decided that we would meet at the hospital as planned.

It was hot and uncomfortable in the street outside. I went into the lobby and found myself sitting outside the Emergency room next to anxious relatives. It seemed to me that the Hindu gods were not well disposed towards a Tamil Brahmin meeting up with someone who had challenged the basic tenets of the faith.

Within minutes, Ilaiah showed up and walked briskly up the steps of the hospital to shake hands. He's a short, slightly built man with a professorial air about him. We took the elevator up to the hospital room. Ilaiah sat on the hospital bed and motioned me to one of the chairs nearby.

I am somewhat flustered and vexed by the confusion of the past half an hour. It's rather warm inside the room. The fan whirring above offers little comfort. I tell Ilaiah that I would have been happy to call off the meeting, given that he has a serious medical problem on his hands. Ilaiah brushes aside my concern. 'No, no. My brother has had a long-standing valve problem. He has been in and out of hospital often.'

I begin by asking him about one of his pet themes, spiritual equality. By this, Ilaiah means that the lower castes must have the same spiritual rights as the upper castes, especially the right to become priests. It's an idea that looms large in *Post-Hindu India*. Ilaiah launches a no-holds-barred assault on Brahmins, whom he calls 'spiritual fascists'.[25]

Brahmins, he says, used their position as the priestly class to exclude a large number of people from the realm of God, something that no other religion does. They defined knowledge in narrow religious terms, not in the broader term of knowing the world in which we live. They chose to exclude the masses from education. They created the system of untouchability. Spiritual fascism is the equivalent in the spiritual realm of political fascism. It's about a minority controlling and subjugating the majority by colonizing the minds of the latter.

I ask him why it is such a big deal for a Dalitbahujan to become a priest—I don't particularly care whether I or my son can get to recite the Vedas or the Upanishads in some temple. 'But you have a choice,' he counters. 'That matters.'

I am not convinced. 'Don't you think other things matter more today, such as political empowerment? After all, it's the economic advancement of Dalitbahujans that we are interested in. There are things other than becoming a priest that could be helpful to Dalitbahujans. Reservations in the private sector, for instance.'

Ilaiah grants that other means of uplifting Dalitbahujans have their uses. 'But religion is crucial to philosophy,' he insists. 'Brahmins denied religion to the lower castes. That has stalled their growth.' Spiritual equality matters, he says emphatically. 'Let a Dalit be appointed as a priest in the Tirupati temple. At one stroke, untouchability will vanish.' Ilaiah says he compared the introductory pages of the Rig Veda, the Bible and the Koran. The Bible alone recognizes workers fully, he says, the Koran to a lesser extent. The Rig Veda not at all.

The absence of spiritual equality doesn't seem to have turned Dalitbahujans away from Hinduism, I tell Ilaiah. I tell him about a Dalit student who had come to see me the previous week. He was doing his doctorate in the US and he stayed with his parents in a slum in Ahmedabad when he visited India. I asked the student whether he and his fellow Dalits felt they were not part of Hinduism. He said he didn't think so. They were very much part of Hindu festivals, for instance.

That Dalits and OBCs are getting into the IITs and IIMs and landing prized jobs seems far more important to me than the spiritual equality that Ilaiah aspires for. Ilaiah seems not to have noticed this phenomenon or given it the importance it deserves. He has railed against the IITs and IIMs, saying that these do not cater to the needs of Indian society or the Indian economy. They are only vehicles for the advancement of the upper castes:[26]

> We should close down the IITs and the IIMs as they pander to the upper-caste economy of the country. Those who pass out from these institutes use their technical and managerial skills to earn dollars abroad. Are they using their skill sets to the benefit of the agro-based economy of the country? Tell me, with rising incomes of our B-school graduates are farmer suicide rates coming down? So what is the use of such education if it cannot be put to any use within the country or for the uplift of the majority of the population who live in villages?

The IITs and IIMs have had reservations for SCs/STs since their inception. Reservations for OBCs commenced about a decade ago. When it comes to jobs, the preferences of the SC/ST/OBC students are no different from those of the upper castes. They tend to opt for the same highly paid jobs that the upper-caste students do. I tell Ilaiah that he is wrong in supposing that the preferences of IIT/IIM students are caste-specific.

I cite the case of an OBC student whom I met over a pre-convocation dinner at IIM Ahmedabad. She introduced me to her parents. Her father was a tailor from a remote village in Andhra Pradesh. Her mother stood bashfully by his side. The girl had got off to a flying start with a job in London. I tell Ilaiah, 'You will agree that is quite a transformation for the family. Isn't it wonderful that the IIMs should be part of such a transformation?' Ilaiah is silent—he seems to see my point.

In *Why I Am Not a Hindu*, Ilaiah writes that despite their lack of access to formal education or knowledge, Dalitbahujans have accumulated knowledge and expertise about farm productivity, cross-breeding of seeds, herbal medicines, the making of leather, shoes, ropes, etc. Physical labour was never separated from mental labour.

This is not true of upper castes, he says. They tend to look down upon manual labour of any sort and are solely preoccupied with mental labour. Brahmins are to be found today as priests and members of what we might call white-collar vocations: teaching, politics, bureaucracy, medicine, engineering, etc. Seldom are they seen in 'productive work' (by which he means work that involves manual labour), such as the production of food, washing of clothes, milk production, etc. Brahmin knowledge is divorced from any creative interaction with nature.

The delinking of the two has implications for the development of science and technology. 'Hindus [by which Ilaiah means upper castes] do not have the life experiences that lead them to experiment or to take risks, without which scientific knowledge cannot develop. Experimentation and taking risks become possible only when consciousness is grounded in a variety of real-life tasks . . .'[27]

There is some merit in Ilaiah's contentions. Many have commented on the lack of creativity amongst Indians in matters of science and technology, the failure to come up with original, world-class products, for instance. Yet, to ascribe this entirely to cultural factors may be an exaggeration. Upper-caste Indians who migrate to the West have been in the front rank of a variety of creative fields, including science and technology. Some of the world's leading information technology companies are headed by upper-caste persons of Indian origin. The fact that they did not grow up doing manual labour does not seem as serious a limitation as Ilaiah makes out.

Similarly, lack of manual training does not prevent scientists, economists, historians, mathematicians and computer experts—the people who can be said to be the Brahmins of every society—elsewhere in the world from being creative. It is not as if members of the knowledge economy must soil their hands before coming to grips with theoretical concepts.

I bring up this point with Ilaiah. I suggest that it's a little odd that he should regard only manual labour as 'productive'. By that token, the economies of the Western world in which services dominate (and most of these are white-collar jobs) must be regarded as unproductive. And yet it is high productivity that accounts for their high income levels.

Ilaiah is unfazed. 'Man and nature are linked through production,' he tells me solemnly. And yet the Hindu texts give little importance to production. 'They give centrality to procreation and protection,' he says. 'This is not true of Jewish religious texts.' *Post-Hindu India* makes the point that the education of every Jewish student involved knowledge of some manual art. Ilaiah believes this is the reason the Jews have produced some of the foremost thinkers in the world. 'The contribution of Jews is far greater than that of Brahmins,' Ilaiah tells me triumphantly.

* * *

When you read the chapter 'Social Smugglers' in *Post-Hindu India*, you understand why the book evoked such a fierce reaction from the Vaishya or Bania community. The chapter is one long diatribe against the community.

Ilaiah explains why Banias may be justly characterized as smugglers. Smuggling is the act of taking something secretly and in defiance of rules and regulations. Trading or business in other societies is open to all. In India, however, the Brahmins assigned this role exclusively to one caste, the Vaishyas. This was not a contract that had the sanction of the other communities. Ilaiah implies this is a violation of commonly accepted societal norms and hence qualifies as 'smuggling'—the Vaishyas or Banias were given exclusive licence to 'smuggle' grains, commodities and the like. It seems a rather extravagant interpretation of the word.

There is another sense in which Ilaiah seems to regard Vaishyas as smugglers. There is the long-standing practice in the community, he says, of *Guptadhana* or wealth that is kept in hiding in order to avoid tax. He says the practice began when there were Sudra kings in several places in the country and it has continued since. It has served two functions. One, it helped the Vaishyas bribe state officials and enjoy privileges in the villages. Two, it became a source of usury or moneylending.

Ilaiah contends that the Hindu religion, unlike Islam or Christianity, has no restrictions on usury or the interest rates charged on loans. Usurious lending ensured that peasants could never accumulate capital. He sees the Nehruvian state as one based on collusion between the Brahmins who controlled the state apparatus and the Banias who controlled the economy.

Ilaiah also sees the Bania community as the principal source of corruption in the country. He says even the British officials were not immune to the corrupt ways of the Banias. Ilaiah writes:[28]

> . . . there is no business community in the world that can match the Baniyas in corrupting the state machinery and operating businesses by 'walking over the law'. Even now, they are masters of this practice. The Indian capital is finding it difficult to overcome corruption as the Baniya capital in our markets has made it a systemic process.

One should not be surprised that the mobs went after Ilaiah.

There is a third sense in which Ilaiah refers to Banias as social smugglers. He says that Banias have 'perfected the art of using "lies" as an instrument of business'.[29] They never make the purchase price public, for instance—it varies from customer to customer. They quote lower prices to the lower castes while buying and higher prices while selling. They cheat on weights. And so on.

Ilaiah is clearly getting carried away. Sharp practices in business are the norm worldwide. Manipulation of accounts, money laundering, tax evasion, violations of laws and regulations—these have come to be associated with some of the biggest names in business worldwide. Think WorldCom, Enron, Volkswagen, the collapse of banks in the financial crisis of 2007–08. To suggest that unethical business practices are the monopoly of the Bania community in India does seem an exaggeration.

There are other passages where Ilaiah's prejudice shows clearly. He says that Banias have spent a large amount of business capital on propitiating the gods through elaborate spiritual rites. 'But no amount of spiritual expenditure and wastage of humanly useful wealth could save the epicentre of the Baniya exploitative capital—Gujarat—from the disastrous earthquake on 26 June 2001 . . . The Brahman-Baniya state of Gujarat did not possess the internal strength to withstand such calamities.'[30] The earthquake of 2001 in Gujarat did cause enormous devastation. However, the state showed enormous resilience in overcoming its effects, contrary to what Ilaiah says.

It is Ilaiah's comment on the assassination of Gandhi by Nathuram Godse that takes the cake. He says Gandhi stood for truth and simplicity. His stand was resented by the Brahmin-Bania combine, both of which favour lies and expensive living. 'He was killed by the Brahmanic forces of India for preaching the un-Hindu ethics of simplicity and truth-telling.'[31] This is indeed news to many of us. We thought that Gandhi was assassinated because right-wing extremists didn't approve of his attitude towards Muslims and the state of Pakistan.

* * *

In *Post-Hindu India*, Ilaiah lists other failings of the Hindu religion, failings for which he holds Brahmins responsible. Hindu temples are not places of prayer alone; they are the means of accumulating wealth through donations and offerings to the gods. They are not accessible to the Dalitbahujans who built them in the first place. (This is not entirely true today. Important temples, such as the Tirupati temple in Andhra Pradesh, host pilgrims from across the entire social spectrum.) Their sacred books talk of killing and the pursuit of pleasure. There is no mention of healing the sick, caring for the old, human achievement and failure, compassion or equality. They are written in a language, Sanskrit, that is alien to ordinary people. Prayer is not a public affair, as in other religions, but something that is done in secret (again, a questionable proposition, given the public manner in which major Hindu festivals are celebrated today). The gods interact exclusively with Brahmins, unlike the god in Christianity or Islam who is accessible to all. These are all facets of the 'spiritual fascism' that Hinduism has come to represent.

Ilaiah's contention that Hinduism is alone among religions in glorifying war and warrior gods and that this is what explains the latent violence in Hinduism is a little hard to digest. It may well be, as he contends, that killing has no role among the gods of Islam or Christianity. But whatever the texts of these religions may say, countless wars have been fought in their name (and in the name of other religions). The religions may not glorify violence but its adherents have not eschewed violence.

Ilaiah's point that Brahmins have fostered a system that has failed to harness the creative energies of the majority of the population is well taken. His contention that Hindu religious literature has been used to perpetuate the domination of the Brahmins is compelling. His observation that the writings of Raja Ram Mohan Roy, Aurobindo Ghose, Vivekananda and S. Radhakrishnan are notable for their complete silence on untouchability and, indeed, on the very existence of the

Dalitbahujans is damning. However, he does spoil his case with statements that appear too sweeping.

Here is an example. 'The social process of reading books, of interpretation of the words and sentences written in the books handed down by the positive prophets in the process of evolution of different religions is totally absent among the Hindus and also the Dalitbahujans.'[32] This is patently incorrect. Few books have been read, quoted and dissected as much as the Ramayana, Mahabharata and the Bhagavad Gita. These books have had a profound influence on the everyday lives of Hindus.

In another place, Ilaiah talks of the sari as an 'undignified' dress, one that leaves parts of the body uncovered. He sees it as an aspect of the fascist attitude of Hinduism.[33] Well, the burka, as he grudgingly concedes, is no less oppressive. Christianity, as we know, allows dresses that expose a great deal more. Using the dress code, past or present, to judge a religion can be highly misleading.

Ilaiah also has a tendency to ascribe all of India's ills to the Hindu religion when, in fact, many of these are aspects of a low level of economic development and are independent of religion. He writes, 'The Hindu society has not produced any major scientist or thinker whose research has influenced the global knowledge system.'[34]

This is just not true. One can think of scientists such as C.V. Raman and S.N. Bose who made an impact at the international level. If one includes non-resident Indians, that is, Indians who were born and educated in India and then pursued higher studies abroad, there is a galaxy of leading Indian researchers in science, economics, finance and technology. If India's impact on global knowledge has not been greater, it is because India is still a low-income economy. Buddhist Sri Lanka, atheistic or Confucian China, Christian South Africa and Islamic Pakistan have not produced a host of great thinkers in modern times, that is, thinkers who made a global impact. To my mind, this has to do with lack of economic development, not with a nation's religion.

True, to the extent education is made available to larger numbers of people, the quality of scientific and other output can be expected to go up. But this is a long-drawn-out process. Communist China's early investment in education and its rapid economic growth in the past three decades have yet to make it a world leader in scientific research. The end of Hinduism or the reform of Hinduism as Ilaiah envisages are unlikely to propel India into thought leadership in quick time. Thought leadership is a function of economic development, and there are factors other than cultural change that are crucial to economic development. Ilaiah must be careful not to overstate his case.

* * *

How do the Dalitbahujans free themselves from upper-caste domination and come into their own? Ilaiah believes there are two options. Either the upper castes opt for major reform and confer spiritual equality on the lower castes. Or the Dalitbahujans walk out of the Hindu fold.

In *Post-Hindu India*, Ilaiah seems to think that the chances of major reform within Hindu society are rather bleak. The conditions are ripe for a major confrontation, perhaps a violent one if the upper castes persist with their ways. 'India,' he writes ominously, 'is moving towards a major civil war . . . one that the Brahmanical forces have avoided for centuries.'[35]

He does not see this as a problem or a matter of regret. Societies throughout the world have often undergone upheaval and change through civil wars. That is how the existing order is overthrown and a new order is born. Ilaiah remarks candidly,

A civil war with progressive ideology is a necessary evil of every upward moving society. Social upheavals with a vision of change to establish better human relations and equality as an essential goal of human beings are necessary evils. The evil of civil war is preferable to the evil of caste degradation of the society.[36]

Sudras have gained entry into temples but they cannot qualify as priests. The Sudras have access to a church, a mosque or a vihara (a Buddhist place of worship) and they can also become priests in those religions if they choose to convert. Yet that very freedom is denied them in the Hindu religion. 'The position of Shudras in Hinduism,' Ilaiah writes trenchantly, 'is like that of a peon in an office.' He has no rights to promotion, even if he has money of his own or commands power in his own vocation. In the Hindu office, the Sudra is a subservient nobody.[37]

Ilaiah believes that, following the mass conversion to Buddhism under Ambedkar and the leadership provided by some Dalit intellectuals, Dalits are reasonably well placed to emancipate themselves by walking out of Hinduism. However, the Sudras or OBCs have not had a leader of the stature of Ambedkar and continue to be intellectual slaves of the upper castes. They lack consciousness of their own contribution and of their prolonged slavery. The upper castes have exploited the many layers of castes that obtain among the Sudras in order to prevent unity amongst them. Ilaiah urges the Sudras to rise in revolt against the upper castes in order to assert their right to equality in the spiritual realm. He spells out how they might do so.

The OBCs need to challenge the basic premises of Hinduism and to assert all that is good in the Dalitbahujan culture and that has been suppressed in the texts written by the upper castes.

The anti-Brahmanic civil war has to attack all that is Brahmanic and Hindu, because the entire cultural idiom of Hinduism is built in the image of the Brahman man-woman life and relations. All the Brahmanic modes of life were standardized to humiliate the productive culture and further the hegemony of the parasite culture. The image of the productive mass, their

idiom, their man-woman relations, their dress code, food habits
and linguistic expressions—all were constructed as spiritually
unworthy and culturally unfair. The civil war must put the
culture of the productive mass at a hegemonic position and
degrade all that is Brahminic.[38]

To put it simply, the Dalitbahujans must regain their pride. That
is what the Self-Respect movement in the south in the late 1920s,
started by E.V. Ramaswamy Naicker, was about and it did change
equations among the castes in the south quite a bit.

Ilaiah does not see political democracy and the political
empowerment of Dalitbahujans as solving the problem of spiritual
inequality. He is convinced that the institutions of democracy
have been manipulated by the upper castes so that the nature of
Hinduism remains unchanged.

Now the only alternative left for the religion is to die, as such
spiritual fascism does not contribute to the transformation and
development of the Dalitbahujans of India . . . The civil war
that will take place in India will perhaps be the last major civil
war in the world, which will involve the liberation of about
seven hundred million people from the most primitive form of
slavery, that is, spiritual slavery.[39]

Ilaiah sees the decline of Hinduism as inevitable. Hinduism has
yielded to Buddhism, Islam and Christianity in the past thanks
to its deep-seated internal divisions. Out of the original Indian
subcontinent, three Islamic countries have been born, Afghanistan,
Pakistan and Bangladesh. He believes the hold of Hinduism will
continue to weaken in the years to come.

It wasn't clear to me what Ilaiah meant when he said
Hinduism would die. Did he mean that Hindu temples, gods,
scriptures, festivals would all cease to be and that people would
cease calling themselves Hindu? This seemed pretty far-fetched.

Even if Dalitbahujans walked out of Hinduism, there would still be practising Hindus left. Or did he mean that Hinduism would undergo radical reform, meaning castes would not exist or at least inequality among castes would not exist? Or would we end up having a broader narrative of Hinduism, one that included the culture of the Dalitbahujans?

I posed these alternatives to Ilaiah by email. He wasn't willing to make any firm prediction and, indeed, he seemed to leave open the possibility of reform and inclusion in Hinduism.

Ilaiah wrote back:

> Any social scientist's prediction does not move in one direction. The fact is that the Hindu system is not spiritual democracy. As of now it operates as spiritual fascism. Its transformation may take any direction based on the direction of the oppressing Brahminism. It can avert civil war or it may lead to a civil war. With BJP in power symptoms of civil war are deepening as it approves [of] spiritual fascism . . . Reform direction, if there was any, is getting derailed. Spiritual democratic values are being dubbed as foreign . . . My writings could be understood by any reader in one's own perspective. You could come to any conclusion.

Ilaiah's response suggests to me that, for all the strident tone of *Post-Hindu India* and its call to civil war against the Brahminical order, he was still leaving the door open for Hinduism to reform itself. Reform or perish—that seems to be his message to the upper castes.

* * *

Like Ambedkar and, indeed, like many rationalists who would like a place for religion in their lives, Ilaiah has been drawn to Gautam Buddha. His doctoral thesis, as we mentioned earlier, was about Buddha's political philosophy. It was later developed and published as a book, *God as Political Philosopher: Buddha's Challenge to Brahminism*.[40]

Buddha is seen by most people as a saint and a religious reformer. Ilaiah portrays him as a political thinker, who preceded Greek thinkers such as Aristotle, Plato and Socrates. Ilaiah shows that Buddha thought through the ideas of the state, society, democracy, justice, class and caste and the role of women in ways that were astonishingly ahead of his time.

Buddha's understanding of the state was quite different from the Hindu view. The Hindus believed that the state was divine in origin. The Hindu thinkers, Kautilya and Manu, were of the view that human beings were selfish and depraved in nature. God created a ruler to maintain order in society. Some of the Hindu scriptures make it clear that the ruler's duty is to respect and protect the Brahmins and to use force to punish those who threatened the existing order.

Buddha, in contrast, thought of the state as emerging from a social contract amongst people. In doing so, he anticipated Western thinkers such as Rousseau and Locke. Buddha gives a simple illustration of his point. Disputes may arise amongst people, say, over some person taking rice from another. Then, the question of giving punishment to the thief arises; in other words, the need for a governing agency. The people then decide that they would choose from amongst themselves individuals—not any one individual—who are the 'largest, the handsomest, the strongest' and allow them to rule over the rest.

Note the elements in the above formulation of a state: entrusting rule to a class of people (and not to any one ruler); election through a democratic process; and the importance of attributes other than strength in the choice of rulers. Ilaiah also highlights the fact that Buddha thought highly of the tribal republics and urged the monarchies that surrounded them not to attack the former. Buddha was thus pro-republican and anti-monarchical by instinct.

Not just for his time but even by contemporary standards, Buddha was thus revolutionary in his thinking.

Ilaiah contrasts Buddha's idea of justice with that of the Hindu idea of justice. Dharma or justice in the Hindu scheme of things was the performance of one's duty or role in accordance with the varna system. This was to be ensured through coercion if required. Buddha's dhamma emphasized equality and non-violence. His singular achievement was the creation of the sangha, the body in which he gave expression to his ideas of how society should be organized.

Admission to the sangha was open to all and was based on approval by vote of the existing members. The sangha even had a returning officer (a person who conducts elections and announces the results) who was duly elected by the members. It had elected committees to whom work was delegated. Thus, democracy was the essence of the sangha's functioning.

Ilaiah gives vivid illustrations of how Buddha sought to inculcate a democratic culture in the sangha. When a woman sought admission, Buddha refused. One of Buddha's disciples, Ananda, then pleaded the case for women, quoting Buddha as saying that women too could attain nirvana. If so, how could they be denied admission? The matter was debated and the sangha decided to admit women into its fold. No preference was shown to Buddha's own son or his cousin—administrative positions were assigned based entirely on merit. Ilaiah quotes Ambedkar as saying in India's Constituent Assembly, 'Buddha was the torchbearer of democracy and an ardent exponent of liberty, equality and fraternity.'[41]

Buddha was equally forward-looking when it came to property rights. He was opposed to both state ownership and private ownership of property. He could see that state ownership led to benefits being conferred on the ruling class. Private property inevitably leads to accumulation by a few and destitution of the vast majority. Buddha opted, therefore, for communal ownership of property. The sangha had no landed property but it had other property conferred on it by patrons. Buddha himself took the lead in enacting laws on the regulation and maintenance of such property.

Ilaiah makes the interesting point that Buddha, for all his emphasis on equality and opposition to discrimination, could not ignore the compulsions of the times in which he lived. In opening the sangha to all irrespective of caste, he took the Brahminical order head-on. However, he did bar soldiers in service, debtors and slaves seeking asylum.

The bar on debtors seems surprising given that these must have been the very poor seeking to escape the tyranny of creditors. Under the law obtaining then, a creditor had claims to the very body of somebody who had defaulted on his debt obligations. Buddha seemed to compromise on this issue given the pressures he faced from powerful elements in society. Similarly, he may have not pressed the issue of slaves joining the sangha as they were crucial to the requirements of production.

Western scholars have long suggested that political thought originated in the West with the Greeks and that ancient India had nothing to offer other than religious dogma. Ilaiah's book on the Buddha shows that they are mistaken. Buddha predated Western political thinkers by offering what is, even by today's standards, a modern political philosophy. It is a humanistic philosophy that places man and worldly arrangements at the centre of things. Ilaiah also shows that Indian scholars, who attempt to portray Buddha's thinking as part of Hindu thought, are thoroughly mistaken. Buddha's thinking was a revolt against Hindu thought and the caste system on which it was premised.

I have earlier mentioned Ilaiah's propensity to overstate his case. While chronicling the story of Buddha's life, Ilaiah talks of the moment in which Buddha attained enlightenment. By almost all accounts, the moment of enlightenment, which happened under the sprawling tree at Gaya, was a mystical moment in which the

Buddha's separative identity dissolved and he became one with the universal consciousness, so to speak. Ilaiah ventures to suggest that the moment of enlightenment was one in which Buddha could see clearly the political system the world needed! This is a leap that will confound admirers of both Buddha and Ilaiah.

* * *

I was curious to know about Ilaiah's views on Ambedkar and Gandhi. He hasn't written at great length on either. His views on the two leaders are to be found mostly in assorted newspaper and magazine articles.

Ambedkar is today a national icon. The two major national parties, the BJP and the Congress, have both been eager to appropriate him, with an eye to the votes of the Dalits. Ambedkar statues have proliferated all over the country. A collection of his works is being brought out decades after the publication of the works of Gandhi and Nehru.

Ambedkar was a great scholar and a prolific writer. He combined many roles in politics—leader of the Dalits, member of the Viceroy's Council, chairman of the Drafting Committee of the Indian Constitution and minister in Nehru's cabinet, and yet found the time for numerous publications, many of enormous depth. It is astonishing that whole generations of Indians after Independence have gone through school and college without having encountered any samples of Ambedkar's work. It is only amongst the Dalits that his works are known and shared zealously.

In an introduction to a recent edition of Ambedkar's book, *Riddles in Hinduism*, Ilaiah explores Ambedkar's disillusionment with Hinduism, culminating eventually in his converting to Buddhism along with half a million other Dalits.[42] Ilaiah quotes Ambedkar as saying in 1935, 'I had the misfortune of being born with the stigma of an Untouchable. However, it is not my fault; but I will not die a Hindu, for this is in my power.'

To Ilaiah, it is a mystery that Ambedkar should have regarded himself as a Hindu at all. As we saw earlier, Ilaiah does not think that there is anything Hindu about Dalitbahujans. Ambedkar himself was of this view early in his political career. In 1919, he had argued before a British committee that a British census of 1911 had regarded the 'Untouchables' as a separate category from the Hindus. By 1916, the term 'Depressed Classes' had been used to categorize them. In 1935, under the Government of India Act, they became the Scheduled Castes.

Of the British census of 1911, Ilaiah writes:

> The basis adopted by the census commissioner for separation is to be found in his circular, in which he laid down certain tests for the purpose of distinguishing these two classes. Among those who were not 100 per cent Hindus were included castes and tribes which: a) deny the supremacy of the Brahmins; b) do not receive the mantra from a Brahmin or other recognised Hindu guru; c) deny the authority of the Vedas; d) do not worship the Hindu gods; e) are not served by good Brahmins as family priests; f) have no Brahmin priests at all; g) are denied access to the interior of the Hindu temples; h) are said to cause 'pollution' by touch or within a certain distance; i) bury their dead; j) eat beef and have no reverence for cow.

Ambedkar argued that even if one of these criteria were not met, a person could not be regarded as 100 per cent Hindu. In *Annihilation of Caste* (to which I have alluded in my essay on Arundhati Roy), Ambedkar was clear that Hinduism was incapable of evolving into an egalitarian religion. Why, then, did his formal repudiation of Hinduism and his conversion to Buddhism happen only towards the end of his life?

Ilaiah suggests that, in his early years as an activist, Ambedkar believed that Hinduism was capable of reform, that he could appeal to the reason of upper castes. Ilaiah thinks this was an error of judgement on Ambedkar's part. After making the statement quoted above (about not dying as a Hindu), Ambedkar should have immediately converted to Buddhism or even to Islam or Christianity. Instead, Ambedkar stayed for long within the Hindu fold and helped draft a Constitution that categorizes Buddhists, Sikhs and Jains as Hindus. This mistake of Ambedkar's has allowed Hindus to co-opt Buddhists. Buddha himself has come to be absorbed into Hinduism as one of the ten avatars of the Hindu God, Vishnu.

In the early 1950s, Ambedkar made a valiant attempt to reform Hinduism by piloting the Hindu Code Bill as law minister in Nehru's cabinet. The fierce opposition to the bill from various quarters seems to have convinced Ambedkar of the futility of his efforts. He resigned from Nehru's cabinet and eventually shed his Hindu identity as well.

Recent years have seen an enormous revival of Ambedkar— Ilaiah says that Ambedkar has been discovered by most Indians only post 1990.[43] He credits Kanshi Ram, the founder of the BSP, for the higher profile that Ambedkar has acquired post-1990. Ilaiah also thinks that former Prime Minister V.P. Singh helped enhance Ambedkar's image by implementing the Mandal Commission report on reservations in government institutions for OBCs (mostly the Sudra caste). The OBCs then began to see Ambedkar as their great saviour—after all, the idea of advancing disadvantaged sections of society through reservations was his.

Three other events served to boost Ambedkar's image to its present level. He was awarded the Bharat Ratna, India's highest civilian award, in 1990 by the V.P. Singh government. His birthday came to be declared a national holiday. The Congress government under Rajiv Gandhi enacted the Scheduled Caste and Scheduled Tribe (Prevention of Atrocities) Act, which came to be implemented by the V.P. Singh government. Amongst Dalits, Ambedkar's stature has risen so high that the slightest insult to his memory (such as defacement of any of his statues) risks sparking a riot.

Ilaiah sees the BJP's attempt to appropriate Ambedkar as entirely opportunistic. He believes that had the BJP been in the Congress's position in 1946–47, it would never have got Ambedkar to help draft the Indian Constitution. The RSS and the Hindu Mahasabha, which are the political mentors of today's BJP, had no use for Ambedkar's vision. 'They were looking backwards to *Manudharma.*' (Ilaiah is alluding to the laws laid down by Manu in ancient India.) Ilaiah writes caustically, 'The BJP's ownership is quite recent and artificial. As a radical Hindu party, controlled by a fundamentalist organization like the RSS, it cannot really own Ambedkarism as a philosophical and social ideology. His mode of Buddhism can never be reconciled with radical Hinduism of the RSS type.'[44]

Ilaiah thinks that Modi's espousal of Ambedkar is driven entirely by the need for Dalit and OBC votes. Without those votes, he would never have become prime minister. 'But he has not taken a single concrete step to expand Ambedkarism and advance the position of Dalits/STs/OBCs.'

Ambedkar awakened the Dalits to their oppression. He showed them how the upper castes had been exploiting them. Says Ilaiah, 'That is the greatest service that Ambedkar rendered to this nation. He made the wretched of the Indian earth stand up and fight as they did on April 2, 2018. Nobody can set the clock back now.' (In April 2018, thousands of Dalits all over India protested against an order of the Supreme Court on the Scheduled Caste and Scheduled Tribe [Prevention of Atrocities] Act which they perceived as diluting the protection offered by the Act. In the violence that followed, ten people died and hundreds were injured. In October 2019, the Supreme Court recalled its directions of March 2018.)[45]

On Gandhi, Ilaiah has said different things at different times. His views seem to have evolved over time. In an undated piece that appears to have been written some years ago, he had scathing remarks to make about Gandhi. He wrote:

The majority of educated dalits do not accept the epithet 'the father of the nation' for Gandhi. Instead, they address Bhimrao Ramji Ambedkar as the 'father of the nation'. Is that because we live in two different nations: India and Bharat? . . . For the liberal, globalised intellectual of India, Gandhi is the solution to all problems. However, in village India he is a faint memory, with dilapidated statues here and there, and a customary lesson in some school textbooks.[46]

Ilaiah quotes Ambedkar as saying about Gandhi, 'Unfortunately, the Congress chose Mr Gandhi as its representative. A worse person could not have been chosen to guide India's destiny.' He adds,

Gandhi did not prove him wrong when he said, 'The Congress has from its very commencement taken up the cause of the so-called "untouchables".' He saw untouchability in 1931 as 'so-called', not real, and the untouchables as people who deserve to be referred to in quotes. Ambedkar understood the diabolism of Gandhian linguistic engagement with Dalits.

Like many other Dalit commentators, Ilaiah seemed to view Gandhi's gestures towards Dalits as mere tokenism. Gandhi was in favour of abolishing untouchability but was not willing to go beyond that. He certainly did not favour Dalits becoming priests in temples. Ilaiah concludes, 'For many illiterate villages, he is the *thathaa* (grandfather) of *tamashas*.'

I have seen Ilaiah lash out against Gandhi in a TV discussion on the relevance of Gandhi today. Gandhi's semi-naked appearance, he suggested, had no meaning for Dalits who had been semi-naked for centuries. Gandhi wrote important works such as *Hind Swaraj* in Gujarati; what the Dalits needed was English. For Gandhi, *Ram Rajya* (the rule of Lord Rama) was the ideal; for Dalits, it was something of a nightmare as it was a world full of violence.[47]

In Ilaiah's introduction to a collection of his articles, he has rejected the idea of Gandhi as a prophet of non-violence. How could that be when Gandhi operated within the framework of the Ramayana and the Bhagavad Gita, both of which built their philosophy around war and violence, he asks.[48]

At some point, however, Ilaiah seems to have changed his position on Gandhi. In an article in the same collection, Ilaiah sings a very different tune:[49]

> Unlike Vivekananda, Gandhi was critical of Hinduism since he actually shared a lot with Ambedkar on the question of the removal of untouchability and the granting of reservations. Their appreciation and criticism of each other was democratic . . . Gandhi and Ram Manohar Lohia were two upper caste persons who took a stand on reforming the caste system in a radical way, as Ambedkar did. Both belonged to the Bania caste and knew from their own experience, as persons coming from the third group in the social hierarchy, that caste as an institution would never allow democracy to survive. No Brahmin leader felt as strongly as Gandhi and Lohia about transforming the caste system.

These comments came as a surprise to me. I doubt that many other Dalit writers would agree that Ambedkar ever appreciated Gandhi's views or that Gandhi wanted a fundamental transformation in the caste system.

I asked Ilaiah about the contradictory positions he has taken. He admitted that his views about Gandhi had changed with time. 'During my student days, I thought Gandhi was a ruling class agent. I thought his motives were diabolical and that he stood for the caste system. Later, I came to appreciate his positive contributions.'

Ilaiah went on, 'Gandhi was neither a Brahmin nor a Dalit. He was a Baniya. He positioned himself somewhere in the middle when it came to reform of the caste system.' Gandhi, he said, was keen to reform the caste system but he was also conscious of his position as a 'money-mobilizer' for the Congress, a role for which he needed the support of the upper castes.

This conforms to the mainstream view of Gandhi as a cautious and pragmatic reformer. Gandhi was mindful of the inequity of caste but did not want to push for reforms at a pace that would upset the upper castes and jeopardize the primary objective of obtaining freedom from British rule.

I thought it interesting that Ilaiah, who rebels against the mainstream view in so many respects, should be in agreement with it when it came to Gandhi. To me, his changed stance on Gandhi indicates a moderation in his position on Hinduism over time. For all his vehement denunciations of Hinduism and its inequities, he seems willing to settle for gradual reform as long as the intent is genuine. But the coming to power of the BJP at the centre in 2014 may have caused another rethink in his position.

Ilaiah worries about the resurgence in 'cow nationalism', the projection of the cow as a national animal under the present BJP government. He asks why the cow has come to assume so much importance to upper-caste Hindus in a way in which the buffalo has not. There is talk of an Anti-Cow Slaughter Bill but no mention of protecting the buffalo. This, despite the fact that the buffalo produces most of the milk in India. The buffalo's contribution in terms of providing meat, draft power, fuel and fertilizer is also much greater than that of the cow. Yet the Hindu scriptures, while venerating the cow, make no mention of the buffalo.[50]

Gandhi used cow nationalism as part of the anti-British narrative. However, in a historical sense, it had an anti-Dalitbahujan connotation as the buffalo is very dear to Dalitbahujans. It soon acquired an anti-Muslim connotation as well. Ilaiah writes, 'This nationalism metaphor was aimed at constructing the vegetarianism of Brahmins and Baniyas as the superior food culture and more particularly to build an anti-beef position as beef was considered part of the Muslim culture . . . Cow nationalism is a dangerous anti-Dravidian and anti-Dalitbahujan ideology.'

Ilaiah notes that the cow is not exclusive to India; the Euro-American continents survive on the economy of the cow. The buffalo, however, is exclusively Indian. Buffalo nationalism is thus a more authentic and inclusive expression of Indian culture than cow nationalism. Dalitbahujans must, therefore, work towards the construction of buffalo nationalism.

Most of Ilaiah's important works have been published by relatively obscure publishers. They did not get much media coverage when they first came out. Nevertheless, they have come to be widely sold and read. He is today something of an international celebrity. His books are prescribed in foreign universities. He has been invited to leading American universities and to important conferences in Europe and elsewhere. When he came under attack in Andhra Pradesh for calling Banias 'social smugglers', a member of the US Senate spoke up for him. Ilaiah's dissent has come to be heard.

It's a different matter that events have not quite panned out the way Ilaiah had visualized. Not only is the traditional Hindu order not on the verge of dissolution, the forces of Hindutva seem to have the upper hand. Far from walking out of Hinduism, Dalits and OBCs seem to be flocking towards the BJP. The BJP could not have won a majority in Parliament in the elections of 2014 and again in 2019 if the appeal of Hindutva had not transcended the traditional caste divides.

Ilaiah may want the Hindu order to break up but it doesn't seem to be happening in a hurry. His cry for an insurrection against Hinduism has failed to find resonance amongst the toiling masses of India. The rise of Hindu extremism alarms him. If it takes an ugly turn, Ilaiah may well jettison his moderate stance and leap into battle with the forces of reaction.

Ilaiah is important not because he is always right but because he gets us to revisit basic premises about Hinduism. He shines a light on a vast section of Hindu society that has remained in darkness for centuries. As in the case of Ambedkar, his very scholarship and wide-ranging reputation are a rebuke to any notion that the Dalitbahujans are inferior to the upper castes. He is living proof of what the long-suffering Dalits and OBCs are capable of achieving. He is a warning to the Indian elite not to take the masses for granted and a symbol of hope and achievement for the Dalitbahujans.

The Hindu right wing may be furious at the challenges he has thrown to the traditional Hindu order but they dare not harm him. His celebrity status amongst his own people is his protective charm. 'I am safe today,' Ilaiah told me with an air of quiet satisfaction, 'not because of the Indian state but because every village in India has a Bania store. The upper castes know what will happen to them if I am harmed.'

4

David Irving: Maverick Historian

When I included David Irving in the proposal I sent to my publishers, it drew a hostile response. Not Irving!—they seemed to say.

Irving has produced several accounts of World War II that have earned him the title of 'historian'. It's a title that many professional historians dispute. Irving does not have a degree from a university, much less a doctorate, nor has he held any academic position. Moreover, his views on some matters are considered so outrageous that many historians are not willing to take any of his work seriously.

I made out a case saying that, however outrageous one might find some of Irving's views, he has value as a chronicler of World War II. It's a test of liberalism, I wrote, whether we can hear out the Irvings of this world. In a way, that was the point of the book I had proposed. My publishers relented.

Irving provokes widespread revulsion primarily on account of his views on the Holocaust, the extermination of an estimated 6 million Jews during World War II. Irving does not deny that millions of Jews died in concentration camps. He differs from the accepted narrative in two respects. One, he believes that most of the deaths occurred on account of starvation and disease, not in gas chambers. Two, he rejects the idea that the deaths were the result of a systematic plan approved by Adolf Hitler. He believes that Hitler was kept in the dark by his minions and that he got to know about the deaths of Jews in large numbers only towards the end of the War.

To deny that 6 million Jews were killed in an act of genocide is a crime in sixteen countries of Europe. It's called 'Holocaust denial' and the perpetrator is labelled a 'Holocaust denier'. Several civil rights advocates have criticized these laws as repugnant to the spirit of free speech. They say that it should be possible to contest the details of the official version of the Holocaust. And yet to suggest that the number of deaths of Jews was significantly lower than 6 million may be construed as 'Holocaust denial'.

In 2006, Irving was convicted and sentenced to jail for three years in Austria on the charge of Holocaust denial. Irving appealed to the highest court in Austria and got his sentence reduced from three to two years, with one of those two years to be served on probation—in effect, a one-year jail sentence.[1]

* * *

The serious setback to Irving's standing as a historian had come many years before the jail sentence in Austria. In 1992, Irving signed a contract with the publishing house Macmillan for a book on Joseph Goebbels, minister of propaganda in Hitler's cabinet during the War. Jewish community leaders were outraged and lodged protests with Macmillan. A member of the Yad Vashem Trust, which works to preserve the memory of the Holocaust, said, 'How can you entrust the writing of a biography of a key figure in history to a person who denies the existence of a period in history, in the face of eyewitness testimony of thousands of people who were there? Anything that gives Irving more respectability by a renowned publisher or newspaper is to be deprecated.'[2] Macmillan cancelled the contract.

In 1995, St Martin's Press of New York City agreed to publish the book. Again, various Jewish organizations got in on the act. St Martin's Press came under pressure not to publish the book. Among those involved in lobbying against the book was Deborah Lipstadt, a historian specializing in Jewish studies and the Holocaust.

St Martin's Press' decision to drop the book came in for criticism from serious historians and writers. An eminent British historian, Hugh Trevor-Roper, called the decision 'craven'. An American professor of history, who did not quite appreciate the conclusions that Irving had drawn in the book, nevertheless felt there was enough serious history in the book to merit publication.[3]

The writer Christopher Hitchens observed, 'St. Martin's has disgraced the business of publishing and degraded the practice of debate. David Irving is not just a Fascist historian. He is also a great historian of Fascism.'[4] Hitchens argued that Irving deserved a hearing. He quoted British historian John Harris as saying, 'Few contemporary scholars of the Third Reich have his depth of knowledge, virtually none has met as many of its leading figures and nobody, surely, has unearthed more original material—a private archive known as the "Irving Collection", always generously made available to other researchers, which weighs more than half a ton.' Hitchens added, 'His studies of the Churchill-Roosevelt relationship, of the bombing of Dresden, of the campaigns of Rommel and others, are such that you can't say you know the subject *at all* unless you have read them.'[5]

Hitchens sought the opinion of Raul Hilberg, a historian at the University of Vermont, who was acknowledged as an authority on the Holocaust. Hilberg told him, 'If these people (that is, people such as Irving) want to speak, let them. It only leads those of us who do research to re-examine what we might have considered as obvious. And that's useful for us. I have quoted Eichmann references that come from a neo-Nazi publishing house. I am not for taboos and I am not for repression.'

Following the rejection of his book by two major publishers, Irving decided to publish his book on Goebbels on his own in 1996. *Goebbels: Mastermind of the Third Reich* was reviewed in the *New York Review of Books*, the *Washington Post* and the *New York Times*, among other publications.

Writing in the *New York Review of Books*, a respected Stanford University historian, Gordon A. Craig, remarked, 'Silencing Mr. Irving would be a high price to pay for freedom from the annoyance that he causes us. The fact is that he knows more about National Socialism than most professional scholars in his field, and students of the years 1933–1945 owe more than they are always willing to admit to his energy as a researcher and to the scope and vigor of his publications.'[6]

Craig added, 'It is always difficult for the non-historian to remember that there is nothing absolute about historical truth. What we consider as such is only an estimation, based upon what the best available evidence tells us. It must constantly be tested against new information and new interpretations that appear, however implausible they may be, or it will lose its vitality and degenerate into dogma or shibboleth. Such people as David Irving, then, have an indispensable part in the historical enterprise, and we dare not disregard their view.'

Craig rejects, as many have done, Irving's attempt to portray Goebbels as responsible for all that was wrong with the Third Reich. Indeed, he suggests that Irving's book points to the contrary, namely, that Hitler was the central figure in all the key decisions of the Third Reich. He also rejects Irving's contention that Hitler did not want the extermination of the Jews and that he only wanted them removed to the East.

In the same vein, a reviewer in the *Washington Post*, wrote:

Sometimes while reading this book, I thought Irving was just plain crazy, and if we were in a room together, I would have gone for his throat. He is a thoroughly repulsive character, and if I were a book publisher, David Irving would never be on my list. But we cannot get to the point where the Holocaust, which is a historic event, gets to be treated like a biblical story—beyond criticism and shielded from hostile scholarship. Yet this book, which has been written about in *The Post* and *New York Times*, the *Nation* magazine and *Vanity Fair*, has effectively been banned in the United States. Whatever its merits or faults, you have been deprived of the right to judge for yourself. That's not censorship in this case. It seems merely to be timidity.[7]

This is not the view that prevailed. With the pressure brought on publishers not to go ahead with Irving's book on Goebbels, the ostracism of Irving had begun in earnest. The turning point in Irving's career came with the publication in 1993 of a book by Lipstadt (the academic referred to above) titled, *Denying the Holocaust*. In the book, Lipstadt characterized some of Irving's writings and public statements as Holocaust denial and called him a bigot.[8]

Irving sued Lipstadt in the UK for defamation. British law places the burden of proof on the defendant—Lipstadt had to justify that her statements were correct and not libellous. Both sides presented experts to give testimonies. One of the witnesses on Lipstadt's side was Richard J. Evans, professor of modern history at Cambridge University. His statements on Irving were scathing:[9]

Not one of [Irving's] books, speeches or articles, not one paragraph, not one sentence in any of them, can be taken on trust as an accurate representation of its historical subject. All of them are completely worthless as history, because Irving cannot be trusted anywhere, in any of them, to give a reliable account of what he is talking or writing about . . . if we mean by historian someone who is concerned to discover the truth about the past, and to give as accurate a representation of it as possible, then Irving is not a historian.

Irving and some of the witnesses on his side argued that Jewish organizations had systematically sought to suppress writings that were at variance with their own narratives. During the trial, Irving created a sensation by referring to the judge as 'Mein Fuhrer'. In fairness, it must be said that the judge referred to Irving once or twice as Hitler.[10] The judge rejected Irving's charge of libel and, in the process, dealt a crushing blow to his standing as a historian.

However, it's important to be clear that the judge, while faulting particular aspects of Irving's writings, did not dismiss Irving's qualities as a military historian in their entirety. Let me cite the relevant part of the judgment cited by one writer:[11]

As a military historian, Irving has much to commend him. For his works of military history Irving has undertaken thorough and painstaking research into the archives. He has discovered and disclosed to historians and others many documents which, but for his efforts, might have remained unnoticed for years. It was plain from the way in which he conducted his case and dealt with a sustained and penetrating cross-examination that his knowledge of World War 2 is unparalleled. His mastery of the detail of the historical documents is remarkable. He is beyond question able and intelligent. He was invariably quick to spot the significance of documents which he had not previously seen. Moreover he writes his military history in a clear and vivid style. I accept the favourable assessment by Professor Watt and Sir John Keegan of the calibre of Irving's military history . . . and reject as too sweeping the negative assessment of Evans . . . [Richard Evans, a historian who testified for the defense, had stated that Irving has had 'a generally low reputation amongst professional historians since the end of the 1980s and at all times amongst those who have direct experience of researching in the

areas with which he concerns himself; although not noted by
Judge Gray, Evans also reiterated Lipstadt's charge that Irving
was not a historian at all.]

But the questions to which this action has given rise do not
relate to the quality of Irving's military history but rather to the
manner in which he has written about the attitude adopted by
Hitler towards the Jews and in particular his responsibility for
the fate which befell them under the Nazi regime.

The above excerpt from the judgment deserves to be read carefully
because Irving's critics have interpreted the judgment to mean that
Irving is devoid of any merit as a historian. That's not what the
judge is saying. He grants that Irving is to be taken seriously as a
military historian. However, he is emphatic on one point: Irving
is wrong in contending that Hitler bore no responsibility for the
Holocaust.

The distinction is important. Along with arguments made
by other writers whom I have cited above, it's the reason I have
chosen to include Irving in this book. Let me make my position on
Irving clear enough. I too reject Irving's view that Hitler bore no
responsibility for the Holocaust and that he was kept largely in the
dark on the subject. I do not buy Irving's view that gas chambers
played little or no role in the Holocaust. I also accept the criticism
of historians such as Richard Evans that Irving has taken liberties
with some of the material he has come across.

However, I do believe, as the judge did and many historians do,
that Irving has much to offer purely as a military historian looking
at the War from Hitler's point of view. The calculations underlying
the major military initiatives that Hitler took, his grasp of the
totality of the war situation, his assessments of the leading German
generals and of the evolving political situation—on these matters,
Irving does contribute to our understanding of World War II.

There are those who say that Irving is not terribly original
on many of these matters. His sole original contribution is his

defence of Hitler in relation to the Holocaust. Once this particular contribution is rejected, his critics say, he has little to offer. It is possible to disagree. I found interesting and useful Irving's rebuttal of the general belief that Hitler was an amateur whose big blunder was to impose his views on his generals instead of following their professional advice. Irving argues persuasively that many of the crucial decisions that Hitler made during the War were militarily sound and had the support of many of his top generals. In some instances, his generals developed an appreciation of Hitler's decisions after they produced successful outcomes. It's a different matter that after the Germans lost the War, many of the generals wrote self-exculpatory memoirs in which they distanced themselves from Hitler's decisions.

Irving's biographies of various German generals, his exploration of various themes related to the War (such as the Germans' half-hearted pursuit of nuclear weapons) and his account of the Nuremburg trials also offer valuable material. Irving is a gifted storyteller who can be read easily by lay persons with an interest in World War II. To read Irving is to get a sense of the atmosphere in Hitler's inner chambers, to have the many great battles of the War come alive. It is to appreciate that there's another side to the story of the War.

Irving is, therefore, worth reading even while we disagree with his views on Hitler and the Holocaust and accept that there is a right-wing agenda that he has pursued. He is a dissenter who deserves our tolerance.

* * *

David Irving was born in 1938 in Sussex, England, the son of a naval officer and commander in the Royal Navy. His father's ship was attacked and badly damaged during World War II. His father survived but thereafter cut off all links with his family.[12]

Irving seems to have had an urge to shock right from his schooldays. He once hung a 12-foot hammer-and-sickle flag over the front entrance of his school. He won a prize for art appreciation. When asked what he would like as a prize, he asked for a copy of Hitler's *Mein Kampf*.[13]

Irving went on to study physics at Imperial College, London, in 1956. He had to drop out after about three years for want of funds. He worked briefly for a British developer before taking up a job with Thyssen, the well-known steel company, in the Ruhr region of Germany. Next, he moved to Spain where he worked as a clerk at an airbase. He met his first wife, a Spanish lady, and had four children.

While working in Germany, he came to know about the savage bombing of the city of Dresden during World War II. After researching the subject, he wrote a series of articles for a magazine on the bombing during the War. Around 1961, he signed a contract with a publisher to write a book on the bombing of Dresden. The book, *The Destruction of Dresden*, was published in 1963.

From 1961 to 1963, he was enrolled for a course in political science and economics at University College, London. Since he had become a well-paid professional author by then, he chose to drop out.[14]

Irving courted controversy at college as well. As the editor of a campus magazine at the University of London, he added a secret supplement to the magazine which called Hitler 'the greatest unifying force Europe has known since Charlemagne'. In another article, he wrote that the British press was owned by Jews. The magazine carried a cartoon that was viewed as racist. The supplement was later removed and destroyed.[15]

The Destruction of Dresden became an international bestseller and launched Irving as an amateur historian. The book was about one of the bloodiest bombing campaigns of World War II— Irving calls it 'the worst single massacre in European history'.[16] In February 1945, Allied planes dropped bombs on the town of Dresden, close to the war frontier with the Soviet Union, in three waves. The first wave came around 10 p.m. The next was an hour past midnight. The third one came the next day. The three bombing raids—all in a space of fourteen hours and for which the city was unprepared—reduced the city to rubble. Thousands were cooked alive in the firestorm that swept through the city.

The general public had heard little of the savage bombing of Dresden until Irving's book was published. Irving argued that the town was of little military importance. The Allied leadership had chosen to bomb it mainly to terrorize the German population and undermine support for Hitler. Some have also suggested that the Western powers wanted to send out a message of support to the Soviet Union.

The deaths in the bombing remain a matter of controversy. Irving has been accused of grossly inflating the number in the initial editions of his book and later revising it downwards in the face of criticism. In the 2005 edition that I have read, Irving says that, in his first edition of 1963, he had accepted the figure of 135,000 as the best estimate.[17]

Irving says that, in 1966, he received a document from the director of the Dresden city archives. The document, prepared by the then police chief of Dresden, mentioned an interim death toll of 28,000 identified victims. Irving underlines the fact that, on top of the identified dead, the police chief referred to an estimated 35,000 missing people. Adding the two, the number of casualties goes up to 60,000. There is also the fact that in such incidents, whole families get wiped out, leaving nobody to report the missing. Putting all this together, Irving suggests that the bombing raids could have claimed anywhere between 60,000 and 100,000 victims. An independent commission set up by the Dresden city council in 2005 estimated the maximum number of deaths at 25,000.

But the central point about Irving's book was not the number of deaths in the bombing raid. It was that the raid on a city of no great industrial or military importance was unwarranted and against all civilized canons of war. In a foreword to the 1963 edition of the book, a retired air marshal, who was deputy to the commander-in-chief of the bomber command, wrote, 'That it was really a military necessity few, after reading this book, will believe. It was one of those terrible things that sometimes happen in wartime, brought about by an unfortunate combination of circumstances.'[18]

Some have challenged Irving's contention about the lack of military importance of Dresden. One writer makes the point that Dresden was an important communication centre for the German Army. The intent was not just to terrorize the public but to sever German Army communications and disrupt the flow of reinforcements to the war front.[19] A member of the bomber crew disputes this view. He says that, whatever the military and industrial importance of Dresden, the personnel taking part in the raid had been asked to specifically target the marketplace where civilians would be gathered.[20]

The debate on Dresden remains inconclusive. The striking fact about Dresden is that the horrific results compelled Churchill to say that 'the question of bombing of German cities simply for the sake of increasing the terror, though under other pretexts, should be reviewed'.[21] Irving can be said to have made an important contribution by bringing Dresden to the attention of the public in the first place.

Following Dresden, Irving's output has been prodigious. He has produced some two dozen books and two translations. He has also given numerous commentaries and speeches, many of which are available on YouTube. His books are voluminous: some of the shorter ones run to about 400 pages. It is impossible in the course of an essay of this sort to cover his output, much less do justice to it. In this essay, I will make a brief mention of some of his works and then focus on three of these, *The Trail of the Fox*, *Hitler's War* and *Nuremberg: The Last Battle*. My intention here is not to provide a comprehensive review of his output but to capture his abilities as a military historian.

The Mare's Nest, published in 1964, is about the German quest for unconventional weapons for bombing the enemy's cities, in particular, London. Two of these came into use: the V-1, which was a flying bomb, and the V-2, which was a missile. Reviewing the book in the *New Statesman*, historian Paul Johnson commented, '. . . David Irving's excellent book can be read with profit by statesmen on both sides of the Iron Curtain.'[22]

Irving shows that British intelligence did not believe that the German rocket project was feasible, and the British side became aware of the rockets only after they began to be launched. The British worked on the assumption that the rockets would carry large warheads and hence would require large launching sites. Since no such sites were detected, the rockets were assumed not to exist. Once the launches began, the British were quick to identify the production and launch sites and neutralize them through effective bombing.

On the German side, the work on the missiles resulted in a significant diversion of financial and human resources from conventional fighter aircraft (which could have proved useful in defending Germany from Allied bombing raids). They did not lead to the creation of any significant destructive capability. Thus, the rocket project, far from turning the course of the War to Germany's advantage, contributed to the German defeat. Irving's account is considered authoritative and it is also uncontroversial.

In 1967, Irving published *The Virus House,* an account of the German nuclear energy project. The book again underlined Irving's prowess as an indefatigable researcher. It was praised by the *New York Times Book Review* and the *Times Literary Supplement,* among other publications. He uncovered thousands of documents and interviewed numerous individuals in the course of writing the book.

Irving contends that the German effort was not successful because the German scientists failed to bring home its importance to the Nazi leadership, in particular, the armaments minister,

Albert Speer. The two scientists, who came to head the project in succession, were not men of vision or drive. The second head of the project was not even motivated by the desire to win the nuclear race. He saw nuclear research as a way of keeping German physics alive if some of the best scientists were to fall on the battlefields. Only on the day the Americans dropped a bomb on Hiroshima did he come to realize the enormity of his lapse. Irving concludes that, during the course of war, science can never be safely left to scientists.

Irving highlights an important detail which led to the derailment of German efforts to produce a nuclear bomb. The production of uranium for use in a nuclear bomb requires the use of a moderator. In respect of a moderator, two possibilities were open to the Germans: graphite and heavy water. A German scientist incorrectly concluded, based on his experiments, that graphite could not be used. That left the Germans with heavy water as the sole possibility. The only plant that produced the heavy water they required was the Vemork High Concentration Plant at Rjukan, Norway, then under the control of the Germans.

Through their intelligence, the Allies realized the importance of Vemork to the Germans and tried to sabotage it on two occasions. The first attempt was unsuccessful. It led to the Germans increasing security measures around the Rjukan plant. The second attempt, made in February 1943, was a perfect piece of sabotage. It was done in such a way so as to not hurt Norway's post-War developmental needs. It ended up delaying Germany's uranium research programmes by several months. The delay was to make a huge difference to Germany's attempt to produce a nuclear weapon.

Among Irving's other notable works are *Churchill's War*, *Goebbels: Mastermind of the Third Reich*, *Goering, a Biography*, and *The Rise and Fall of the Luftwaffe*.

* * *

In 1977, Irving came out with *The Trail of the Fox*, a biography of
Field Marshal Erwin Rommel. The book received many favourable
reviews. The *Christian Science Monitor* called it 'a brilliant biography,
almost a great one'. General Matthew Ridgway, former chief of
staff of the US Army, said it was 'a superb character study . . .
a fine work'. Irving gives us an idea of the formidable research
that went into the writing of the book. '*The Trail of the Fox* leads
from vaults in West Germany to government files in Washington,
from a military museum in South Carolina to presidential libraries
in Kansas and Missouri, from the drawing rooms of Rommel's
surviving comrades to the musty attics with their tantalizing boxes
and files of papers as yet unopened by the widows and families of
the comrades who died.'[23]

Irving captures the essence of the Rommel mystique, one
that gripped the imagination not only of Germany but the Allied
forces. 'He was, most spectacularly, a battlefield general, eagerly
flinging himself into the fray, oblivious to danger. No enemy
shell could cut him down, though men to his right and left were
shot away; no mine could shatter his body, no bomb would fall
near enough to kill him. He seemed immortal.'[24] The mystique
endured in post-War Germany. A warship was named after him.
There were 'Rommel barracks' in the German Army and Rommel
streets.[25]

Rommel, rising up the ranks, came to Hitler's attention. In
September 1936, he was made responsible for Hitler's security
arrangements for the Nazi Party rally in Nuremberg. One day Hitler
wanted to go for a drive. He told Rommel that not more than six
cars should follow him. Rommel did exactly as ordered. He let the
first six cars pass and then stood on the road to halt the rest. The
party VIPs seethed but Rommel told them that he had arranged
for two tanks to block the road. Later, Hitler sent for Rommel and
congratulated him on carrying out his orders so well.[26]

Soon, Rommel came to be appointed commandant of the
Fuhrer's headquarters during the attack on Poland. This gave

him direct access to Hitler—and a seat at Hitler's dining table. Rommel did not disguise his admiration for Hitler, whether in person or in writing to his own family. The reward came in due course: Rommel asked for and was given command of a panzer division although he was an infantry officer and knew nothing about tanks. The appointment, like several other appointments that Hitler made in the armed forces, says something about Hitler's remarkable ability to assess the capabilities of individuals. Hitler had judged that Rommel would learn and adapt to tank warfare. His judgement was to prove well founded.

The legend of Rommel was created during the invasion of France in May 1940. Irving provides a thrilling account of Rommel's drive through the western defences right up to the Channel coast. Over a period of nineteen days, Rommel thrust forward boldly, ignoring the risks to his flanks and rear. Rommel calculated that his thrust would create so much confusion in the enemy ranks that they would not be able to regroup and attack effectively. He was proved right time and again.

Rommel was that rare commander who led from the front all the time. He took impossible risks. Once, he stood on top of a railway embankment and directed the attack even while enemy snipers picked off his men. Deadly shells claimed the lives of his aides but Rommel himself remained unharmed. For weeks on end, he and his tanks ploughed on, Rommel sleeping for just a couple of hours or not at all. In the final dash towards the Channel coast, Rommel averaged 40 to 50 miles a day. Towards the end, he covered 100 miles in a day; 200 miles on the next day.[27]

Irving does not gloss over Rommel's shortcomings. He was apt to claim all the credit for himself and deny his colleagues their due. He was seen by his superiors as impulsive and lacking in judgement. He tended to favour the Nazi commanders under him. He was not always scrupulous in his dealings with his subordinates.[28] Nevertheless, he succeeded magnificently in France.

Hitler picked Rommel to lead the German campaign in Africa. The campaign was intended to help his ally, Italy's Mussolini, whose foray into Africa was facing fierce resistance from the British. Hitler reasoned that in difficult terrain and inhospitable weather conditions, the military commander should be somebody who could inspire his men. Rommel fit the bill. Rommel's limited brief was to contain the British effort to throw the Italians out of Libya. During his years in Africa, Rommel repeatedly violated his brief and the orders of his superiors. He pushed forward along the Mediterranean coast all the way from Tripoli to Benghazi and farther beyond to Tobruk, not far from the Egyptian border. Rommel reckoned that the port at Tobruk would provide a means to directly supply his forces in the region instead of supplies being sent from Tripoli or Benghazi.

It is the little details that Irving weaves into his account that make it stand out. The British had broken the German communications code. By a strange irony, this explained Rommel's early successes as much as his later reverses in Africa. Intercepted German communications told the British that Rommel had clear instructions to stand fast at Benghazi. The British never imagined that Rommel would violate his orders and proceed farther. Thus they were unprepared for his offensives.

In planning his attack on Tobruk, Rommel had counted on reinforcements arriving from Germany. He had been kept in the dark about Operation Barbarossa, the planned invasion of the Soviet Union. Once the war in the East began, it left very little room for reinforcements to be sent elsewhere. Rommel's assault on Tobruk ended up extending his supply lines by more than 700 miles.[29] The expected reinforcements failed to arrive. The attack on Tobruk failed.

The British forces massed in Tobruk counter-attacked. Rommel had to retreat. However, from his new defensive line, he regrouped and attacked again. Tobruk finally fell to Rommel on 21 June 1942. Rommel then set his eyes on Egypt and the Suez

Canal. Hitler, who shared Rommel's penchant for taking big risks, seemed enamoured of this objective: seizing the canal would help Germany cut off a key supply route to the British Empire.

The route from Libya to Egypt passed through the town of El Alamein. Rommel attacked in force but the attack was repelled. He had the option to withdraw into Libya or to stay put and attack at a later point. Rommel chose the latter option. He built a formidable defensive line some distance from El Alamein behind which his troops dug in. At this time, a momentous change occurred on the British side. In August 1942, the commander of the British forces, Claude Auchinleck, was replaced by Bernard Law Montgomery, who would go on to become commander-in-chief of the British Army.

Irving notes that Rommel's forces were inferior in numbers of men and equipment but this was not something new to Rommel. He now suffered from two more serious shortcomings. One was an acute shortage of fuel. The other was that, thanks to the British code crackers, Montgomery got to know about the plans to supply Rommel by sea. Rommel watched in despair as tanker after tanker proceeding to Libya to provide him fuel was sunk. Montgomery also knew of Rommel's plans for attack and could plan his defences accordingly. Not least, he had got to know that Rommel was not keeping in the best of health.[30]

Rommel took the fateful decision to go ahead with his attack on El Alamein as planned on 30 August. It met with far more fierce British resistance than Rommel's intelligence had led him to believe. Rommel decided to call off the attack and withdraw to his jumping-off position. Montgomery had won a great psychological victory.

Rommel left for Germany in late September to recoup his health. When Montgomery launched his expected offensive, Rommel's forces began to crumble. Returning to Africa, Rommel was forced to retreat some 60 miles west to a new line. Irving highlights the fact that Rommel did not convey this decision to retreat clearly enough to Hitler. Hitler's response was swift: Rommel was to stand firm and fight unto 'Victory or Death'.[31]

Rommel could not bring himself to defy Hitler's orders. His troops suffered heavily under the onslaught of a superior army. Eventually, Hitler agreed to yet another request for a retreat. Rommel was able to carry his troops through to the safety of Tunisia. Irving provides a graphic description of the retreat—the 60-mile-long procession of troops and equipment subject to merciless bombarding from the air, paralysed by lack of fuel, Rommel's men starved of food and water and yet fighting their way out.

Irving does not hide Rommel's failures in Africa. He may have retreated too far too fast; both the German and Italian leadership certainly seemed to think so. An Italian general commented acidly that Rommel withdrew as he pleased; for him, every day was a 'desperate battle'. Rommel's boss, Field Marshal Albert Kesselring, felt the same way.[32] At various points in time, Kesselring urged a counter-attack but Rommel was now hell-bent on a quick retreat into Tunisia. Rommel managed to save most of his troops. He was then summoned back to Germany.

Many analysts have seen Hitler's orders to the army to stand and fight on in Africa as a psychological aversion to withdrawal. This is not true, as we shall see later in the invasion of the Soviet Union. Irving contends that Hitler had long concluded that the war in Africa was lost. His priority was to delay an Allied landing in Southern Europe and to prop up his key ally, Mussolini. By making the Allies fight all the way to North-west Africa, he hoped to gain time in which to find the forces to buttress Italy. (The German Army was at the time fully engaged in the battle of Stalingrad in the Soviet Union and hence had little to spare for other theatres.) Rommel and the generals on the ground could not see the larger picture. They tended to perceive Hitler's orders as a reckless disregard for German lives.

Hitler dangled before Rommel the prospect of becoming Supreme Commander in Italy. However, Rommel's lack of optimism in adverse conditions, his poor equations with the generals in the German high command and his inability to get along with Mussolini resulted in Rommel's not getting the job. He was instead given charge of preparing the defence of France under the Commander-in-Chief, West, Field Marshal Gerd von Rundstedt. It was, as Irving puts it, a 'real chance (for Rommel) to gain his lost renown'.[33]

Rommel was of the view that the best way to defend France was to repel the Allied forces at the point of landing, namely, the beaches. Irving devotes several pages to the elaborate fortifications and mines that Rommel planned and implemented. His boundless energy and zest for work were in evidence. He travelled up and down the 1400-mile coastline, pulling up his commanders, toughening the troops, suggesting ingenious ways of making life difficult for the invasion force.

One huge point of controversy was how to deploy the panzer divisions. Irving details the different points of view in the German Army. Rommel insisted that they be deployed close to the coastline in order to beef up the attempt to repel the invasion at the beaches themselves. Rundstedt and his staff were reluctant to do so. They wanted the panzers to be kept in reserve for deployment wherever needed. There was also a view that airborne Allied troops would land deep inside and the panzer divisions must be available to respond.

Heinz Guderian, Hitler's panzer expert, argued that the panzer divisions must be kept well out of range of the enemy's warship artillery. Rommel countered that leaving the panzer divisions too far in the rear would mean they could never move forward—the enemy air force would rip them to shreds in the open. The German high command intended the panzer divisions as a reserve to be used in the East once the attack in the West was fended off.[34] Hitler opted for a compromise: three panzer divisions were given to Rommel and four were kept as inland reserve.

When the invasion began, Rommel was away on leave. Things began to unravel for the Germans very quickly. By the fourth day, Rommel had concluded that the invasion had succeeded. Irving underlines that Rommel still had overwhelming numerical superiority and he had not yet deployed his panzer divisions. Rommel was injured in an air attack and was removed to a hospital in Germany.

By this time, an attempt had been made on Hitler's life and it had failed. Rommel was implicated in the plot. He was given a choice between facing trial and committing suicide by taking poison and getting a state funeral. He opted for the latter. Irving's view is that Rommel may have been vaguely aware of the plot but he was not involved in it. He goes to great lengths to show that the villain of the piece was his chief of staff in France, General Hans Speidel. Irving believes that Speidel was among the plotters and that he implicated Rommel in order to save his own neck. After the War, Speidel rose to become Supreme Commander of NATO.

Irving is balanced in his judgement of Rommel: a great battlefield commander but lacking an appreciation of strategy. He quotes Hitler as saying of Rommel, 'He is not a real stayer.'[35] Throughout the book, Irving shows us another side of Rommel, that of a devoted husband and father. Amidst all the battles he's fighting, he's writing letters to his wife and son, venting his frustrations, giving them advice and reassurance. This is a book that few can quarrel with. It is quite free from political judgement while bringing out the best in Irving as a military historian.

* * *

Hitler's War, first published in 1977, is, perhaps, Irving's most important book. It is not a biography of Hitler. It confines itself mostly to Hitler's years in power as Chancellor of the Third Reich, starting in 1933. Of those years, it is the period of World War II (1939–45) that takes up most of the space.

In a lengthy introduction, Irving makes clear that he is setting out to challenge many of the mainstream views on Hitler. The book was hugely controversial. The fiercest controversy centred on Irving's contention that Hitler never intended the extermination of Jews. Irving says that Hitler used anti-Semitism to ride to power but 'once inside and in power, he dismounted and paid only lip service to that part of his Party creed'.[36]

The extermination of Jews, Irving says, was carried out by Hitler's subordinates—notably, SS chief Heinrich Himmler—without Hitler's knowledge and concurrence. Irving would have us believe that Hitler was a far less omnipotent leader than is generally believed and that his grip on his subordinates weakened with each passing year.[37] He concentrated increasingly on the conduct of the war and neglected affairs of state.[38] Hitler did not even get to know of the extermination programme until October 1943.

Irving concedes the fact that Hitler ordered the deportation of Jews from Germany after they had been deprived of all their political rights. He also accepts that Hitler wanted them deployed as slave labour in the construction of roads. He would, however, have us believe that Hitler was not responsible for what happened to them thereafter. This strains one's credulity. Hitler may have indeed left many matters to his subordinates. However, it is inconceivable that Himmler and others would have carried out the extermination of 6 million Jews on their own. The SS was, after all, an agency created for directly enforcing Hitler's will.

Moreover, as one reviewer of the book mentions, there is documentary evidence that Himmler sent reports of the killing of Jews to Hitler.[39] Another reviewer quotes Himmler as telling an audience of generals that he had 'uncompromisingly' solved the 'Jewish problem'. Himmler is said to have remarked, 'You can imagine how I felt executing this soldierly order issued to me, but I obediently complied and carried it out to the best of my convictions.'[40]

Irving trumpets his offer of a prize of a thousand pounds to anybody who could produce a written order signed by Hitler ordering the extermination of Jews. No such document has surfaced, he declares. He dismisses the suggestion that Hitler might have chosen to give only oral orders on the subject. He writes:[41]

> Why however should Hitler have become so squeamish in this instance, while he had shown no compunction about signing a blanket order for the liquidation of tens of thousands of fellow Germans (the T-4 euthanasia programme); his insistence on the execution of hostages on a one-hundred-to-one basis, his orders for the liquidation of enemy prisoners (the Commando Order), of Allied airmen (the Lynch Order), and Russian functionaries (the Commissar Order) are documented all the way from the Führer's headquarters right down the line to the executioners.

Well, the killing of 6 million Jews was hardly on the same footing as some of the other killings that Hitler ordered—the need for secrecy was clearly greater. Moreover, since Hitler had made his intentions towards Jews well known to his inner circle, it was hardly necessary for him to issue any written order on the subject. His intentions were duly translated into practice and he was kept informed, as mentioned earlier.

Irving makes much of a telephonic message from Himmler to Reinhard Heydrich on 30 November 1941 to the effect that Jews were not to be liquidated.[42] A reviewer points out that this is a serious distortion of fact: the message was about one particular trainload of Jews—it was not an order about halting the liquidation of Jews in general at all.[43]

The reviewer underlines that the order not to liquidate was driven purely by expediency. German officials in Riga in the Soviet Union (the place to which the concerned Jews had been despatched) were upset over the public massacres of Jewish arrivals in the province. The international media was also beginning to show interest in these happenings. The decision not to liquidate one particular trainload was taken against this background.

A second important theme in Irving's book is that Britain was ill-advised to have got embroiled in a war with Germany. It should not have declared war on Germany after Germany's invasion of Poland. It should have at least accepted Hitler's offer of peace after France fell to the Germans. Britain would have then saved its empire, saved precious lives on both sides, and it would have not been left economically weakened as it was by conflict with Germany.

Irving contends that Hitler did not in any way wish to threaten or interfere with the British Empire. Indeed, he regarded the British Empire as a force for good and would have been happy to co-exist with it. Even after his victory over France, Hitler hoped that Britain would come round to a peace agreement with him. Irving writes:[44]

> He had no ambitions against Britain or her Empire at all, and all the captured records solidly bear this out. He had certainly built the wrong air force and the wrong navy for a sustained campaign against the British Isles; and subtle indications, like his instructions to Fritz Todt . . . to erect huge monuments on the Reich's western frontiers, suggest that for Hitler these frontiers were of a lasting nature.

In fairness to Irving, he is not the only person to believe that Britain's involvement in World War II was uncalled for. American conservative commentator Patrick J. Buchanan devotes a whole book to this theme.[45] Like Irving, Buchanan too thinks that Britain should have let Hitler have a free hand in Eastern Europe. It should have let Stalin and his totalitarian regime get its comeuppance. Buchanan does not believe that Hitler had any programme for the conquest of the world.

Well, we don't really know. Once Hitler had conquered the Soviet Union and gained access to its enormous resources, what was to stop him from turning his attention to Britain in due course? The reason that Britain gave up its earlier policy of appeasement was that it had concluded that Hitler simply could not be trusted to live up to his commitments. In the ultimate analysis, it was the two-front war—one against the West, including Britain and the USA, and the other against the Soviet Union—that led to Hitler's defeat and saved the world from domination by Nazi Germany. Had Hitler been allowed by the Western powers to prosecute his war against the Soviet Union without hindrance, he may well have won the war.

A third theme in Irving's book is that Hitler's attack on the Soviet Union was essentially a preventive war. If Hitler had not struck the Soviet Union when it was relatively weak, the Soviet Union would have struck Germany when the former was economically and militarily stronger. This theme too is the subject of considerable controversy. Again, Irving is not alone in his view. Many others subscribe to it. Let me outline Irving's views first and then mention what a few others have to say.

In August 1939, Hitler and Stalin had agreed to a peace treaty known as the Molotov–Ribbentrop Pact. (Ribbentrop and Molotov were the foreign ministers of Germany and the Soviet Union respectively.) The pact committed the two nations not to attack each other or to side with the other's enemy. There was also a secret protocol that outlined how the two parties would carve up the territories of various East European nations between themselves.

The pact is commonly viewed as an act of cynicism on the part of both Hitler and Stalin. Both intended to buy time before the inevitable confrontation between the two powers. Hitler wanted to focus on his war with the West. Stalin wanted to strengthen the Soviet Union's economy and enlarge its boundaries while Germany was busy fighting Britain and France.

Hitler outlined his concerns to one of his generals, Alfred
Jodl, in 1940:[46]

> He [Hitler] explained that he was perfectly aware that Stalin
> had only signed his 1939 pact with Germany to open the
> floodgates of war in Europe; what Stalin had not bargained
> for was that Hitler would finish off France so soon—this
> explained Russia's headlong occupation of the Baltic states
> and the Romanian provinces in the latter part of June. It was
> clear from the increasing Soviet military strength along the
> eastern frontier, on which Germany still had only five divisions
> stationed, that Russia had further acquisitions in mind. Hitler
> feared that Stalin planned to bomb or invade the Romanian
> oil fields that autumn. Russia's aims, he said, had not changed
> since Peter the Great: she wanted the whole of Poland and the
> political absorption of Bulgaria, then Finland, and finally the
> Dardanelles. War with Russia was inevitable, argued Hitler;
> such being the case, it was better to attack now—this autumn.

Elsewhere, Irving notes that news of Soviet preparations for an
attack on Germany were reaching Hitler:[47]

> German Intelligence learned of a meeting of the Supreme
> Soviet on August 2 in which they were warned against trusting
> Germany because 'certain information indicated that after her
> victory in the west she [Germany] would start a war against
> Russia.' 'Indeed,' the officials had continued, 'we must get in our
> attack before our thieving neighbour in the west can get in hers.'

Irving quotes Hitler as saying in 1945:[48]

> I didn't take the decision to attack Moscow lightly, but because
> I knew from certain information that an alliance was being
> prepared between Britain and Russia. The big question was,

Should we hit out first or wait until we were overwhelmed at some time in the future?

There is more in this vein in the book. Irving's critics say this is just one of many attempts on his part to whitewash Hitler's actions. They make the point that an expansion of the German nation eastwards was integral to Hitler's long-term vision. Hitler saw the expansion as providing the needed space to the German population. He believed the resources of the Soviet Union were required to build a strong German nation. He was keen to establish control over the Balkans. He wanted to undermine Bolshevism in its native land. The intelligence Hitler received about the Soviet Union's preparations to attack Germany may have dictated the timing of his own attack on the Soviet Union. However, the basic decision to attack the Soviet Union had long been taken.

This seems plausible. But it's worth pointing out that Irving has plenty of company in respect of his thesis about a preventive war. In 1985, a former Soviet intelligence officer (who used the pseudonym Victor Suvorov) wrote an article in which he made the same argument as Irving. Later, Suvorov developed the article into a book.[49] Suvorov argues that Stalin wanted to spread communism throughout Europe. He was waiting for Germany and other Western powers to exhaust themselves before he struck. Suvorov contends that Stalin had planned an attack on Germany in the summer of 1941. He says that it was precisely because the Soviet forces were deployed for assault that they were thrown into complete disarray when the Germans pre-empted the Soviet attack. The Soviet forces were simply not positioned for defence.

Another Russian writer, Gabriel Gorodetsky, sought to rebut Suvorov's thesis. Gorodetsky pointed out that the Soviet Army was in no way prepared for an assault on Germany. Least of all in the summer of 1941 when the German Army was at the peak of its powers.[50] Nevertheless, Suvorov's thesis came to be backed by several researchers in Western Europe and North America.

One American historian has even cited the statements of several Russian officials in support of Suvorov's thesis.

Several Soviet scholars came out in support of Suvorov even if they did not accept all that he said. One author suggests that some of this may have been part of a larger attempt to malign Stalin in the Soviet Union in the wake of Mikhail Gorbachev's glasnost. It was intended to fit in with the image of the Soviet Union as evil empire. However, even he grants that Stalin believed that a war with Hitler was inevitable.[51]

There are some who don't accept the view that Hitler's motivation in attacking the Soviet Union was to pre-empt a Soviet attack. As we mentioned above, Hitler had numerous other reasons for wanting to subdue the Soviet Union. However, they are willing to go along with the contention that Stalin was indeed readying to attack Germany. One writer cites the draft of a war plan that is revealing of Soviet intentions although he is careful to add that there is no evidence that Stalin accepted the plan:[52]

> Considering that Germany is currently maintaining its army in a state of mobilization . . . it has the capacity of beating us to the punch in deployment and of launching a surprise attack. To prevent this, I [that is, Marshal Zhukov] consider it essential, above all, not to leave the initiative to the German command, but to forestall the enemy in deployment and to attack the German army while it is still in the deployment stage.

The debate on this matter is inconclusive. But I believe I have said enough to indicate that Irving's position is not as outlandish as it is made out to be.

* * *

Let me turn now to a fourth theme in Irving's book, namely, Hitler's prowess as a military commander. Hitler has often been portrayed as a madman who pursued his fantasies about world conquest with little regard for military strategy. His biggest mistake, it is often suggested, was to override or ignore the views of his highly trained, professional military commanders. This resulted in great military defeats that ultimately turned the tide of the War. If only Hitler had allowed himself to be guided by his generals, the outcomes would not have been as disastrous.

Irving doesn't think so at all. Nor did many of those who served under Hitler. In his memoirs, *Inside the Third Reich*, Albert Speer, Hitler's architect and armaments minister, gives us vivid descriptions of Hitler's grasp of strategy, tactics and detail. He shows how Hitler was often able to put forward arguments that left his generals tongue-tied. Irving himself regards Hitler as a gifted military commander. He believes that some of the important defeats suffered by the German Army happened because the generals did not faithfully carry out Hitler's directives. The generals should have listened to Hitler, not the other way around.

So who's right, Irving or Hitler's numerous detractors? I propose to examine three crucial military decisions taken by Hitler: the strategy of blitzkrieg in the invasion of France; the attack on Moscow; and the decision to seize Stalingrad.

The German invasion of France in 1940 was a stunning success. It not only took the French and the British forces by surprise, it exceeded the expectations of the Germans themselves. The success rested on an audacious plan of attack. The original plan, formulated by the German Army leadership (under General Franz Halder), envisaged an attack along a broad front with the thrust being on the northern wing. Hitler opted for a different plan altogether. Let me outline the conventional narrative of the alternative plan and Irving's version of the story.

The conventional narrative is that an alternative plan was presented by Erich von Manstein, then chief of staff of Army Group A headed by General Gerd von Rundstedt. (Some elements of the plan were contributed by a distinguished tank commander,

General Heinz Guderian.) Manstein, later to become known as the most outstanding general of World War II on either side, proposed a drive through the Ardennes forest in Belgium. The Ardennes area was least defended by Allied forces. The belief among the Allies was that the Ardennes forest and the mountainous terrain provided a natural barrier to any enemy assault.

In Manstein's plan, the main thrust of the German forces would happen at Belgium in the south, bypassing the main body of Allied forces stationed along the border. Thereafter, the German forces would turn northward and proceed rapidly towards the English Channel coast. In the process, the Allied forces would be encircled and their supply lines cut off. Most crucially, the elements of surprise and the swift movement towards the Channel would throw the Allied forces into complete disarray. An attack by the German Army in the north would be intended as a diversion.

This strategy, which later came to be described as blitzkrieg, was named Sichelschnitt ('sickle strategy') by Manstein. It entailed a massive concentration of armoured forces at one point. It was a risky gamble. If it failed, the Germans would be left with very little reserves to deal with an Allied counter-attack.

The conservative German top brass did not view Manstein's plan favourably. He was removed from Rundstedt's Army Group A and posted as commander elsewhere. According to one version, some members of Manstein's staff passed on his plan to Hitler's adjutant, Rudolph Schmundt, who may have passed it on to Hitler. Manstein was given an opportunity to appear before Hitler and present his plan. Hitler then approved a modified version of the plan.

In Irving's telling, Hitler himself had been dissatisfied with the plan for the invasion of France presented by the German Army high command. He was looking for a strategy that would take full advantage of his armoured and mechanized divisions. Hitler had arrived at a plan very similar to that of Manstein, one that favoured a German attack that focused on an area south of the Meuse river (again, the Ardennes region).[53]

Irving says that Hitler's adjutant, Schmundt, had come to know of Manstein's plan on a visit to Rundstedt's army group headquarters. Hitler accosted Manstein at a party held at the Chancellery thereafter. Irving writes, 'Manstein assured him that the new plan was the only means by which to obtain a total victory on land. The next day Hitler sent for General von Brauchitsch and his chief of staff and dictated the new operational plan to them.'[54]

Most accounts of World War II view Manstein as the principal architect of the blitzkrieg strategy. Let us suppose this is correct. It would still be true that the plan prevailed because Hitler was willing to support it over the heads of the German Army top brass. A leader does not have to have all the bright ideas himself. But leadership is certainly about being able to judge which idea to back. Hitler must get credit for backing the right idea for the invasion of France.

The second example of Hitler's abilities as a military commander has to do with the invasion of the Soviet Union. As part of the strategy, the German Army leadership favoured a drive towards Moscow. Since Moscow was the command and control hub of the Soviet Union, the army high command felt that Moscow should be the primary target. Hitler did not think so. He wanted the Russian forces in the Baltic coast and the Ukraine to be destroyed first as that would release German forces for other operations.

More importantly, Hitler favoured targeting Leningrad to the north (as it happened to be a key industrial centre of the Soviet Union) and the oil fields in the south. Supplies of oil were crucial to Germany's domination of the War and they were also crucial to the Soviet Union's ability to fight Germany.[55] In other words, Hitler felt that destroying the industrial bases of the Soviet Union was the key to a quick victory. Moscow was of no particular importance. Irving repeatedly makes this point in his account of Operation Barbarossa, as the Russian campaign was called.

What emerged finally was a compromise between the views of the German Army high command and Hitler. Germany would despatch forces towards Moscow, Leningrad and southern Russia. This dissipation of forces, Irving contends, ultimately proved detrimental to Hitler's objective of a quick victory.

Operation Barbarossa commenced in June 1941. Irving says that even after the initial successes, in August 1941, Hitler was inclined to stick to his original strategy of concentrating on Leningrad and the south of Russia. However, before Hitler could issue the necessary directive, he was laid low by fever. The German generals 'began to go their own way disregarding Hitler's strategic intentions'.

The attack on Moscow was stalled just before winter set in and the German forces were about 20 miles away. Thereafter, the Russians counter-attacked in a big way, pushing the Germans more than 100 miles away from Moscow. The attack on Moscow had resulted in a greatly weakened German Army. Irving writes:[56]

> The Army High Command continued stubbornly with its plans to attack Moscow. Only later was it realised that Hitler's strategy would have offered the better prospects. [Field Marshal] Bock's armies would still be stalled outside Moscow when winter set in, and Hitler's illness bore the blame. 'Today I still believe,' Goering was to tell his captors, 'that had Hitler's original plan of genius not been diluted like that, the eastern campaign would have been decided by early 1942 at the latest.'

There is, however, one aspect of the attack on Moscow that is not disputed. When the Russians counter-attacked in a big way, the German generals opted for a headlong retreat. Hitler refused to countenance one. He insisted that the only way the front could be preserved was for the German Army to stand firm and fight—this was his famous 'no retreat' policy.

Hitler argued that dropping back 30 miles was not going to help matters—it wasn't less cold 30 miles away nor were the transport and supply problems going to change. Moreover, a retreat would mean leaving behind heavy weapons which would erode the army's ability to fight back from the new line.[57]

Hitler moved decisively to dismiss senior generals who balked at his orders to stand firm, beginning with the commander-in-chief of the German Army, von Brauchitsch. (He then appointed himself commander-in-chief.) Even Hitler's detractors accept that the German line was stabilized and a complete rout avoided, thanks to Hitler's steely determination not to permit any further retreat.

Irving's elaborate documentation of these facts is a useful contribution. He quotes Goebbels as saying that Hitler blamed the German Army leadership for the reverses in the Russian campaign:[58]

> The Führer had no intention whatever of aiming for Moscow; he wanted to cut off the Caucasus [from the rest of Russia], thus hitting the Soviet system at its most vulnerable point. But Brauchitsch and his General Staff knew better: Brauchitsch kept hammering on about Moscow. He wanted prestige victories instead of real ones.

A third example of Hitler's abilities as a military commander that we find in Irving's book is the battle for Stalingrad. This battle is widely seen as marking a turning point in the War and paving the way for Hitler's downfall and defeat.

Many mainstream commentators view Hitler's attack on Stalingrad as a battle of egos between him and the Soviet dictator after whom the city was named. They are wrong—it wasn't just that. Hitler viewed Stalingrad as a key strategic objective. It was an important industrial city and a vital rail junction. It was situated on the Volga river across which supplies of valuable raw materials passed to the rest of the Soviet Union. It was also crucial to protecting the flank of the German Army which was proceeding to the south to seize the oil fields of the Caucasus.

Several commentators have argued that Hitler's mistake was to have attempted too many campaigns in the Soviet Union simultaneously. As a result, he ended up spreading his forces thinly. This is a valid criticism. However, it does not apply to his decision to split his forces in the south into two—one headed for the Caucasus and beyond and the other towards Stalingrad.

Irving notes that Stalin had far more divisions and armaments at his disposal than Hitler. The only way that Hitler could prevail was to ensure that Stalin was starved of vital raw materials, including oil, from the south. Hitler's instinct to target the south was thus bang on. As for Stalingrad, it had to be neutralized as otherwise the Russian forces stationed there could pose a threat to the German forces penetrating deep into the south. There is thus a plausible defence of Hitler's basic strategy of targeting the Caucasus and Stalingrad simultaneously.

Hitler entrusted the attack on Stalingrad to the famed Sixth Army and chose General Friedrich Paulus as its commander. Taking Stalingrad turned out to be more difficult and costly than anybody on the German side could have envisaged. The defenders fought stubbornly and exacted a heavy toll on the attackers.

The Sixth Army found the going difficult after entering the city. Stalingrad had been reduced to rubble by weeks of bombardment by the German air force. Thousands of Russian defenders hid in the rubble and harassed the attacking force. The German panzers, which performed magnificently in the open, were hopelessly bogged down within the city. Subjugating the defenders became a matter of hand-to-hand combat fought street by street, building by building. More and more German forces were sucked into the city, leaving the flanks dangerously exposed.

The defenders at the northern edge close to the Volga river fought on tenaciously and the city never quite came under the complete control of the Germans.

All this gave Stalin enough time to build and regroup forces for a counter-attack. The Russian forces attacked the Sixth Army from the north-west as well as the south in a pincer movement. The pincer would soon close thus trapping the Sixth Army inside the city. Hitler has been severely criticized for the decisions that followed. The gist of the criticism is as follows.

As soon as the news came in of the Soviet counter-attack, the German generals advised that the Sixth Army break out through the west. Hitler insisted that Stalingrad be held. He believed that the Sixth Army could be supplied by air until it was relieved by reinforcements sent by the German Army. In this, he was foolishly supported—so Hitler's critics contend—by the Luftwaffe chief Hermann Goering who overestimated the capabilities of the air force. The expected air supplies did not arrive. Nor could the siege be lifted by German reinforcements sent towards Stalingrad.

The Sixth Army at Stalingrad comprising an estimated 300,000 men was ultimately starved into submission. An estimated 90,000 men surrendered including the commander, Field Marshal Friedrich Paulus. A whole army was lost due to Hitler's obdurate insistence of holding Stalingrad against all odds. This paved the way for the German Army's eventual defeat at the hands of the Soviet Union.

Irving presents a different view. Hitler was not alone in supposing that the Sixth Army could be supplied by air. Irving documents the crucial fact that Field Marshal Erich von Manstein, the author of blitzkrieg, was of the same view initially. This has been corroborated by others.[59]

Manstein had been given command of the newly created Army Group Don and asked to mount a relief operation that would help the Sixth Army hold on to Stalingrad. As supplies from the air proved inadequate and the Soviet encirclement of the Sixth

Army grew tighter, Hitler ordered Manstein to break through the encirclement and relieve the Sixth Army in Stalingrad.

Manstein found the going heavy although he managed to get within 30 miles of Stalingrad. Irving notes that two alternatives were now available to Paulus. He could either push a battle group south-west in order to meet Manstein's relieving panzer divisions. Or the entire Sixth Army could attempt to break out, leaving behind thousands of wounded men. Paulus was keenly aware that accomplishing the latter was not easy: large amounts of food and fuel were required and for the Sixth Army to fight its way out leaving behind heavy artillery would be quite a challenge.

From Hitler's point of view, there was a more crucial consideration. The Sixth Army had tied down some seventy Soviet divisions and brigades. If Stalingrad was given up, these divisions and other Soviet divisions would be rendered free and could potentially cut off the 700,000-strong army group that had gone deep into the south. The Russian campaign would then be over. The decision to hold Stalingrad, Irving notes, allowed the German armies in the Caucasus to make an orderly retreat. Hitler calculated that the longer the Sixth Army fought on in Stalingrad, the greater the possibility of stabilizing the other fronts.

The German Army lost the battle of Stalingrad because the fundamentals favoured Russia and these asserted themselves over time. Russia's industrial capability and military strengths had been underestimated. So also the capacity of Stalin and the Russian people to endure enormous casualties in what had been billed the 'Great Patriotic War'. The drive towards Moscow had weakened Hitler's plan to conquer the south of Russia quickly and deprive the Russian military of vital supplies of oil. Allowing the Sixth Army at Stalingrad to break out would have resulted in its annihilation anyway and it would also have hastened the collapse of Hitler's Russian campaign. The loss of the Sixth Army at Stalingrad was a disaster but retreating from Stalingrad would have resulted in an even bigger one. Irving provides a useful counter-narrative to this effect.

* * *

As I have said at the very outset, Irving's attempt to exonerate Hitler of the extermination of Jews by the Third Reich fails pathetically. Where Irving is useful is in providing a corrective to the perception, common even among historians, that Hitler was some sort of 'Devil incarnate'.[60]

Irving makes the useful point that Hitler was a complex personality who carried within himself several contradictions. His ruthlessness and disregard for human life are well known. Not as well known are his restraint and adherence to conventions in some matters. This is a theme that runs through Irving's book. It is, perhaps, best summarized in the introduction itself:[61]

> The sheer complexity of that character is evident from a comparison of his brutality in some respects with his almost maudlin sentimentality and stubborn adherence to military conventions that others had long abandoned. We find him cold-bloodedly ordering a hundred hostages executed for every German occupation soldier killed; dictating the massacre of Italian officers who had turned their weapons against German troops in 1943; ordering the liquidation of Red Army commissars, Allied commando troops, and captured Allied aircrews; in1942 he announced that the male populations of Stalingrad and Leningrad were to be exterminated. He justified all these orders by the expediencies of war. Yet the same Hitler indignantly exclaimed, in the last week of his life, that Soviet tanks were flying the Nazi swastika as a ruse during street fighting in Berlin, and he flatly forbade his Wehrmacht to violate flag rules. He had opposed every suggestion for the use of poison gases, as that would violate the Geneva Protocol;

at that time Germany alone had manufactured the potentially
war-winning lethal nerve gases Sarin and Tabun.

Irving makes the point that Hitler was a shrewd judge of men.
'His assessment of character was instant and deadly.'[62] His
constant shuffling of generals and his choice of them for particular
situations bear this out. To give just one illustration, he made good
use of Field Marshal Manstein in offensive situations, such as the
breakthrough in France. However, following Stalingrad, when the
German Army was in retreat he decided that 'what the southern
front needed was a new name, a new slogan, and a commander
expert in defensive strategy'.[63] Manstein was replaced by Walter
Model who had shown that he could get his troops to dig in and
fend off Soviet offensives.

Hitler conceived of the autobahn programme, the network of
super highways that still mark Germany. He was struck by the fact
that the city folk were worn out from travelling by overcrowded
trains for their Sunday outings. Their lives would be better if they
could travel by road. Within days of seizing power in 1933, he sent
for Dr Fritz Todt, an engineer whose monograph on road-building,
written in 1932, had impressed him. He assigned Todt the job of
building roads. He had a ninety-minute stroll with Todt in which he
showed the grasp of detail that was to be the hallmark of his style of
functioning. Hitler told Todt what routes the road network would
take and also specified the minimum width of the traffic lanes.[64]

Hitler commanded the respect of his generals; at times, he
even seemed to inspire awe in them. General Halder referred to 'his
unusual intellect and grasp, his imaginativeness and willpower'.[65]
General Alfred Jodl maintained until the very end that Hitler was
a great 'warlord'. He remarked, 'Rome destroyed Carthage but
Hannibal is still regarded as one of history's greatest warriors and
always will be.'[66]

Hitler took great interest in the design of guns and warships.
He demanded and got enormous increases in arms production.

When Field Marshal Keitel presented him with details of ammunition expended in the French campaign, Hitler pointed out that the German Army had consumed more of certain types of ammunition each month in 1916. The German Army's office then drew up more ambitious production targets. When a general in charge of munitions objected to the targets set, Hitler decided that a civilian would take charge of armaments production.[67] His first appointment was Fritz Todt and his second, Albert Speer, later to become a legend for the feats of production he was able to pull off.

The idea of constructing an 'Atlantic Wall' in preparation for an Allied invasion in the West was Hitler's. Hitler had commissioned photographs of the coastline. These had shown that the whole coast was vulnerable to an Allied assault. Hitler summoned Albert Speer and his military experts and gave detailed instructions on the defences to be built. He asked for special treatment to be given to submarine bases and naval gun sites. Since any invasion would begin with heavy bombardment, heavy machine guns, tanks and anti-tanks needed to come under cover. He ordered bunkers to be made gas-proof and he also took special steps to protect these against napalm bombs. It's in the recital of such detail that Irving excels.[68]

Irving is also dismissive of the notion that Hitler lost control of his faculties or his mental balance towards the end. He cites the testimony of Hitler's doctors who were questioned on the subject in 1945:[69]

There were virtually no clinical symptoms of abnormality. He showed no mental faults like inappropriate euphoria, incontinence, anosmia (loss of smell), or personality changes. Brain examinations disclosed no 'sensory aphasia' and no 'dream states.' Tests on his reflex centres and spinal root functions revealed no abnormalities. The doctors would put on record that his orientation as to time, place, and persons was excellent . . . 'no hallucinations, illusions, or paranoid trends were present.'

The examples from Irving's book I have cited are merely illustrative. It is impossible here to do justice to the many details of Hitler's personality and his leadership qualities that Irving provides in his writings. Irving asks us to grant that Hitler was a man of considerable ability even while we hold that he put his abilities to destructive use.

* * *

The principal members of the Third Reich were tried at Nuremberg in Germany. The most important trials, which took place between November 1945 and October 1946, were conducted by the International Military Tribunal (IMT) comprising the US, the UK, France and the Soviet Union. These involved the twenty-two top leaders of the Third Reich (including one tried in absentia).

David Irving has written a racy account of the IMT trials.[70] However, this book has proved non-controversial. It comes close to the mainstream narrative. (An exception is a relatively minor portion of the book that questions the sources of information on the basis of which the crimes against the Jews were included in the trials.) Yet, as we shall see, Irving does make a contribution by highlighting aspects of the story that may not have got due attention in other accounts.

The Nuremberg trials were intended to punish the leadership of Nazi Germany for the crimes they had committed. The Allied leaders were not keen on a proper trial of the German leadership at all. Churchill wanted the German leaders to be simply shot. Roosevelt was somewhat ambiguous on the issue. His Secretary of State, Cordell Hull, was in favour of shoot and kill. General Dwight Eisenhower, Supreme Commander of Allied Forces and later President of the United States, added a small nuance to the summary solution: the enemy leaders should be shot while trying to escape.[71]

Apart from favouring swift execution of the German leaders, US Treasury Secretary Henry Morgenthau came up with a truly blood-curdling idea. The now infamous Morgenthau Plan proposed that Germany be reduced to a land of small firms without large-scale industrial enterprises. It also proposed that large numbers of Germans be used as slave labour. Both Roosevelt and Churchill were in agreement with Morgenthau on the matter of the destruction of Germany's industries.[72]

Roosevelt remarked somewhat savagely, 'We have got to be tough with Germany and I mean the German people, not just the Nazis. You either have to castrate the German people or you have got to treat them in such a manner so they can't go on reproducing people who want to continue the way they have in the past.'[73] The US Secretary of War, Henry Stimson, found the proposal revolting and managed to stall it.

It was Joseph Stalin who came in the way of the idea of shooting German leaders outright. Stalin said that there should be no executions without trial as the world would think that the Allies were afraid to try them. If there were no trials, there would be no executions, only lifelong imprisonment.[74]

The Allied view on how to deal with the German leadership began to change with the death of Roosevelt and the arrival of Harry Truman as President of the United States. Truman favoured a trial for the top Nazis but he was quite clear as to the outcome he expected—in Irving's words, 'The Nazis should be given a fair trial first—and then hanged.'[75]

Truman's big contribution to the war crime trials was his decision to offer the job of US prosecutor to a Supreme Court judge, Robert H. Jackson. This was in April 1945. Jackson hesitated briefly as he thought it would interfere with his ambition to become Chief Justice. However, the court was soon to go into recess until October 1945. Jackson felt that the war crimes trials could be completed by then. He was to be proved wrong—the trials dragged on for a year longer than he had calculated.

The Germans were charged on four counts: conspiracy, that is, conspiring to engage in the three other counts; crimes against peace, which was planning and waging wars of aggression; war crimes, which referred to the killing and mistreatment of soldiers and civilians; and crimes against humanity, which referred to inhuman actions against civilians, notably the mass killing of Jews.

Irving underlines the fact that these charges could very well have been brought against the Allies.[76] War of aggression? In 1939, Britain had attacked Poland. Stalin had joined hands with Hitler in slicing up Poland between the Soviet Union and Germany. In 1940, Churchill had had no qualms about ordering the invasion of Norway.

War crimes? In the spring of 1940, the Soviet Union had deported large numbers of Polish prisoners into the Katyn forests in its territory and executed 15,000 officers and intellectuals. (At Nuremberg, the Germans found themselves accused of this crime.) In April 1945, over 400 German soldiers at the Dachau concentration camp were put to death by the Allied liberators of the camp. These were ordinary soldiers who had taken over from the SS guards who had fled.

British officers who gunned down the fleeing survivors of a German ship in 1940 were awarded the Victoria Cross. The Germans had killed Allied commandos and paratroopers who had fallen into their hands. But, then, American soldiers had done exactly the same in Italy.[77] These examples show that all parties in the War had innocent blood on their hands. However, only the vanquished were to be held accountable.

The greatest irony, as Irving shows, was that even after the War had ended, the Allies continued to indulge in the very crimes with which the Germans had been charged. Thousands of Russians captured with Hitler's troops were 'sent back to the tender mercies of Stalin's secret police' after the War.[78] The Soviet Union as well as the Western Allies treated German prisoners harshly and used the civilian population as slave labour in reparation for

German crimes (despite Jackson's efforts to prevent this from happening). The Soviet Union engaged in the ethnic cleansing of Germans in Poland and Czechoslovakia.

Irving is often portrayed as an apologist for Nazi Germany. In his book on Nuremberg, he makes it clear that the crimes of the Allied powers cannot be said to extenuate the horrors perpetrated by the Third Reich. As he puts it felicitously,[79]

> None of this (that is, the crimes of the Allies) can be read, of course, as justifying or even mitigating the Nazi excesses, particularly the horrors inflicted by the S.S. on the populations of eastern Europe. It is pointless to weigh, one against the other, such catalogues of horrors and atrocities. The deeper lesson is that war itself is a crime—and that the real crime of war is not genocide but the far broader bestiality which embraces genocide, and which we can label Innocenticide, the Slaughter of the Innocents.

He adds drily, 'This slaughter was still not at an end, even as Robert Jackson was preparing to undertake his holy crusade against war, because there would soon follow the release by his own country of the atomic bombs above Hiroshima and Nagasaki.' This should give those who have sought to demonize Irving something to chew over.

Jackson was interested in having a trial although he was in little doubt about the outcome. He valued the trial as a spectacle and he also wanted it to serve a much grander purpose: the creation of an international framework that would prohibit wars of aggression. He fondly hoped that the rules that he set out to create for the Nuremberg trials would equally apply to leaders who led their countries into wars in the future. 'The definitions under which we will try the Germans are general definitions. They impose liability upon war-making statesmen of all countries alike.' Irving remarks acerbically, 'They were brave words, but they had not the slightest effect on the statesmen who would wage one hundred wars, large and small, in the half-century after he uttered them.'[80]

Jackson came under tremendous pressure from Jewish groups to focus separately on the extermination of Jews during the War. He refused to oblige. As he put it, 'We are prosecuting these Nazis not because they killed Jews, but because they killed men and women.' He wanted to ensure that the trial did not end up as an act of vengeance on behalf of any particular community.[81]

After a great deal of squabbling, amongst the four Big Powers, a list of twenty-two names was prepared for trial (including one, Martin Bormann, Hitler's private secretary, who would be tried in absentia). The inclusion of Admiral Karl Donitz was particularly controversial as neither the British nor the American officials concerned thought there was a case against him. The desperation to include one industrialist, Gustav Krupp, in the list verged on the hilarious. Every attempt was made to include Krupp, by then senile and quite ill. His name was dropped when a medical team comprising doctors from various countries reported that he was in no condition to be tried.

The rules according to which the trials were conducted evoked a huge controversy, especially in the US. First, the Allies were seeking to convict their enemies under laws that did not exist at the time. In other words, laws were created and applied with retrospective effect. On the retroactive nature of the Nuremberg laws, Justice William O. Douglas of the US Supreme Court expressed widespread concerns when he wrote:[82]

> Hitler and his ilk were guilty of multiple murders and under common law deserved the death penalty. But they were not indicted under the relevant national laws. Before the Nuremberg trials the crime of which the Nazis were convicted was never considered to have been such an act under our criminal laws, nor was it held by the international community to be under threat of the death penalty.

Second, the rules stated that Germans could not argue that the other side had committed the same crimes. By way of illustration, Irving mentions how the lawyers for the defendants were not allowed to introduce a handbook given to British commandos that explicitly ordered them to kill captured German prisoners, often in gruesome ways. The victors could allow themselves the luxury of blatant double standards.[83]

Third, the Germans could not plead that they were carrying out orders that they were bound to obey as soldiers. Irving highlights the extent of manipulation that the Allies indulged in in their attempt to convict the German defendants. Both British and American military laws explicitly stated that members of the armed forces could not be held responsible for carrying out orders given by the government or by their commanders. When it was recognized that this provision could be troublesome in prosecuting the Germans, the particular provision in the British manual was changed in April 1944 and the American manual seven months later!

The dice was loaded against the defendants in more ways than one. The prosecution had access to all the materials seized from the German side. However, they would share with the defendants' lawyers only the incriminating material. They would not allow the defendants access to material that might be used in mitigation or exoneration. The defendants' lawyers faced threats, harassment and even arrest. Witnesses friendly to the prosecution were housed in luxurious conditions whereas hostile witnesses languished in the jailhouse in conditions no better than those of the defendants.

Witnesses sought by the defence were often declared untraceable. One key witness was arrested. Another was committed to a mental asylum. (He was summoned in the case of another defendant when he was able to prove his sanity and was released to a normal prison.)[84] While the prosecution could make an opening statement, not so the defence counsel. At the end, the defence lawyers were permitted a brief closing speech, followed by a lengthy prosecution statement to which the defence counsel could not reply.

The German prisoners, all top generals or members of Hitler's cabinet, were kept in inhuman conditions in the jailhouse in Nuremberg. They were provided meagre rations, given little medical treatment, provided hardly any time for exercise and exposed to severe cold. The commandant in charge of the jailhouse, Colonel Andrus, told the prisoners that the Geneva Convention on prisoners of war did not apply to them as the German state no longer existed. Irving notes coldly that the Geneva Convention had 'provided expressly that no signatory could suppress its provisions for one full year after the cessation of hostilities . . . it was not within the gift of either Eisenhower or his superiors or his junior officers like Colonel Andrus to abrogate it.'[85] The families of the defendants were not spared. The wives were rounded up and lodged in prison while the children were sent to orphanages.

Irving concedes that, despite all of what is stated above, the defence counsel did receive assistance and support of a greater order than might have been expected from lesser occupying powers. The defence lawyers, he says, were 'overwhelmed by the courtesies extended to them by the victors'.[86] He mentions in particular the Defense Information Center that was created in the courthouse to cater to the documentary needs of the fifty defence lawyers.

The proceedings went pretty much the way Jackson wanted until Hermann Goering, Reichsmarschall and number two in Germany under Hitler, took the stand. Goering had been portrayed in the Western media as a 'dope fiend, a physical wreck and a neurotic'.[87] Many in the West were astonished and dismayed as he proceeded to make a powerful case for himself and the Third Reich. His first day, Irving notes, 'produced a debacle which threatened to dismantle the whole edifice that Jackson and his colleagues had painstakingly laboured to erect'.[88]

Jackson had hoped to tame Goering during the cross-examination. That did not happen. Irving says that Jackson's skills were somewhat rusty since he had long ceased to practise as a lawyer. Goering had the advantage of knowing English whereas Jackson had to await the translation of Goering's utterances from German to English. Most crucially, Goering had decided to make one last stand knowing full well what the outcome would be. His intention was to ridicule the entire trial, not to work towards his acquittal. This devil-may-care attitude lent a certain vigour to his defence of the Third Reich. The general reckoning is that the Jackson–Goering duel had resulted in a victory for the latter.

The judges deliberated their judgment over nearly three months. Very little of these deliberations is known except for notes made by the American judge, Francis Biddle. Irving was able to access these notes. The notes, Irving observes, indicate that, after nine months of trial, the judges were 'floundering on even the most essential issues'.[89] The French judge, for instance, was uncomfortable with the charge of conspiracy but was overruled by Justice Geoffrey Lawrence, the British judge who presided over the tribunal.

Of the twenty-two defendants, nineteen were found guilty. Three were acquitted. Twelve of the defendants were sentenced to the gallows. The remaining seven were given jail sentences of varying terms. Four organizations were found to have been criminal in character—the Nazi Party, the SS (a paramilitary organization that reported to Hitler), the Gestapo (Hitler's secret police) and the S.D. (the intelligence arm of the SS). The Reich cabinet and the OKW (the military high command) were acquitted.

Irving does not hide his dissatisfaction over particular judgments. Hjalmar Schacht, minister for economics in Hitler's cabinet, was acquitted because the central banking elite in the West did not want one of their own to be punished. Albert Speer, the armaments minister, got away with a prison sentence because he had turned against Hitler and his former colleagues during the trial. Julius Streicher was sentenced to hang although he had not been involved in Hitler's government after 1939. Alfred Jodl, a professional soldier, was sentenced to death. (In 1953, a German court cleared Jodl of the charges on which he had been convicted and rehabilitated him posthumously.) Some of these anomalies troubled Jackson but he could do little about them.

Irving is at his best when he captures the thoughts of the many actors in the concluding few months of the trial—the Chief Prosecutor Jackson, Judge Biddle of the US, and the twenty-one defendants in the jailhouse—through the notes and memoirs of the people involved. He describes poignantly the last moments of the condemned men, especially their meetings with their families and their interactions with the jail officials. He gives a graphic account of how Goering cheated the hangman by taking cyanide. Irving writes, 'His suicide, shrouded in mystery and emphasizing the impotency of the American guards, was a skilful, even brilliant, finishing touch, completing the edifice for Germans to admire in time to come.'[90]

Finally, out of the charges made against Germany, what did the tribunal accept and not accept? The German attack on Poland was seen as a clear war of aggression. The tribunal rejected the defence contention that the attack on Russia was a preventive war. The tribunal also did not accept that the German invasion of Norway in 1940 was preventive in character but this, Irving says, was because the British would not allow access to their own files that would have revealed Britain's own intentions to invade Norway.

Strikingly, the tribunal did not characterize Germany's wars with France and Britain as wars of aggression. The allegations against German submarine warfare were rejected and there was no mention of the aerial warfare waged by Germany. The tribunal also confirmed that the liquidation operations in Germany were unknown to the German public, thereby making it clear that there was no question of collective guilt for the crimes.

Jackson's fond hopes of outlawing wars of aggression forever evaporated within years of the trials. The Soviet Union waged war on South Korea in 1951. Britain, France and Israel launched an attack on Egypt in 1956. To which one might add that the wars waged by the US and its allies against Iraq, Libya and Syria in recent years have happened without the provisions of the Nuremberg tribunal even being mentioned. The Nuremberg trials have come to be clearly seen for what they were: victors' justice.

Irving's account is gripping and, on the whole, one that accords with the mainstream narrative. His views on the Holocaust, which have discredited him as a historian, take up very little space in this book.

* * *

Irving's ostracism is almost complete today. He speaks to small, carefully selected audiences (presumably in order to avoid heckling and disruption). He takes groups of tourists on paid trips to Nazi concentration camps and to Hitler's headquarters on the Eastern Front, Wolf's Lair. One reporter managed to attend one of his meetings—there were just five people around.[91]

Irving remains unfazed by the scorn heaped on him. He claims to be generating more and more interest among the younger generation. He says that he gets huge amounts of donations. Years after being bankrupted by the Lipstadt trial, he drives around in a Rolls-Royce. One of his critics laments that the Internet, instead of damning Irving conclusively, seems to have had the opposite effect—of rendering Holocaust denial more common.[92]

As I have pointed out, Irving has not denied the atrocities perpetrated by the Nazis. Nor has he denied the extermination of Jews in his books. He disputes the official number, 6 million. He claims that a large proportion of the deaths of Jews occurred due to starvation and disease, not through gas chambers.

Where Irving transgresses the bounds of reasonableness is in seeking to exonerate Hitler of the crime of extermination of Jews in the Third Reich. This one failing has meant that his contributions as a military historian have come to be ignored. Many critics ask with some justification: If Irving has falsified facts in one crucial respect, how can we rely on anything he says?

There is an important, if obvious, lesson to be drawn from Irving's rise and fall. Dissenters must be careful to stick scrupulously to facts at all times. If they take even the slightest chances with their credibility, their efforts to take on the establishment will come to nought.

5

Yanis Varoufakis: Economist as Iconoclast

There's a question that many of us have confronted at some point in our careers. Is it possible to disagree with the establishment view and yet work from within the system? In other words, can a serious dissenter ever be an insider?

Economist Yanis Varoufakis found the answer during his brief stint of about six months as finance minister of Greece. He was appointed to the job to resolve what came to be known as the Greek debt crisis, the problem of servicing the debt owed by the Greek government to various investors.

Quite early into his tenure as finance minister, Varoufakis receives an answer to the question posed above. Larry Summers, economist, former Treasury Secretary of the US and ex-president of Harvard University, provides the answer. The two meet at a bar in Washington. Summers gives him a basic lesson in power politics:[1]

> There are two kinds of politicians, insiders and outsiders. The outsiders prioritize their freedom to speak their version of the truth. The price of their freedom is that they are ignored by the insiders, who make the important decisions. The insiders,

for their part, follow a sacrosanct rule: never turn against other insiders and never talk to outsiders about what insiders say or do. Their reward? Access to inside information and a chance, though no guarantee, of influencing people and outcomes.

Summers then asks Varoufakis, 'So, Yanis, which of the two are you?' He's suggesting that Varoufakis make up his mind whether he wants to be an insider or an outsider. If Varoufakis wanted to be an insider, it was best to fall in line with the others and not speak his mind. Then, he had a chance to be somebody. The costs and benefits of being an insider were pretty clear.

Varoufakis tells Summers that he's willing to play insider as long as Greece can be freed from 'debt bondage'. If the insiders were not prepared to ensure that, he would return to the outside which 'is my natural habitat anyway'.

That's what happened eventually. Varoufakis found himself disagreeing with his comrades in the Greek government on the way forward and resigned as finance minister. He reverted to his natural habitat, the outside. He has since done what comes to him naturally: speaking his mind and taking on the establishment. He's been striving hard to influence outcomes from the outside.

As Varoufakis explains, the choice he made is partly in his genes.

His father Yiorgos was born in Cairo and was brought up in a highly cosmopolitan environment. At the age of twenty, he decided to move to Greece and enrolled as a student of chemistry at the University of Athens. He was elected president of the students' association.

When the university effected a steep hike in fees, Yiorgos met the dean and argued against a fee hike. When he left the dean's office, he was arrested by policemen, roughed up and left in a cold cell for hours. A high-ranking officer then took Yiorgos to his office. The officer apologized for the treatment meted out to Yiorgos and offered to release him if he would sign a statement the officer had kept ready. The statement read: I hereby denounce, truly and in all sincerity, communism, those who promote it, and their various fellow travellers.[2]

Yiorgos calmly told the officer that he was not a Buddhist or a Muslim but would never sign a document denouncing Buddhism or Islam. He was not a communist but he saw no reason why he should be asked to denounce communism. He was beaten up and tortured and found himself in several cells and prison camps over four years. He could have walked out any time by signing a statement but he was not willing to do so.

Signing on a sheet of paper was thus not something in Varoufakis' genes.

* * *

Varoufakis was born in Athens in 1961. Greece had then emerged briefly from its post-War spell of dictatorship. When he was six, a military coup took place, returning Greece to dictatorship. He writes, 'Those bleak days remain with me. They endowed me with a sense of what it means to be both unfree and, at once, convinced that the possibilities for progress and improvement are endless.'[3]

The dictatorship collapsed by the time Varoufakis was at junior high school. When the time came for him to choose his college, the prospect of another spell of military dictatorship was not ruled out. College students were the primary targets of any military regime. His parents decided it was best that he study abroad. In 1978, he went to study in Britain. He enrolled for a degree in economics at the University of Essex.

Within weeks of his joining, his rebellious genes started asserting themselves. He found the lectures and textbooks inane and the mathematics 'third-rate'. He changed his enrolment to mathematics, telling himself, 'If I am going to be reading mathematics I might as well read proper mathematics.'

After graduating from Essex, Varoufakis went to the University of Birmingham for an MSc in mathematical statistics. While looking for a thesis topic, he came across a piece of econometric work. He found it so sloppy that he sought to demolish it. That led on to a PhD in economics and a career in economics departments. Between 1982 and 1988, he taught at the universities of Essex, East Anglia and Cambridge. He writes cheerfully that as an academic, he 'enjoyed debunking that which my colleagues considered to be legitimate "science"'. Even in the early stages of his career, Varoufakis seems to have resolved that he would be an 'outsider'.

When Margaret Thatcher was elected a third time as prime minister in 1987, Varoufakis thought it 'too much to bear'. He decided it was time to leave the UK. From out of the blue, he received an offer to teach at the University of Sydney. From 1988 to 2000, he lived and worked in Sydney. When Australia took a turn towards a conservative government in 2000, Varoufakis decided to return to Greece. This is a man who will leave a country and relocate if he doesn't like the government—even if it's a democratically elected one.

Varoufakis joined the University of Athens. Of his time there he says with some pride, 'The better students in Greece, and the better amongst my colleagues, were intellectually and ethically head-and-shoulders above the majority of the better students, and colleagues, elsewhere.' Varoufakis was to leave Greece in 2012, again because he was willing to stand up for what he believed in. Of that more later.

* * *

The Greek debt crisis of 2010 was one of the defining moments for the global financial system after the financial crisis of 2007. How it unfolded and how it came to be resolved is a gripping story. In what follows, I will keep the exposition simple but some understanding of basic economics is required.

Greece is a member of the eurozone, the nineteen European countries that share a common currency, the euro. In 2001, when it joined the eurozone, its per capita income was 67 per cent of that of Germany. There was an expectation that Greece's joining the eurozone would raise its income to that of Germany over time. This triggered a huge flow of capital into Greece as investors were eager to cash in on the high growth they expected.

From 2001 to 2009, Greek per capita income rose, fuelled by a rise in Greek debt, public and private. The boom was unsustainable. A high level of borrowing from abroad means a high current account deficit—capital inflows finance a deficit in the current account. It can also mean a high fiscal deficit—governments need to borrow when they can't balance their expenditure with revenues. The fiscal deficit peaked at 15.6 per cent at the end of the period. Greece's public debt to GDP ratio rose from 100 per cent at the beginning of the period to 130 per cent. Labour costs rose and Greece's competitiveness against other economies deteriorated.[4]

The high level of public debt frightened lenders. They responded by cutting off further loans and seeking repayment of the existing ones. Greece was in no position to service its debt. By early 2010, the Greek state was bankrupt.

When a borrower cannot service his debts, he declares insolvency. The lenders then agree to restructure his debt. This involves many elements. A key element is to write off some of the debt. There are other elements, such as stretching the payment of the remaining debt over a longer period, reducing the interest rate on debt, etc. The intention is to reduce the debt burden so that the borrower is better placed to service debt.

The borrower, in turn, agrees to reduce costs, say, by laying off some workers. He may also agree to sell off unproductive assets or investments he may have in order to generate income that will help service his debt. Thus, the burden of adjusting to bankruptcy is shared by both, lender and borrower.

This did not happen in the case of Greece. The Greek debt problem was dealt with by the troika of the International Monetary Fund (IMF), the European Commission (which is the executive arm of the European Union [EU]) and the European Central Bank (ECB). The troika organized a loan of €110 bn to Greece to enable it to service its existing debt.

Instead of reducing the debt burden on Greece, the troika chose to increase it. This came to be characterized as the 'rescue' or 'bailout' of Greece! The loan was given on the condition that Greece would agree to a package of 'austerity' measures—cuts in government spending (with the axe falling heavily on pensions and public health programmes), higher taxes, privatization of Greek government assets, etc.

Thus, the burden of adjustment fell entirely on Greece. This agreement was incorporated in a Memorandum of Understanding (MoU) signed by the Greek government and the troika. In the years that followed, the troika would not budge from the commitments made by Greece in this MoU and in the one that accompanied a second bailout in 2012.

In his book, *Adults in the Room*, a scathing account of what went on behind the scenes, Varoufakis details the measures imposed on Greece, its outcomes and his own failed attempt to negotiate a way out of the crisis after he became finance minister in 2015.[5] The title is based on a remark made by Christine Lagarde, the IMF managing director. At one point during the negotiations between Greece and the troika, Lagarde said in exasperation that if the drama was to be resolved, they needed 'adults in the room'.

The 'bailout' of Greece in 2010, Varoufakis points out, was meant for the French and German banks that had lent to Greece. These banks were holders of Greek government bonds. Greece was not in a position to service these bonds. Had it declared bankruptcy, the governments of Italy, Ireland, Spain and Portugal would have followed suit (the five economies were together somewhat uncharitably labelled the PIIGS economies). The

German and French governments would then have had to rescue their banks at a cost of over €1 trillion.

France and Germany had already infused enormous amounts to save their banks after the sub-prime crisis of 2007. It would have been difficult for them to justify to their parliaments and their people another large infusion of capital into their banks. Greece had to be saved from bankruptcy in the interest of French and German banks.[6]

The participation of the IMF in the bailout was intended to give the feeling that this was an international effort aimed at saving the international financial system. The €110 bn bill was not being footed entirely by France, Germany and the IMF. Other EU countries would contribute in the name of showing solidarity with their fellow Europeans, the Greeks.

French and German banks immediately benefited from the Greek 'bailout'. The French banks reduced their holdings of Greek government bonds from over €100 bn to nil by December 2012. The German banks reduced their exposure to Greek government bonds from around €120 bn to €795 million by March 2012.[7]

In 2012, the troika decided that Greece needed another loan—of €130 bn—in order to keep servicing its debt. Unlike in 2010, they were willing this time around to write off some of Greece's debt. However, the troika was clear who would bear the brunt of the write-offs of debt. It would be Greek pension funds, Greek semi-public institutions and Greek savers who had invested in government bonds; not foreign investors.

This was not all. Greek public debt would go up and hence the burden on the people of Greece. However, the loan of €130 bn would be used not to increase their future income—say, by investing in infrastructure—but to take care of various foreign lenders to the Greek government. The bulk of the €130 bn would not go to the Greek state. It would go to Greek private banks, to Greece's foreign private lenders and towards servicing the loans made by the EU and the IMF in the first bailout.[8] This was billed as the 'second bailout' of Greece!

The loan came with several humiliating conditions. Greek private banks would be bailed out but the state would have little control on them. The head of the state revenues and customs department would be appointed with the approval of the troika and could not be fired without the troika's approval. Greek privatization would happen under the auspices of an authority controlled by the troika.

The Greek government went along because the alternative was too frightening to contemplate. Greece would be kicked out of the eurozone and would have to produce its own currency. It would be cut off from the financial markets. Greek banks would be closed down as the ECB would cut off access to its funds which were keeping the bankrupt banks afloat.

As Greece entered a period of turmoil, Varoufakis met Alexis Tsipras in early 2011. Still in his mid-thirties, Tsipras had emerged as the leader of the left-wing party, Syriza. Varoufakis told Tsipras that one of three outcomes was possible in dealing with the troika. The best one was restructuring Greece's debt accompanied by economic reform. The worst was continuing on the existing basis, which meant that Greece would be in debtors' prison forever. In between was Grexit, the option of leaving the eurozone.

Tsipras seemed to think that Grexit was the best outcome. Varoufakis explained that for Greece to do without the euro as its currency, it needed to have enough currency of its own. Printing its own currency would take months. It was best to negotiate the restructuring of Greek debt. Over the meetings that followed, Tsipras seemed to come round to Varoufakis' thinking.

Throughout 2011 Varoufakis wrote and spoke extensively about the true nature of the two bailouts—whom it was intended to benefit and how the Greek political system had been complicit in a bailout of private lenders. He received a post-midnight call one day warning him that his teenage son would not be safe if he continued to write his articles. In early 2012, his partner Danae and he decided to move to the US. Varoufakis initially worked as economist-in-residence at Valve Corporation. Then he took up a teaching position at the University of Texas's Lyndon B. Johnson School of Public Affairs.

* * *

Greece had its general election in May 2012. It threw up an unstable coalition government. Another round of elections followed in June 2012. A coalition government was formed between the leading conservative party and a centre-left party. Syriza remained in the Opposition but with more seats than before.

As the Greek government pushed ahead with austerity measures, its unpopularity rose. By 2014, it was clear that its days were numbered. From the US, Varoufakis kept in touch with Tsipras and the Syriza party. He frequently visited Greece. Tsipras and his colleagues suggested that Varoufakis take the job of finance minister and lead the negotiations over Greek debt in the event the Syriza government came to power.

Varoufakis wanted Tsipras and his colleagues to agree to his plan for resolving the Greek debt crisis and also his negotiating strategy. His plan involved six key elements. One, Greek debt must be restructured. Two, the primary surplus in the government's budget should not exceed 1.5 per cent of national income. Three, there would be reductions in sales and business tax rates. Four, there would be strategic privatizations subject to worker interests being protected. Five, a development bank would be created that would use the remaining public assets to generate domestic investment. Six, all shares and management of private Greek banks would be transferred to the EU so that the Greek government did not have to finance them any more.[9]

As for the negotiating strategy, Varoufakis had to reckon with one powerful weapon the troika wielded in the negotiations with

Greece. Greece's bankrupt banks depended on a cash infusion from the ECB in order to keep going. The ECB could threaten to shut down Greek banks by withholding liquidity support. There would be a run on the banks as depositors rushed to withdraw money. The ensuing chaos would cause the government of the day to collapse.

How could the Syriza party prepare for such an eventuality assuming it would come to power? Varoufakis proposed that Greece should threaten a delay or a haircut (meaning, a reduction) in the payments owed on ECB bonds held by Greece. He felt such a threat would profoundly unsettle the troika. Varoufakis outlined why.

The ECB chief Mario Draghi had given the assurance that he would do 'whatever it takes' to keep the euro alive. This assurance came at a time when the financial markets were wary of any further exposure to the debt of the problem-ridden economies of the eurozone. If the members of the eurozone could not raise debt to finance themselves, they would choose to exit the euro. Draghi's assurance meant that he was willing to purchase vast amounts of debt floated by the eurozone members.

There was a problem with living up to this assurance. A German court had ruled that the ECB could purchase eurozone bonds subject to its not facing any losses on these. Any Greek threat to impose losses on ECB bonds would thus put the brakes on the ECB purchase of such bonds. That, in turn, could cause the collapse of the euro, as we mentioned above. This was the trump card that Greece held in its negotiations with the EU and the IMF. By signalling that it would take steps that could cause the collapse of the euro, Greece could get the IMF, the EU and the ECB to negotiate a compromise with Greece.

Varoufakis also suggested that Greece prepare itself to put in place a parallel payments system if the troika decided to shut down Greece's banks. He offered Tsipras a detailed blueprint of such a system. Having a parallel payments system would help Greece stand up to the troika if they threatened to oust Greece from the euro.

Varoufakis was very clear in his mind that a Syriza government must stick to its terms even if threatened with Grexit. Tsipras and his colleagues agreed. Varoufakis set one more condition. He would serve as finance minister only if elected to Parliament. Tsipras was aghast as Varoufakis had never contested an election before. Varoufakis would not back off:[10]

> If I am to face up to Wolfgang Schauble [Germany's finance minister] in the Eurogroup, a seasoned politician who has received his people's backing for decades, I need to go in there with thousands of votes backing me too. Otherwise, I would lack the necessary legitimacy.

Tsipras agreed.

As a candidate for the elections, Varoufakis had a chance to spell out details of how he would like Greece's debt problem to be resolved. He wanted Greece's public debt to be split into four components:[11]

i.   ECB debt
ii. Debt owed to the rest of Europe (60 per cent of total debt)
iii. Debt owed to the IMF (about 10 per cent of the total)
iv. Debt owed to private investors (about 15 per cent of total debt)

Varoufakis proposed that (iii) and (iv) be honoured in full. Private investors had already taken a 90 per cent haircut and there was no point in provoking them further. The US regarded the IMF as its own and it was not worth antagonizing the US.

As for (i), ECB debt, it would be converted into perpetual debt with a small interest rate. Debt owed to Europe's taxpayers would be swapped with new thirty-year Greek bonds with two provisions. One, annual payments would be suspended until the country's income recovered to beyond a certain threshold. Two, the interest rate would be linked to the growth rate of the Greek economy. The idea was that lenders would become partners in Greece's growth instead of being responsible for the decline of the Greek economy.

The Greek establishment reacted with alarm to these proposals. A prominent Greek banker told Tsipras that Greek banks' ATMs would not function the day after the election if Varoufakis was made finance minister. Tsipras asked the banker how old he was. Sixty-five, came the response. Tsipras replied: If you overthrow me, I am young enough to rise again. You are not![12]

Tsipras gave his backing to Varoufakis' plan for resolving Greece's debt crisis.

* * *

In January 2015, Syriza swept to power, securing a near majority on its own. Varoufakis was elected to Parliament with the highest number of votes anybody got in the election. Huge crowds gathered to celebrate in front of the Syntagma Square where the government offices are located.

Varoufakis was sworn in as finance minister. He met Tsipras a little later in the prime minister's office. Alexis told Varoufakis:[13]

Listen! Don't get comfortable in here. Don't learn to love the trappings of office. These offices, these chairs, are not for us. Our place is out there, on the streets, in the squares, with the people. We got in to get a job done on their behalf. Never forget that this is why we are here. For no other reason. And be ready. If the bastards find a way to stop us from delivering what we promised, you and I must be ready to hand back the keys and get out on the streets again, to plan the next demonstration.

Varoufakis' spirits soared. He was ready to fight the big fight that lay ahead.

On 20 February, the new government sought and obtained from the troika a four-month extension of the bailout. They had until 30 June to enter into negotiations with the troika. A group within the eurozone, known as the Eurogroup, was formed to negotiate with Greece.

Varoufakis secured agreement to a three-step process. In step one, by 23 February 2015, Greece would submit a list of reforms that was different from the toxic reforms proposed in the MoU. In step two, the troika would study the proposed reforms and communicate on 24 February through a teleconference whether the reforms were sufficiently comprehensive. In step three, in mid-April, an assessment would be made of the progress made by Greece. If successful, it would lead to the release of funds with which to repay the amounts due to the IMF. Following these three steps, a fresh agreement could be concluded with the troika by June 2015, one that would replace the existing MoU.

On 23 February, Varoufakis emailed the reforms that Greece would carry out. His email was delayed until thirteen minutes past midnight, thanks to a delay in the troika officials responding to a draft sent earlier in the afternoon. The media promptly seized on the delay: Varoufakis Misses Deadline.

On 24 February, Varoufakis got a shock. The troika conveyed to him that his proposed reforms could not replace anything in the MoU! The troika was not willing to abide by the understanding reached on 20 February. In retrospect, Varoufakis thinks he should have called off the negotiations at that very moment. He did not do so. He clung to the hope that, over the next four months, a compromise could still be worked out.

An even greater shock was in store. The problem was not just with the troika but within his own government. The Greek government was to have sent a request to the troika to extend the bailout. On 26 February, Varoufakis learnt that the troika had sent a template of the request to the Greek government on 21 February by email. The email had mentioned that the deadline for making any changes to it was 23 February. One of his deputies, George Chouliarakis, the Chairman of his Council of Economic Advisers, was among those marked in the email. Chouliarakis had not passed on the communication to Varoufakis. Unknown to Varoufakis, the deadline for making changes to the troika's letter had expired!

Varoufakis was outraged. He told Chouliarakis that he would lose his present assignment. To which Chouliarakis replied coolly that he would join the Greek central bank whose governor, known to be a troika favourite, had a position for him. Varoufakis conveyed the news to Tsipras. He expected Tsipras to erupt in rage. To his surprise, Tsipras was unfazed. This was an early sign that Tsipras' commitment to the stated position of Syriza, the plank on which it had been voted to power, had begun to falter.

However, Varoufakis was reluctant to acknowledge the fact in the initial months of his tenure. He repeatedly made excuses for Tsipras' lack of consistency:[14]

> Again and again during the weeks [that followed an initial indication that Tsipras could not be trusted to take a principled position], instead of recognising his evident duplicity, I would find excuses for Alexis' backtracking from our covenant. I would blame it on fear, depression and inexperience, relying eventually on sheer faith that the moment would come when he [would] bounce back, shake off the tentacles, reactivate his belief in our cause . . .

Varoufakis told himself that the people of Greece had reposed faith in the two of them and he should not let them down.

He was in for a huge disappointment.

* * *

In the months that followed, Varoufakis engaged in hectic parleys with leaders in Europe and the IMF in an attempt to get the troika to move away from the MoU and accept the Greek government's proposals on the debt crisis. He flew from one capital in Europe to another, pleading, cajoling, at times taunting his interlocutors.

Pictures of Varoufakis wearing a black leather jacket and riding his motorbike became famous. In Germany, a TV news anchor gushed that Varoufakis reminded her of the actor Bruce Willis. One magazine gushed about Varoufakis' 'classical masculinity'. His tieless appearance and his preference for not tucking in his shirts and leaving their tops unbuttoned evoked comment and admiration. 'What makes Yanis Varoufakis a sex icon' was the headline in a German newspaper.[15]

Varoufakis once showed up for an official meeting in Paris wearing a tight blue shirt and a leather overcoat. It created a splash in the media. Varoufakis suggests the sensationalism was misplaced. He had travelled without any change of clothes. Upon arrival in Paris, he had found that most shops were closed. The best he could do was to pick up two 'vaguely suitable' shirts and borrow a coat from Greece's ambassador to France.[16] To the world, it seemed that Varoufakis was trying to advertise his status as a maverick and outsider to the European establishment.

Varoufakis obtained support for his plans from American economists Jeffrey Sachs and Jamie Galbraith. He had the broad sympathy of former US Treasury Secretary Larry Summers. He was able to reach across to and win over Norman Lamont, the conservative former Chancellor of the Exchequer of the UK, and France's economics minister and future President, Emmanuel Macron.

The key negotiators within the eurozone, including German finance minister Wolfgang Schauble, would make appreciative noises about Varoufakis' approach and even say a few positive things in public. In private, the head of the IMF in Europe went so far as to propose a write-off of €53 bn of debt—Varoufakis wondered whether he was dreaming.

When it came to the crunch, however, the officials of the eurozone were not willing to move away from the troika's basic position: Greece must practise extreme austerity in order to repay the debt it had been saddled with. None of the arguments that Varoufakis could muster, none of his appeals for reasonableness changed this reality one bit.

Tsipras nursed the hope that he could look beyond Europe for help—to the US and Russia. One proposal was that Greece could do a swap with the US Federal Reserve whereby the Fed would provide dollars in exchange for a new Greek currency. (This would have helped the Greek government confront the troika with the threat of Grexit.) Another was that Russia would provide €5 bn for the construction of a pipeline. Both these hopes were dashed by March 2015.

Tsipras met Germany's Chancellor Angela Merkel on 20 March. Merkel went over Greece's proposals in great detail. Then, she came up with an idea. Since the Greeks detested Schauble and Varoufakis was seen by the Eurogroup as a problem, why not let the two 'cancel' each other? Merkel and Tsipras could then do a deal with each other.

Tsipras fell for the idea. A new group was created for carrying out negotiations. In the weeks to come, it was even insinuated—through inspired leaks—that Varoufakis and Schauble were plotting behind the backs of their leaders to get Greece out of the euro! Merkel had managed to drive a wedge between Tsipras and Varoufakis.

Varoufakis recounts an unsettling cabinet meeting on 3 April. Varoufakis had met Tsipras before the meeting and told him that, since there had been no progress in talks, it was time to announce that Greece would default on repayments to the IMF. Tsipras told him that the time had not yet come for a default. At the meeting, however, Tsipras changed his stance dramatically:[17]

Greece is still a sovereign country and we, the cabinet, have the duty to say, 'Enough!' . . . Not only are we going to default but you [Varoufakis] are going to get on a plane, go to Washington and tell the lady [Christine Lagarde] in person that we shall default on the IMF.

It was arranged that Varoufakis would meet Lagarde over the Easter holidays. Even as Varoufakis was leaving the airport in Washington, he saw a text message from Tsipras on his mobile asking him to call. When Varoufakis called, Tsipras told him, 'Look, Yani, we've decided that we're not going to default, not yet.'[18] Yet another volte-face!

An astonished Varoufakis asked him what he should then say to the IMF chief. Tsipras told him that he should go ahead and threaten a default. The threat of a default would get Lagarde to call the ECB president and get him to relax the liquidity squeeze he had imposed on Greece.

Varoufakis duly conveyed the message to Lagarde. He received no assurance from the IMF chief that she would lean on the ECB to ease the liquidity situation in Greece. Lagarde suggested coolly that it was up to the ECB president to decide how to respond. On yet another trip to Washington, Varoufakis got conflicting signals from the US government. President Barack Obama was friendly but offered nothing more than a homily about Greece compromising with the institutions and meeting them halfway. The US representative at the IMF was more helpful. He asked Varoufakis to prepare his own plan for the IMF instead of a modified version of the MoU.

This was followed by another meeting with the Eurogroup in Riga in Latvia on 24 April. Varoufakis was told bluntly that there was no alternative to implementing the MoU in full. No interim measures or compromises could be considered. The media kept up a steady drumbeat of criticism against Varoufakis. Bloomberg reported:[19]

Euro area finance chiefs said Varoufakis' handling of the talks
was irresponsible and accused him of being a time-waster, a
gambler and an amateur . . .

A Reuters report said:[20]

While other ministers were feted by their entourages with food
and warm clothing during the meeting in Riga, Varoufakis was
seen alone at almost *every* turn, eschewing aides or any security
detail. 'He is completely isolated', a senior Eurozone official
told Reuters on condition of anonymity.

In the meantime, the German Chancellery leaked the news that
Merkel had given Tsipras the cold shoulder. Sensing that Tsipras
was not as committed to their position as he was earlier, Varoufakis
offered to step down. Tsipras assured Varoufakis of his continued
support:[21]

Yani . . . They are aiming at your undoing to undo me. They
want to get you to get at me. We are not going to let them,
right? We are going to stand together. I do not want to hear
again about this nonsense [about resigning]. Stay strong. We
have a war to win.

Barely two days later, at a cabinet meeting, Tsipras was singing a
different tune. He said he was replacing Varoufakis' deputy with
Chouliarakis. He said he had to offer the Eurogroup something
as they had demanded Varoufakis' head. Those who spoke at the
meeting supported Tsipras. Varoufakis' isolation in the cabinet
was complete.

Varoufakis met Tsipras later that day with his resignation
letter in his pocket. As he waited for Tsipras, he noticed a few
papers lying on his table. One number on one of the pages caught
his attention. Tsipras was committing himself to a primary budget

surplus of 3.5 per cent for the next ten years. Tsipras intended to junk Syriza's position that the surplus could be 1.5 per cent at the most!

Tsipras offered the feeble defence that he was making the concession in the expectation that the troika would offer something in return. Incredibly, even at this point, Varoufakis could not bring himself to resign. He still clung to the hope that when Tsipras was confronted with the reality that the troika would not offer anything in return—when he faced complete ignominy—he would be moved to defiance.

One episode that Varoufakis mentions stands out. He calls Jeffrey Sachs and tells him that his government is finally ready to default on its repayment on the IMF repayment. Half an hour later, Sachs calls him up. He says that five minutes after he hung up, he got a call from the US National Security Council asking whether Varoufakis had meant what he said. Varoufakis' phone had been tapped and the spooks were making no bones about it!

This should have alerted Varoufakis to the possibility that the Americans and the Europeans knew full well what was going on within the Greek government. They would have known that Varoufakis had been isolated in his cabinet. They would have also known that the Greek government's threats about Grexit were one big bluff.

* * *

The endgame unfolded rapidly. At a meeting in Brussels in early May, Schauble made clear the choice facing the Greek people: they could stay within the eurozone while accepting the MoU in toto—or they could choose to exit the eurozone. A month later, Varoufakis asked Schauble bluntly whether he would sign the MoU if he were in Varoufakis' place. His answer came as a pleasant surprise. 'As a patriot, no. It's bad for your people.'[22]

Towards the end of June, Tsipras decided he would hold a referendum on 5 July. The people of Greece would vote whether they wanted to go with the troika's MoU or not. When the referendum was held, 61.3 per cent voted 'no'. Tsipras was not inclined to honour the vote. He hinted vaguely at a coup that would overthrow the government if he defied the troika. He offered Varoufakis some other ministry so that negotiations with the troika could continue. At last, Varoufakis put in his papers.

On 13 July, Tsipras finally acceded to the troika's demands. In Parliament, Varoufakis was blamed for the failure to reach an agreement with the troika. Some even wanted him to be tried by a special court. In mid-August 2015, a third bailout agreement was approved by the Greek Parliament. The overwhelming majority voted in favour. Only thirty-two Syriza MPs voted against. Twenty-five MPs split to form a new party. Having lost his majority, Tsipras resigned as PM and called for fresh elections. In September 2015, he was voted back to power. All the major political formations in Greece now wanted to toe the troika's line.

Thus ended the drama of the first three Greek bailouts. A fourth bailout followed in August 2018. Greece is committed to austerity until 2060. It must generate a primary budget surplus of 3.5 per cent until 2021 and 2.2 per cent in 2022–60. The complexion of the government has made no difference to the final outcome.

The questions remain. Could Greece have done anything different? Should the troika have done anything different?

There are limits to national sovereignty in a globalized world. Economic sovereignty is circumscribed by the financial markets. The limits to sovereignty are even more pronounced within the eurozone. The use of a common currency leaves no scope for monetary policy independence. No eurozone economy can inflate its way out of a debt crisis by printing more money; only the ECB is authorized to do so.

A eurozone economy cannot devalue its currency or use monetary stimulus to deal with a crisis. If it cannot access the financial markets either, it would be in no position to defy the diktats of the EU and the ECB. This is the reality that Tsipras and the people of Greece eventually accepted.

Adam Tooze, the economic historian, makes a crucial point. In 2010, the decision to save French and German banks under the guise of saving Greece had the support of the US. Any restructuring of Greek debt would have meant losses for French and German banks. After the sub-prime crisis of 2007, the last thing the US wanted in 2010 was an implosion of banks in Europe. The IMF, which was a member of the troika, was merely reflecting the preferences of the Americans. If Greece had chosen to defy the troika, it would have been up against virtually the entire international community.[23]

Varoufakis wanted Greece to respond to the troika's stubbornness by threatening to move to a parallel payments system in anticipation of a Grexit and imposing a haircut on bonds held by the ECB. Would these threats have worked? To take the first, the calculation underlying Grexit was that financial markets would lose trust in all the troubled economies of the eurozone. This would devastate those economies and ultimately bring about the demise of the euro. Germany would not want such an outcome and would try to prevent a Grexit.

This overlooks the fact that the ECB president, Mario Draghi, had committed himself to support government bonds in the eurozone at all costs. The risk of contagion from Greece was thus quite small. It is unlikely that the leaders of the eurozone would have been cowed by the prospect of Grexit.

What about the threat to impose a haircut on bonds held by the ECB? As mentioned earlier, any write-down of government bonds held by the ECB had the potential to attract an adverse verdict from the German constitutional court and put an end to the ECB's purchase of government bonds. That would certainly have impacted Italy, Portugal and others in a big way and thrown Europe and the world economy into turmoil. It would have meant grave consequences for the Greek economy as well while also spelling Greece's political isolation from Europe and the US.

What about the EU's treatment of Greece? Once the rescue of French and German banks was accomplished in 2010, why did the EU not restructure Greece's debt in, say, 2012? Well, the problem for Germany was not just Greece but other troubled economies such as Portugal, Spain and Italy. Germany's concern was that any leniency shown to Greece would trigger defaults in other debt-ridden countries and saddle the EU with an unmanageable problem. Germany was especially mindful of the impact on France, which too had not done a good job of balancing its budget. Varoufakis acknowledges this fact:[24]

> The harsh and failed policies imposed upon Greece had nothing to do with our country. The threat to close down Greece's banks . . . had nothing to do with our banks. They were Wolfgang's signal to Paris: if France wanted the euro, it must forfeit sovereignty over its budget deficits.

More broadly, Germany believed that the time had come for Europe to rein in the welfare state that emerged after World War II. By making an example of Greece, it wanted to make this message amply clear. Austerity in Greece was a means for achieving broader political and economic goals within the EU.

Tsipras' ultimate surrender sprang from an unwillingness to step into the abyss. Varoufakis, the principled dissenter, believed that the Greek government should live up to the mandate of the people, whatever the risks involved. The system chose to eject him.

We have the answer to the question we posed at the outset. Dissenters may be able to influence the system from the outside but they cannot be effective from within—unless they swallow their dissent and choose to be 'insiders'. When confronted with this reality as finance minister, Varoufakis chose to be an outsider, as he had clearly told Larry Summers he would.

* * *

The Greek crisis of 2010 was part of a larger crisis in the eurozone. Shortly before Varoufakis became finance minister, he commenced work on a book on the eurozone project. He completed the book after he had exited the government.

The book is titled *And the Weak Suffer What They Must?*[25] The title is borrowed from Thucydides' book on the Peloponnesian War. The book quotes Athenian generals as saying that 'the strong actually do what they can and the weak suffer what they must'.[26] In other words, the world is run on the basis of brute force; there isn't much room for fairness or respect for others' rights.

Varoufakis contends that the present crisis in Europe—of which Brexit or Britain's decision to quit the EU is a manifestation— has been shaped by three events: the breakdown of the post-War system put in place at Bretton Woods in the US; the creation of a common currency, the euro, for some countries of the EU; and the financial crisis of 2008.

The Bretton Woods system emerged following meetings between the famous British economist John Maynard Keynes and Harry Dexter White, an American economist and America's nominee in the negotiations to create a new international financial system. Europe's currencies had been battered in the War and needed support. Keynes and White agreed that Europe's currencies were best supported by a system of fixed exchange rates under which those currencies could be converted into a worthwhile currency at fixed rates.

Keynes saw clearly that, in a fixed exchange rate system, trade imbalances would get worse over time. To see why, let's first accept that some countries will have trade surpluses and others will have trade deficits. If the exchange rate is allowed to float, that is, it is not fixed, the currency of a country with a trade deficit will tend to weaken. Exports will then rise and imports will fall, thus allowing the deficit to be corrected over time.

Not so in a fixed rate system. Banks in countries with current account surpluses will tend to lend the money they accumulate to economies with deficits, allowing the latter to import even more. Thus, the surpluses in the system get recycled through private lenders. Economies with surpluses don't have to worry about the currencies of economies with deficits devaluing as exchange rates are fixed.

As the borrowings of the deficit economies keep going up, a point would come where lenders would begin to think that their debt was not sustainable. Private lenders would then stop lending. The deficit economies or borrowers would face what is called a balance-of-payments crisis—they would not have the foreign exchange needed to keep importing or servicing their loans. They would have to cut back on consumption and investment. Their incomes would drop. Lenders from the surplus economies would be left with loans that cannot be serviced (or non-performing loans). There would be an international economic crash.

How do we prevent a crash in a fixed exchange rate system? Keynes and White both understood that the system would need to have a mechanism to recycle surpluses once private lenders stopped doing so. That's how they conceived of the IMF, an institution that would help economies in times of balance-of-payments crises.

Where Keynes and White disagreed was on the currency to which all other currencies would be pegged, that is, the stable currency into which the weak currencies of Europe would be converted. Keynes wanted an international currency called 'bancor'. White preferred to have the dollar as the international currency. The dollar would be convertible into gold at $35 an ounce.

Keynes also wanted the IMF to be the world's central bank. The IMF would be managed by a governing committee with the

US among its members. White demurred. He wanted the US Federal Reserve to perform the role. He was very clear that the US must call the shots in a world in which it was the dominant power. America was running huge trade surpluses at the time. If American surpluses were to be recycled to Europe, then America would decide how. Again, a case of the strong doing whatever they liked. White's view prevailed.

The system of exchange rates pegged to the dollar was sound as long as America ran trade surpluses with the rest of the world. Things changed dramatically towards the late sixties when the US trade surpluses turned into deficits. When Europe sold more to the US than it bought in dollars, it was Europe that was flooded with surplus dollars, not the US. The dollar pile in Europe reached a level where a fraction of it could purchase all the gold in America's vaults.

The moment speculators realized this, they also realized that America could not afford to trade gold at $35 an ounce. It was bound to allow the price of gold to rise. So the speculators borrowed dollars and bought more and more gold. Once gold prices rose, they could sell the gold and get more dollars than they had borrowed, thus making a tidy profit on their speculative trades.

If the US still wanted to protect the Bretton Woods system— that is, to trade gold at $35 an ounce—America's current account deficit needed to be reduced (so that dollar surpluses in Europe would fall). For this to happen, America had to accept austerity— cut government expenditure and private consumption (and hence imports) and settle for slower growth. That would have meant compromising its economic hegemony. The US, under the presidency of Richard Nixon, was not willing to accept such an outcome. It chose instead to abandon the Bretton Woods system. The fixed exchange rate system, which had sustained Europe and its currencies, was pronounced dead.

* * *

Western Europe, long used to the stability provided by fixed exchange rates, was now exposed to the fluctuations inevitable in floating exchange rates. France and Germany (but not the UK) decided that they should substitute the Bretton Woods system of fixed exchange rates with a system of fixed exchange rates in Europe.

Western Europe had been moving towards such a system over a long period of time. A common market had evolved starting with the European Coal and Steel Community. Varoufakis says this was essentially a cartel comprising the two industries in France and Germany. This later became the European Common Market.

Germany's emergence as Europe's industrial powerhouse in the years following World War II meant that the Deutschmark (DM) was the strongest currency in Europe. Germany produced and exported, giving it enormous surpluses, while France was in deficit (as were other countries in Western Europe). This created a tendency for the franc to depreciate with respect to the DM. Frequent devaluation would be humiliating for the French. A continuous rise in German surpluses would push up the DM to a level where the surpluses would no longer be sustainable. It was in the interest of both France and Germany to have some stability in exchange rates.

Another concern was that, without stable exchange rates, it would be difficult to maintain stable prices of coal, steel and agricultural products across Europe. Price stability was essential for maintaining the cartel that had come into existence. If exchange rates fluctuate, producers in Europe might engage in price wars that would prove destabilizing to the cartel.

Europe's first response to these concerns was to create a 'snake in a tunnel'. It was a system in which exchange rates would be pegged to the DM and float within a narrow band—like a snake in a tunnel. This experiment, Varoufakis points out, gave rise to the same problem as Bretton Woods. In the absence of a mechanism for recycling surpluses, it was difficult for economies with chronic deficits to maintain their exchange rates.

France found that, in order to keep its exchange rate within the permitted band, it would have to raise interest rates (which would attract foreign capital) and cut back on government spending and private consumption. But these measures would result in France sacrificing economic growth in order to stay within the 'snake'.

The alternative was not attractive either. Letting a weak currency float would mean a sharp depreciation and high inflation. Not just France but Belgium, the Netherlands and Italy opted for the latter. Perhaps they reckoned that the first choice was more expensive. The experiment with the 'snake' had failed. Despite its failure, however, the very elites that took the decision to exit the 'snake' have opted for variants of the same in the years that followed. How does one explain this?

Varoufakis has a cynical explanation. He says that the 'snake' was abandoned because it had no particular attractions for the European elite. It had none of the perks that later versions were to bring with them, namely, new institutions and cosy bureaucratic jobs for the European elite. Varoufakis writes:[27]

> A more convincing answer [for why the Europeans abandoned the 'snake'] has to do with the snake's failure to offer worthy job prospects to the ambitious graduates of France's grandes écoles and the alumni of other European nurseries bringing up the next generation of Brussels-based bureaucrats. The snake came with no institutions dedicated to it; there were no buildings with its logo, no army of bureaucrats whose livelihood and perks relied on it, no impressive titles for functionaries whose life's work would be to sing the serpent's praises. In short, the snake was unloved by the elites and thus doomed from the start.

In place of the 'snake' came the European Monetary System (EMS) in 1979. (The UK joined the EMS only in 1990 and exited after a short period of time.) The EMS also sought to keep exchange rates of the twelve member countries within a band, as in the 'snake'. The particular mechanism used for this purpose was the European Currency Unit (ECU). The ECU was a currency unit arrived at based on a basket of currencies of member countries based on suitable weights for each currency. Fluctuations between the member state currencies and the ECU were to be minimized.

Like the 'snake', the EMS didn't quite address the basic problem for Germany, the surplus nation in the group. The DM would keep strengthening relative to the franc and other currencies, given German's propensity to accumulate surpluses. The way to prevent this was for the German central bank, the Bundesbank, to keep buying francs (in exchange for DMs). But this would mean increasing the DMs in circulation and raising the inflation rate in Germany, something that the Bundesbank abhorred. The then German Chancellor Helmut Schmidt chose, nevertheless, to overcome German apprehensions on this score and push ahead with the EMS. What prompted him to do so?

Varoufakis has an unusual explanation. After the collapse of Bretton Woods, the US was faced with the question of how it could maintain its dominance of the international financial system even as it ran up huge current account deficits. Paul Volcker, a banker who became Chairman of the US Fed, had an answer. He would raise US interest rates sky-high. This has been widely understood as an attempt to crush the rate of inflation which had been running high in the US. Varoufakis believes that it was intended more to attract surplus capital flows from other economies to the US. The US would run trade deficits and yet draw in the surpluses of Europe through high interest rates. American hegemony over capital flows would be preserved. Varoufakis writes:[28]

> . . . if America cannot recycle its surplus [Volcker argued], having slipped into a deficit position back in the mid-1960s, it

must now recycle other people's! But how, one may reasonably
ask, can a deficit nation recycle other nations' surpluses? . . . The
trick, he [Volcker] believed, was to persuade foreign capitalists
to send their capital to Wall Street . . . The way to do this
was . . . [to] push American interest rates through the roof . . .
[and] ensure that Wall Street offered a more lucrative market
for investors than its equivalents . . .

High interest rates in the US seemed to offer a solution to German
Chancellor Schmidt's problem of how to deal with a surplus of
DMs in the system. The surpluses would now be sucked into the
US by the high interest rates there! The EMS seemed to combine
fixed exchange rates with an answer to the problem of German
trade surpluses.

In the EMS, the participating countries agreed to maintain
their exchange rates within a range of 2.25 per cent (narrow band)
and 6 per cent (wide band). Periodic adjustment was done to raise
the values of the stronger currencies and reduce the values of the
weaker currencies.

France faced an early challenge to its staying within the EMS
within two years of its formation. In 1981, the leftist government of
François Mitterrand came to power in France. Leftist governments
are associated with high public spending, which would mean a rise
in the current account deficit and a weak currency. Speculators
responded to Mitterrand's coming to power by taking their money
out of France. This caused the franc to plunge.

Mitterrand was confronted with a difficult choice. He could
exit the EMS within a week of assuming power or stay with it.
He chose the latter. This meant ensuring that the franc did not
weaken which, in turn, meant a combination of high interest rates,
cuts in government spending and high taxes. Varoufakis notes that
this was, perhaps, the first time that a government elected on an
anti-austerity platform chose to discard it. (As we have seen above,
the Syriza party was to repeat this formula in Greece later.)

The Mitterrand government had a strange logic for its volte-face. It argued that anti-austerity policies could not be practised at the national level as speculators would always defeat these. These could only be practised in the entire EMS area. Germany had to be won over to anti-austerity policies once the economies of Europe embraced a broader union. So austerity had to be fought by first embracing it![29] Given the way events have shaped up since, this must seem utterly delusional. Germany has not been won over to anti-austerity policies. Instead, it has administered stiff doses of austerity to its partners in the former EMS.

The EMS worked as long as the economic conditions in the countries (growth, inflation, etc.) were broadly similar, which was the case in the period 1981–86. However, in the face of the global recession of the early 1990s, it became difficult to maintain fixed exchange rates. Economies that are not doing well need to sharply devalue their currencies in order to sustain growth. Italy, for instance, devalued its currency by 7 per cent in 1992 and withdrew.

There were other sources of stress in the EMS. France was keen to stick to the band specified in the EMS. It was an economy that was running a current account deficit. It could stay within the band only through austerity. It ended up sacrificing growth and unemployment.

In contrast, the German government was in a mood to boost employment. It was also dealing with the costs of reunifying West Germany with East Germany. It ran up a large deficit. The ultra-conservative Bundesbank responded by raising interest rates sky-high. One of the partners in the government then demanded austerity. The combination of austerity and high interest rates saw the DM shoot up in value.

The UK could stay within its band only by raising interest rates to as high as 15 per cent. Speculators (led by the famous financier, George Soros) felt that this was unsustainable and they bet against the pound. The speculators won. The pound could not be defended. The British government announced that it was exiting the EMS.

The countries that stayed within the EMS opted for a new arrangement: currencies would be allowed to fluctuate within a band of 15 per cent around the rates fixed in the EMS. When the band is as broad as that, what we have is a pretence of fixed exchange rates. The economies in the EMS had come to recognize that fixed exchange rates could no longer be maintained.

The alternative now was to abandon the EMS and opt for a common currency, the euro. Then, the problem of managing exchange rates would go away once and for all. The euro came into being on 1 January 1999. Monetary policy within the eurozone would be thereafter managed by the ECB. The economies of the eurozone had opted for monetary union.

Varoufakis believes the euro was doomed to fail. He makes a point that many others have: monetary union can be effective only if there is fiscal union, that is, there is a system for raising resources and distributing these, based on the needs of various parts of the union.

Why so? Let's suppose that one of the countries within the union has a banking crisis. It will need to pour money into banks in order to save them. Its external debt would shoot up. Beyond a point, the financial markets would not be willing to provide funds. The banking crisis would continue and the economy would find it difficult to recover.

One route for an economy to recover is to devalue and increase exports but this is not possible with a common currency. The only other way to boost exports would be to cut wages and other costs but this can be extremely painful for the economy. If there is fiscal union among the economies of the eurozone, resources can be transferred from the richer parts of the union (such as Germany) to the poorer ones (such as Greece).

This is only one example of the problems that arise when there is monetary union without fiscal union. Another problem is one that we have mentioned repeatedly in the context of fixed exchange rates. Private banks will confidently channel capital from the surplus economies to the deficit economies without the fear of currency depreciation. This will happen until the debt of the latter becomes unsustainable. Then, the flow of capital will be cut off. The deficit economy then has to sharply reduce government spending and raise taxes in order to be able to access the financial markets again.

In a fiscal union, there can be a political mechanism for recycling surpluses from one part of the union to another. Think of what happens in an economy such as India. There are states that are growing fast and states that are laggards. The centre collects taxes. In distributing these among the various states, the centre gives some weightage to the backwardness of a state, that is, how badly it needs the funds in order to develop. Otherwise, the backward states have little hope of catching up.

To his credit, Varoufakis had anticipated the problems with the euro long back. He writes:[30]

How could so many top journalists, academics, functionaries and politicians believe that they could sustainably bind together the French franc and the Deutsche Mark, let alone the Italian lira, the Spanish peseta and the Greek drachma, without a political mechanism for recycling German and Dutch surpluses and managing private and public sector deficits? . . . How did they expect the Eurozone, bereft of any mechanism for coping, to handle the preordained bursting of these bubbles?

Varoufakis suggests that some leaders, such as former French President François Mitterrand, sincerely believed that a monetary union would eventually pave the way for a complete political union. They thought that, perhaps, a financial crisis would make a political union inevitable. The late British Prime minister Margaret Thatcher opposed a monetary union precisely for that reason. She feared that a monetary union was a 'Trojan Horse' for smuggling in a complete federation.

If Mitterrand had been right, then the global financial crisis of 2007–08 should have been just the right trigger for a move towards a political union. Alas, it wasn't. Varoufakis argues that this is because Mitterrand and others created a situation where politicians accountable to the people have been replaced by faceless technocrats who wield real power in the eurozone:[31]

> Inadvertently, Mitterrand and Kohl [former German Chancellor, Helmut Kohl] contributed to a technocracy revolving around a monetary union that eradicated the type of political leadership necessary to step in during a crisis and complete their creation. Adding a political amalgam to the monetary union that Schmidt [another former German Chancellor] and Giscard [another former President of France] began and took so much further requires leaders that their monetary union weeded out. It is not therefore a simple case of heirs and successors proving unequal to the task bestowed upon them by the pioneers. It is, rather, a case of pioneers who put into place monetary institutions which at once needed future politicians to complete them, while at the same time ensuring that this calibre of politicians would be driven out of politics. The stuff of tragedy had been woven into Europe's monetary union from the outset.

Following the financial crisis of 2007, the eurozone has created a European Stability Mechanism for providing capital to states that lose access to the capital markets. It has also taken halting steps towards a banking union—the ECB has been given powers to oversee the eurozone's largest lenders.

Other steps towards a fuller union, such as a Europe-wide common deposit insurance scheme, a common European bond for raising funds for member countries and joint programmes for taxation and spending, still seem remote at the moment. Germany does not fancy itself as bailing out its poorer partners in the eurozone. Many people in the eurozone do not relish the idea of losing national sovereignty in fiscal matters. The European project, which posits the creation of a European entity that can serve as a worthy rival to the US, is still work-in-progress. Nearly two decades after the creation of the euro, Varoufakis, the incorrigible optimist, continues his campaign for the project to fructify.

* * *

Varoufakis' revolt against the establishment is not just about the Greek crisis and the problems in the eurozone. It has to do with modern capitalism and how it has subverted democracy everywhere. He strongly believes that policies are framed by an elite that has scant regard for the priorities of the wider public.

Varoufakis writes about these broader concerns in a book he produced for his daughter in the space of just nine days, *Talking to My Daughter About the Economy: A Brief History of Capitalism.*[32] The book is one long diatribe against markets. Varoufakis does not say that markets are not required. He says that it's okay to leave things such as coffee to markets. However, the big things in economics—technological change, money, the environment— cannot be left entirely to the workings of the market. If we do so, we are likely to get terrible outcomes.

Varoufakis talks of 'experiential value' as distinct from 'exchange value'. In the former, something is valued for its sheer experience. When his daughter dives into the sea to fix the anchor for the boat of a friend of his, it's for experiential value. She would not like it if his friend offered to pay for the service, that is, she would not do it for exchange value. Similarly, organ donors offer their organs because of the feeling of doing good. Putting a price on the organs would probably discourage them. Again, experiential value is preferred to exchange value.

Yet, we have moved into a world in which almost everything has come into the market. This is a relatively new development in human history. There was not much of a market for the important factors of production—labour, capital goods and land—until a few hundred years ago. In the age of feudalism, there were masters and serfs. The masters took a large part of the produce of serfs by the threat of force. The serfs—or craftsmen who worked for the serfs—produced tools. Land was almost entirely inherited.

A great change came about with the development of shipbuilding and the global trade in goods that followed. Some goods, such as wool, spices, silk and steel swords became goods with great international value. Merchants who traded in these goods became fabulously wealthy.

Seeing the change in the merchants' fortunes, landowners in England and Scotland decided to stop producing food items and switch to wool instead. They threw out the serfs who had toiled for them for centuries and started rearing sheep on their lands. The serfs who were thrown out had no choice but to market their labour in order to survive. Soon, they would provide hands to factories as the Industrial Revolution got under way.

Some landowners decided that instead of rearing sheep themselves, they would rent out their lands to others who wanted to do so. Thus, a market for land developed. Some of the land was rented by the former serfs themselves.

Was this a change for the good? We are accustomed to think so. The creation of markets for labour, capital and land ushered in the Industrial Revolution which, in turn, has created an era of unprecedented prosperity.

Varoufakis isn't so sure. He writes, 'The triumph of exchange values over experiential values changed the world for the better and for the worse.'[33] On the one hand, the serfs were liberated from service to their masters. On the other hand, the landless cultivators became industrial workers or farmers paying rent to landowners. A new form of servitude had come into being. 'While the waged

labourers were free to do as they pleased, they were now entirely
at the mercy of the markets . . .'[34] Workers' new-found freedom
made sense only as long as they could find employment or buyers
for their wool.

Varoufakis is right about the initial decades that followed the
Industrial Revolution. Terrible suffering was visited upon workers,
including children. They toiled for long hours under wretched
conditions. Sudden changes in global demand brought great
suffering to those dependent on traded goods. However, over a
longer period of about two and a half centuries, Varoufakis' doubts
about the emergence of markets for land, labour and capital appear
misplaced. The market economy has brought about an enormous
rise in the standard of living.

Varoufakis' complaint is that capitalism (he prefers to use
the expression 'market economy') is beset with serious problems.
The distribution of wealth is highly skewed. The vast majority of
jobs have tended to get more and more mechanized. Capitalism is
prone to recurring bouts of crises.

Varoufakis' criticism of capitalism is well taken. But when he
questions the worth of the profit motive, one begins to wonder.
Greed was always there, he explains, and people always wanted
to amass riches. But profit is something different. It came about
after the serfs had been kicked out of their land and had to rent
it thereafter for rearing sheep or growing crops. In order to use
their land, they needed some money to start with—for paying
rent, wages, for seeds, etc. This money was lent by the landowner
himself or by local loan sharks and it came with interest. In order
to repay the interest, the serfs needed to earn a profit after their
costs had been met.

Debt and profit thus went hand in hand. In order to repay
their debt, the borrowers had every incentive to keep their wages as
low as possible. The lenders of money, on the other hand, amassed
huge amounts of wealth. So we had immense riches and we also
had unspeakable poverty. Varoufakis writes, 'In market societies,

all wealth is nourished by debt and all of the unimaginable riches created over the past three centuries ultimately owe their existence to debt. Debt . . . is to market societies what hell is to Christianity: unpleasant yet indispensable.'[35]

Varoufakis' suggestion that debt and the interest it carries are something evil is hard to stomach. The interest that the borrower pays is simply the price of debt and that price is set in a competitive market. It is no more evil than the rent on land or the wages of labour that the entrepreneur pays. Moreover, it's not just lenders who have become wealthy. So have those who borrowed. Debt by itself is no more evil than any other input into production. As Varoufakis acknowledges, without debt, 'the economy of market societies would come to a complete standstill'.[36]

Nor is it true that profit is required only to service debt. If there were no debt and only equity (either the entrepreneur's own capital or capital borrowed as equity), equity too would carry an expected return that would need to be serviced through profit. Profit, in other words, is required to service the cost of capital, whether equity or debt. If neither debt nor equity had been available and if we had not had firms with limited liability, it would have been impossible for firms to grow as big as they are today.

Where Varoufakis is bang on is when he talks about bankers creating *too much debt*. Excess debt inevitably leads to crashes and enormous suffering for everybody except the bankers themselves. Varoufakis is also right in saying that excess debt arises because of inadequate bank regulation. Bank regulation is inadequate because bankers finance politicians and afford cosy post-retirement jobs to regulators. We need to find ways to tackle excess debt. But that is not the same as saying that debt is evil.

Varoufakis touches on a range of other matters of topical interest—the notion of private wealth, the role of expectations in the economy, the impact of automation, central bank autonomy and managing the environment.

Market economics justifies private wealth by ascribing it to individual ability. Why grudge individuals the fruits of their talent and effort? Varoufakis refutes this notion. Wealth creation, he points out, happens against the background of support provided by the state—for maintaining law and order, providing health and education, roads and other infrastructure, etc. Moreover, all wealth happens through collective effort:[37]

> If you think about it, all wealth has always been produced collectively—through recycling and through a gradual accumulation of knowledge. Workers need entrepreneurs to hire them, who need workers to buy their goods. Entrepreneurs need bankers to lend to them, who need entrepreneurs to pay interest . . . Inventors cannibalise the inventions of others and plagiarise the ideas of scientists. The economy relies on everyone. Again, this should not be taken to mean there should be no private wealth at all. It is an argument against allowing large inequalities in wealth.

Varoufakis' exposition of the role of expectations is also interesting. We are often told that price adjustments are the answer to problems such as high unemployment or low investment. Is there too much unemployment? Let workers accept lower wages and they will get jobs. Is investment too low? Let interest rates fall and investment will rise. Varoufakis points out that the outcomes are no longer as certain once we bring in expectations.

When wages fall, employers may not necessarily hire more workers. They may conclude that falling wages are a sign of depressed economic conditions and lack of demand in the economy. They may conclude that hiring more workers in such a situation and producing more is fraught with risk. Similarly, businessmen may not invest more because interest rates are falling. They may interpret a cut in interest rates announced by the central bank as a sign of weakness in the economy.

The answers that seem obvious are not the right answers once expectations enter the picture.

Automation and the impact this would have on jobs and incomes is a major concern today. Varoufakis believes that Karl Marx is being proved right on how capitalism would evolve. As more and more jobs get automated, three things happen. Costs are driven down. Fierce competition pushes prices down—at some point, below the costs of production. Demand for goods falls as workers are replaced by robots that don't need food, clothing and shelter. Marx had predicted that wages would fall to a point where there would not be enough demand for goods. The capitalist system would then plunge into a crisis.

The saving grace, Varoufakis believes, is that, in a time of acute crisis, wages would fall so steeply that businessmen would find it cheaper to use workers instead of machines. Demand would then revive. Capitalism would be saved in the nick of time.

Varoufakis suggests that there should be a better way of keeping jobs alive than by pushing wages down so steeply. Let a share of profit accrue to workers. Even when wages are driven down, they would have the means to buy goods and services through their share of profit. Profit-sharing, he believes, is the only way in which technological advance can happen without destroying the lives of large numbers of people. Alas, the owners of capital are in no mood to share their profit with workers (except in the case of a few senior managers).

Varoufakis takes on the notion of independent central banks, one that was treated as gospel until after the financial crisis of 2007–08. Central bank independence enshrines the idea of high-minded technocrats taking decisions on monetary policy independent of democratically elected governments. Technocrats will take the long view in a detached way, unlike politicians who can only think of getting votes in the next election—so goes the gospel. We in India became familiar with the debate about technocrats versus politicians during the tenures of Raghuram Rajan and Urjit Patel as governors of the Reserve Bank of India.

Varoufakis rejects the notion that decisions taken independent of politicians are apolitical in nature. No, they remain intensely political except that they are guided, not by the elected representatives of people, but by the 'unelected few: the oligarchy and the bankers'.[38] Varoufakis believes that the notion that money can ever be apolitical is a 'fantasy'. Since money is 'inescapably political', we have to democratize control of it. For that, we need to democratize our states first. But that, he concedes, is a 'tall, tall order'.[39]

How do we manage the environment? Those in favour of markets would like to create a market for pollution. They want pollution rights to be bought and sold in the marketplace. Everybody would be given the same polluting rights to start with. Those who are efficient—that is, pollute less than they are permitted by their rights—would sell their excess rights to others who are not so efficient. The not so efficient—that is, those who exceed the pollution rights allotted to them—would have to bid for rights sold by others. The highly inefficient would find the price unaffordable and be driven out of business.

Thus, by having incentives for creating less pollution, a market for pollution rights would help improve the environment. Since government can't be trusted to take care of the environment, why not leave it to the markets? Varoufakis points out the fallacy in the solution. It is the government that will decide how much pollution rights everybody should be given. Government will monitor. Government will punish. How can the government be trusted to perform these roles if it can't be trusted with the environment in the first place?

Varoufakis contends that a better answer is to democratize the management of the environment: let the people decide how the earth's resources are to be managed. Whether it is technology, money or the environment, his answer is the same: democratize decisions; don't let the markets decide. And why would democratization work better? Because in a democracy, every person has one vote. In markets, the rich have more votes, so the decisions will favour them at the expense of the many.

Varoufakis clearly favours the state in the debate of state versus markets. He glosses over the fact that democracies work through politicians and political parties, both of which depend on funding by businessmen and the wealthy. Whether you leave it to markets or to the state, the role of money power in influencing public policy cannot be ignored. The democratic solution that Varoufakis urges is an abstraction—it doesn't happen in practice.

In another instance, he concedes that the sort of authentic democracy he's talking about, one where people are empowered to influence major policies, is something we have never had so far.[40] Varoufakis doesn't quite tell us how the goal of authentic democracy is to be achieved. All he can say is that radicals must 'arrest the free fall of capitalism in order to buy the time we need to formulate its alternative'.[41]

Now out of office, he's trying hard to present voters with a party that will do just that.

* * *

Varoufakis will not stop short at writing and giving speeches. He's determined to work towards a new international order. After stepping down as finance minister in 2015, Varoufakis launched the Democracy in Europe Movement 2025 (DiEM 25).

DiEM 25 argues that it's not enough for national parties to cooperate in the European Parliament. What is needed is a pan-European movement that works towards halting the disintegration of Europe. It aims to create a European Constitution by 2025, one that would replace existing European treaties. DiEM contested the elections to the European Parliament in May 2019. It failed to win a single seat, falling just shy of the 3 per cent vote required to win any seat. Varoufakis will stand for election in Germany. A German will contest elections in Greece. 'Because if you are going to do transnational politics, you have to do transnational politics.'[41]

DiEM 25 does not wish to overthrow capitalism. Nor does it intend to dismantle the EU. In respect of the latter, it differs sharply from Left parties in Europe that want a return to national sovereignty and national currencies. DiEM 25 believes in the free movement of goods and people. It's also a fervent believer in reform from within. It is of the view that the 'lives of the majority of people can be improved in the short run under existing rules and with the current institutions'.[42]

DiEM 25 has put forward proposals that would help translate what Varoufakis has long preached into practice. Europe would invest €2 trillion in green energy. The European Investment Bank would raise €500 billion in bonds annually for four years to finance the investment. The profits of the ECB and the twenty-eight central banks in the EU would be used to fund an Anti-Poverty Fund.

The eurozone's public debt would be restructured. Big businesses operating in the EU would have to transfer some of their shares to a new European Equity Fund. (Since the companies don't own the shares, perhaps Varoufakis means that they would have to issue fresh shares to the European Equity Fund.) The dividends from these shares would be used to provide a Universal Basic Dividend to every European citizen independent of other welfare payments. Varoufakis doesn't quantify these benefits. Elections to the European Parliament were held end of May 2019. DiEM 25 managed to win just one seat. Clearly, it has a long way to go in catching the imagination of EU voters.

Varoufakis wants to propagate his ideas beyond Europe. In November 2018, DiEM 25 joined hands with Bernie Sanders, a presidential candidate in the American elections in 2016 and a contender in the elections due in 2020, to launch the Progressive International. The objective is to counter the rise of nationalist forces. Varoufakis argues that nationalist strongmen such as Donald Trump in the US, Jair Bolsonaro in Brazil, Rodrigo Duterte in the Philippines and Viktor Orban in Hungary 'are scapegoating minorities and facilitating widespread corruption for their family and friends'.[43]

The forces of nationalism want to undermine international institutions, such as the UN, the IMF, the World Bank and the ILO. The so-called liberals think we need to persist with these institutions in their present form in the belief that they still do good work. Progressive International seeks a radical overhaul of these institutions. For instance, the UN Security Council would comprise not just government representatives but ordinary citizens. The ILO would have the right to investigate countries like the US and corporations such as Amazon and sanction them for suppressing unionization and non-compliance with international labour standards.

The UN has, over the years, escaped even the most modest reform, such as an expansion of the permanent members of the Security Council. So also the IMF and the World Bank. If Varoufakis thinks that public opinion can be awakened to usher in reform of the sort he envisages, one can only wish him luck.

* * *

Varoufakis' battle with the establishment does not stop short with present-day capitalism, austerity or the international economic order. He's a fighter for varied and, often, forlorn causes. He has spoken up for Julian Assange, the WikiLeaks founder, who recently lost his sanctuary at Ecuador's embassy in the UK. He has stood up for the rights of Palestinians in their long-standing struggle against the state of Israel. He has criticized America's withdrawal from the nuclear deal with Iran and its policy of imposing sanctions on nations that continue to do business with Iran. On Brexit, Britain's proposed exit from the EU, he has urged a people's debate on what relationship the people want with Europe. He has thrown his weight behind Jeremy Corbyn, who has led a revival in the fortunes of the Labour Party in the UK.

Like Arundhati Roy, Varoufakis looks at the world around him and finds that almost everything is wrong with it. There is no genuine democracy. Capitalism is seriously flawed. The system of international relations is iniquitous. His charter of demands is a long one.

Whether any of his demands can be realized must be seriously doubted. The sort of peaceful overthrow of the existing order that he wants has rarely happened. What is more certain is that he's unlikely to get a serious chance at becoming an insider ever again. The ruling establishment will make sure he's never vested with office or power.

Varoufakis, the starry-eyed idealist who took on the entire European establishment on the question of Greek debt, is fated to remain an outsider. He is well equipped to excel in that role, trying to rouse ordinary citizens to action, appealing forever to the good sense of rulers. As with Roy, his exertions may help limit the excesses of the present order but they are likely to fall well short of ushering in a brave new world.

6

U.G. Krishnamurti: The Anti-Guru

I stumbled on U.G. Krishnamurti (UG) by the purest accident. I happened to be browsing at a bookshop in Cuffe Parade in Mumbai when I noticed a biography of UG by Mahesh Bhatt, the well-known Bollywood film director.[1] Flipping through the book, I came across a section titled 'Conversations' that was appended to the biography. These were recordings of exchanges various people had had with UG.

I started reading. Here is a sample of what I came across:

Q. We have always been told that mankind has a certain purpose in creation. But ever since I have met you, I have begun to wonder whether this is true.

A. . . . I can say that there is no purpose and if there is any purpose, we have no way of knowing it . . . We are made to believe that we are created for a grander purpose, for a nobler purpose than all the species on this planet. This is not all. We are also told that all creation was created for the benefit of man. That's why we have created all these problems—ecological problems and problems of pollution. Now we are almost at a point where we are going to blow ourselves up . . . We are not created for any grander purpose than the ants that are there or the flies that are hovering around us or the mosquitoes that are sucking our blood . . . I do not see any purpose in life. A living thing, a living organism is not interested in asking the question, 'What is the purpose of life? What is the meaning of life?'[2]

Q. I often ask myself, what are my obligations to my fellow beings?

A. None whatsoever . . . Sorry. All you are interested in is self-fulfilment, the ultimate goal of a Nobel prize and power . . . That's all. I encourage that sort of pursuit . . . But I am not at all taken in by the 'march of progress' and all that rot . . . the same technology that makes fast international travel possible is making ever more deadly military fighter planes . . . You call this progress?[3]

Q. Some would argue that a humanity restored, not through science but through love, is our only hope.

A. I still maintain that it is not love, compassion, humanism, or brotherly sentiments that will save mankind. No, not at all. It is the sheet terror of extinction that can save us, if anything can. Each cell of a living organism cooperates with the cell next to it. It does not need any sentiment or declarations of undying love to do so. Each cell is wise enough to know that if its neighbour goes, it also goes. The cells stick together not out of brotherhood, love and that kind of thing but out of the urgent drive to survive now. It is the same with us but on a large scale.[4]

I read on transfixed. Here, at last, was a voice of honesty and courage. These were not the usual homilies about love, compassion, enlightenment and the betterment of mankind. The man spoke with clarity and what seemed an utter certainty. Nearly an hour passed before I realized that I was in a bookshop. My feet had become stiff. I bought the book and went home. I read it non-stop until I had finished.

My experience is not unique. Many who have come in contact with UG, whether through his writings or in person, have found themselves hooked. UG grabs your attention. His utterances shake you up. They leave you dazed—and pining for more. There is an explosive honesty about his views that blows away much that you have accumulated over time. All the familiar ideas about God, religion, enlightenment and the rest fall by the wayside, leaving you lighter and refreshed.

UG, who passed away in 2007, is the anti-guru of our age, a man who consistently lobbed grenades at the flourishing spirituality industry. He is far less well known than the gurus and godmen of our time, such as J. Krishnamurti (JK), Rajneesh (Osho), Sai Baba and Sri Sri Ravishankar. That is because UG had no organization, gave no speeches, provided no darshan, authored no books, did not profess to have any message to offer to the world.

What we know about him is based on books written about him and recordings of exchanges that people have had with him, either in groups or individually. These books and recordings mostly happened against UG's own wishes. He was unwavering in his belief that there was nothing of value he could ever communicate to his listeners.

If, nevertheless, books and videos on him have emerged, it is because he chose to indulge his fans in a good-humoured way. These books and videos have been a great hit. Many of the books have been translated into several European and other languages. A large number of clips of his interviews and exchanges can be found on the Internet and on YouTube.

Who was this man? Why has he proved so popular and influential despite his shunning the mantle of guru?

* * *

UG was born in July 1918 in a small town in Andhra Pradesh.[5] His mother died seven days after she gave birth to him. UG's father soon remarried and left UG to be cared for by his maternal grandparents. Before his mother passed away, she had predicted a great future for him. His maternal grandfather, a wealthy Brahmin lawyer, took the prediction seriously and devoted himself to lavishing care on the child.

UG's grandfather was an important member of the Theosophical Society founded by Annie Besant. UG spent many of his formative years around the headquarters of the society at Adyar in the city of Chennai (then Madras). There was an atmosphere of intense religiosity and spirituality at home. UG's grandfather was host to numerous swamis, gurus and religious scholars. As a young child, UG was made to listen to readings from various Hindu texts such as the Upanishads and the commentaries on these texts. By the time he was seven, UG could recite passages from most of these texts. He was taken to holy places and centres of learning all over India.

One incident early in his childhood set UG on his quest for truth. His grandfather had a meditation room where he used to meditate for hours. Once, during his meditation, his great-granddaughter, a little baby, started to cry. Furious at having his meditation disturbed, UG's grandfather came out of his room and gave the baby a thrashing. This caused UG to wonder about the business of meditation. There must be something shallow about it, he thought, if his grandfather could behave the way he did.

Other incidents reinforced UG's scepticism about religion and meditation. Every year on the death anniversary of his mother, he was made to fast. He could only eat at the end of the day after the priests who conducted the function had eaten. On one occasion, UG caught the priests eating heartily at a nearby restaurant even while the function was on. He was furious. He ran home to his grandfather and broke his sacred thread. It was a harbinger of a comprehensive revolt against the norms imposed on him by culture and tradition.

UG embarked on his quest for moksha or liberation by practising all sorts of austerities and religious practices. He spent seven summers in the Himalayas studying yoga with a well-known guru, Swami Sivananda. One day he found the swami devouring pickles, forbidden for yogis, in secret. The young UG was shocked at the deception. He gave up his yoga practice and left Sivananda.

At the age of twenty-one, UG enrolled as a student at the University of Madras. He studied psychology and philosophy, among other subjects. He was curious to understand the human mind. One day he approached his professor and asked him, 'We are talking about the mind all the time. Do you know for yourself what the mind is? All the stuff I know about the mind is from these books of Freud, Jung, Adler and so on, that I have studied. Apart from these descriptions and definitions that there are in the books, do you know anything about the mind?'[6]

The professor replied, 'These are dangerous questions. If you want to pass your examinations, memorise what there is in the books and repeat it in your examination papers. You will get your degree.' UG said he wanted to know about the mind; he was not interested in a degree. He did not bother to appear for the examination. He was to say later that the professor was one of the few honest men he had met.

A friend suggested that they go and see Ramana Maharshi, the famous sage of Tiruvannamalai in Tamil Nadu. When he came face to face with the sage, UG asked him three questions. He received answers to all of them.[7]

'Is there anything like enlightenment?'
    'Yes, there is,' replied the master.
    'Are there any levels to it?'
    The Bhagavan replied, 'No, no levels are possible. It is all one thing. Either you are there or you are not there at all.'
    Finally, UG asked, 'This thing called enlightenment, can you give it to me?'

Looking the serious young man in the eye, Ramana replied,
'Yes, I can give it, but can you take it?'

The encounter convinced UG that there was indeed a special
state that Ramana Maharshi was in. However, he would have to
discover by himself what that state was.

During his student days, UG lived in Adyar and worked for
the Theosophical Society of India. He later became joint general
secretary of the Indian section of the society. This position was
later abolished and he became national lecturer for seven years.
In that capacity, he spoke at almost every college in India. He
also lectured extensively in Europe. It occurred to him that he was
wasting his time. There was a certain shallowness to his talks—
anybody could gather the same information and throw it out. He
decided to leave the Theosophical Society sometime in the late
1940s.

In May 1943, UG had got married to a Brahmin girl, Kusuma
Kumari, selected by his grandmother. He was to say later, 'I awoke
the morning after my wedding night and knew without doubt
that I had made the biggest mistake of my life.' They had three
children, including one boy who came to be afflicted with polio.

In 1953, UG and his wife went on a six-week visit to Europe.
In London, UG met Bertrand Russell. He told Russell, who led
a worldwide protest against atomic weapons, that it was futile to
talk of peace without disbanding the many subtle forms of violence
in the world. UG is said to have told Russell, 'The H-bomb is an
extension of the policeman! Are you willing to do away with the
policeman?'

Russell replied, 'One has to draw the line somewhere.'

UG told him, 'If we settle for lesser evil, we will end up only
with evil.'[8]

In 1955, UG decided to take his son to the US for treatment.
He took Kusuma along but left behind their two daughters in the
care of her elder sister. He had just enough money to pay for his

son's treatment. The doctors told him that his son would be able to walk in a year's time. UG had to find the money to support his stay. He decided to give lectures on his own. He gave nearly sixty lectures in the US on a wide range of subjects: philosophy, education, politics, international affairs, etc. He was paid $100 per lecture.

After a year of lecturing, UG lost interest. His manager was shocked. UG had by then become hugely popular and there was easy money to be made. UG was, however, adamant about not continuing with the life he had lived thus far. He conveyed his decision to Kusuma and handed her his last hundred dollars. He told her that she would have to manage on her own thereafter. He then walked out of his house. As he was walking along, he ran into a stranger, Dixon, who had come out of the building of the Theosophical Society of Chicago close to UG's flat.[9]

Dixon was a retired auditor general and former theosophist. He stopped UG and told him that he had had a dream the previous night in which an evolved soul of the Theosophical Society had appeared. The evolved soul had told Dixon that he would run into somebody from India who was in great trouble and that Dixon should help him. Dixon offered to pay UG $200 every month forever out of his pension. UG accepted his offer. He had spent most of the fortune he had inherited and had little choice if he wanted to stay on in the US and continue his son's treatment.

With Dixon's help, UG also managed to get Kusuma a job as a research fellow at the World Book Encyclopaedia. UG had long wanted Kusuma to have a job and be independent so that he could go his own way. She had acquired two postgraduate degrees by then, one in Sanskrit and one in English. She was placed in the Indian section of the Encyclopaedia and had to make notes and respond to queries on Indian religion and culture. UG helped her with her work. He now stayed at home attending to household chores and looking after their handicapped son.

The family carried on in this way for nearly two years with support from Dixon. Kusuma did not much like staying on in the US—she didn't get along very well with Americans. They had their fourth child, a boy, during their stay. Kusuma was worried about the future of the two boys and she was also keen to get back to her two daughters whom they had left behind in India. She was also concerned about the changes in UG's personality and was afraid of losing him.

UG received offers from the UN and the New York Press Association but did not evince any interest in these. He gave a few more talks, perhaps out of a need for money. After his last talk in Texas, a wealthy woman invited him home. UG slept with her. The news reached Kusuma. She was now determined to leave the US with her children. She begged UG to accompany them. UG refused. He gave her the tickets for her flight back to India and handed over whatever money he had. This was towards the end of 1959.

UG now needed a sponsor in order to stay on in the US. He found one in the World University which offered him a job. UG made a trip to India on behalf of the university. He went to Adyar to wind up matters. When Kusuma heard about his arrival, she went to his hotel along with his children in a desperate attempt to get him to join the family. UG would not hear of it. He never saw his wife again. Some members of Kusuma's family and UG's elder daughter never forgave him for his hard-heartedness.

UG's friends from the Theosophical Society took him to meet Dr S. Radhakrishnan, then ambassador to Russia (and later to become President of India), in Delhi. UG is then believed to have met Prime Minister Nehru in connection with his work at the World University. He came to be included in a cultural delegation being sent to the then Soviet Union. After a month's stay in the Soviet Union, UG visited several East European countries as a tourist. Finally, in 1961, he landed in London just as winter was setting in. The stay in London was to set in motion a remarkable transformation in UG.

* * *

UG had little money with him when he arrived in London. He didn't feel like doing anything particular. He describes this period as a 'withering away of the will'. To escape the London cold, he spent the day in the London Library. In the nights, he wandered the streets. He earned a little money by giving lessons in Indian cooking.

One night, while sitting in Hyde Park, UG was warned by a policeman that if he didn't leave, he would be locked up. Something told him to go to the local Ramakrishna Mission. UG took a train as far as he could go with the five pence he had. He walked the rest of the distance to the mission. It was 10 p.m. when he reached there. The staff refused to let him in but the swami in charge himself emerged.

UG showed the swami his scrapbook of news items about himself and his lectures. He asked the swami for permission to use the meditation room for the night. The swami said he could not allow that as it was against the rules. However, he gave UG some money to stay at a hotel for the night and asked him to come back the next morning.

When UG showed up the next day, he was invited for lunch. It was the first proper meal he had had in days. At the swami's request, UG agreed to work on a special issue being brought out on the occasion of Swami Vivekananda's centenary. He was paid five pounds. He would work at the mission until afternoon and then go off to see a movie.

After three months, UG decided to leave. The swami gave him fifty pounds. UG wrote a letter to his wife ending their relationship. About two years later, his wife died. UG wrote to his children expressing his sympathy for their loss. He learnt from one of his daughters that his wife had gone into deep shock after their separation. She was hospitalized and received electric shock treatment. A few weeks after she was discharged, she slipped, broke her neck and passed away.

From London, UG moved to Paris. He returned the airline ticket he had for India and got paid $350. He stayed in a hotel and wandered around for ninety days. He then went on to Geneva with 150 francs in his pocket. He continued to stay in a hotel even after he had run out of money.

When the hotel produced the bill, UG approached the Indian consulate for help. He asked the consulate to send him home to India. He showed the vice-consul his scrapbook containing opinions about him from S. Radhakrishnan (the former President of India) and Norman Cousins, a well-known American editor. The vice-consul was impressed but made it clear that the Indian government could not pay for his return to India. However, he offered to put up UG at his own place until he could get some money from India.

At this point, the hand of destiny showed itself, so to speak. A Swiss lady, Valentine de Kerven, had been witness to the exchange between UG and the vice-consul. She was a translator at the consulate. She offered to put up UG at her place until the vice-consul worked out something. She had a small inheritance and a pension which were enough to take care of the two of them. UG agreed. Valentine quit her job at the consulate, and she and UG took to travelling in and around Switzerland. Later they began spending their winters in India. UG did nothing for the next four years other than reading *Time* magazine and going for walks with Valentine.

UG and Valentine started spending their summer months in the beautiful valley of Saanen overlooking the Swiss Alps. UG was approaching his forty-ninth birthday. For many years now, he had been experiencing terrible headaches and taking large amounts of coffee and aspirin to cope with the pain. UG calls it

the 'incubation' period, a time when the body was getting ready to
undergo major changes.

Some years earlier, in 1963, when he was staying at the
Ramakrishna Mission, UG had experienced a strange movement
within. He had understood this movement as the stirring of the
kundalini or serpent power that is part of Indian mysticism. In the
years that followed, there were other developments that suggested
his body was undergoing physical changes. Whenever he rubbed his
palms on any part of his body, there was a sparkle, like a phosphorus
glow. When he rolled on his bed, there would be sparks.

Two months before his forty-ninth birthday, UG happened to
attend a performance in Paris at the well-known Casino de Paris.
While watching the show, UG could not make out whether it
was the dancer who was dancing or he was on stage. There was
no separation between the dancer and himself—he felt a strange
movement within. A week after this experience, while in a hotel
room in Geneva, he had a dream. He dreamt that he was bitten
by a cobra and died instantly. His body was carried on a bamboo
stretcher to a cremation ground. As the flames leapt up, he was
awakened. UG also developed occult powers. If a person came
into the room, he could read the person's entire past. He could
look at a man's palm and tell his future.

In August 1967, J. Krishnamurti (JK), the well-known
philosopher, came to Saanen to give a series of talks. UG and
JK went back a long way. Both had been connected with the
Theosophical Society. JK had parted company with the society
and started his own Krishnamurti Foundation. UG had listened
to several of JK's talks in Madras (now Chennai). He had had
several conversations with JK, often demanding to know what
state exactly JK was in. UG had not got satisfactory answers.
Throughout UG's stay in the US and his wanderings in London,
JK had kept in touch with him.

In 1953–54, UG happened to listen to JK talk about death in
one of his talks in Madras. UG said out loud to himself, 'Apart from

all the discussions I have heard and my own so-called experience of death in the area of experiencing, apart from all these, you have been talking about death, I really . . .' He wanted to complete the sentence by saying, 'I really do not know . . .' But the words 'do not know' disappeared from his consciousness and he found something happening to him, 'something like a fading out'.

JK looked at him but didn't say anything. The talk and the discussion about death went on for another hour or so but UG was completely out of it. UG felt that the episode had created some change in him. It had led to an indifference to family and money matters and caused him to look at everything very differently.[10]

In 1966, UG had attended JK's talks at Gstaad in Switzerland. The moment JK talked about the art of listening, there would be no listening on UG's part. The words seemed to just hit him and go back. Still, there was a sort of 'watchful expectancy' in him. He often felt weak. At times, he got the feeling that his head was missing above the eyebrows. His friends remarked that he seemed to be operating at a different level of consciousness. He struck some as being free from anxieties and worries.[11]

The encounter with JK in Saanen in 1967 was to carry forward the changes in UG over the past few years and mark a clean break with UG's past. As UG listened to JK's talk, he got the feeling that JK was describing his own state! This realization hit UG in a big way. 'What the hell have I been doing these thirty or forty years, listening to all these people and struggling, wanting to understand his state or the state of somebody else, Buddha or Jesus? I am in that state.'[12] He then walked out of the tent and never looked back. In a later section, we dwell further on the relationship between UG and JK.

The question then transformed into another question, 'How do I know that I am in that state, the state of Buddha, the state I very much wanted and demanded from everybody? I am in that state, but how do I know?'

The next day, which happened to be UG's forty-ninth birthday, he sat on a bench under a wild chestnut tree overlooking Saanen with its seven hills and seven valleys. The question, 'How do I know that I am in that state?' went on whirling around in his mind until it disappeared. It's best to characterize the moment in UG's own words:[13]

> The question disappeared. The whole thing was finished for me and that was all. From then on, never did I say to myself, 'Now I have the answer to all those questions.' That state of which I had said, 'This is the state'—that state disappeared. The question disappeared; finished. It is not emptiness; it is not blankness; it is not the void; it is not any of those things; the question disappeared suddenly and that's all.

The transformation, UG emphasizes, was a physiological phenomenon. 'It was a sudden "explosion" inside, blasting, as it were, every cell, every nerve and every gland in my body.'

At that very moment and in the years that followed, UG's body underwent profound changes. Immediately after the 'explosion', his head tightened. It was as if his brain cells were getting squeezed together. The explosion seemed to shatter every cell, every nerve in his body. He had terrible pain in his head. This continued for three days. While lying on a couch, he felt that his body was missing. He slept well. When he woke up the next morning, it was as if he was waking up for the first time in his life.

There were many other physical changes that UG talked about in later years. He developed a sort of panoramic vision. His skin became soft. He stopped blinking. His senses of taste, smell and hearing seemed to have undergone a change. His hands and forearms changed their structure so that they faced backwards instead of facing the sides.

At those points on the body, which the kundalini yoga calls chakras (energy centres), there were swellings of various sizes and shapes that came and went at intervals. These have been described at length.[14]

> On his lower abdomen, there were swellings of horizontal, cigar-shaped bands. Above the navel was a hard, almond-shaped swelling. A hard, blue swelling, like a large medallion, in the middle of his chest was surmounted by another smaller, brownish-red, medallion-shaped swelling at the base of his throat. These two 'medallions' were as though suspended from a varicoloured, swollen ring—blue, brownish and light yellow—around his neck, as in pictures of the Hindu gods. There were also other similarities between the swellings and the depictions of Indian religious art: his throat was swollen to a shape that made his chin seem to rest on the head of a cobra, as in the traditional images of Siva; just above the bridge of the nose was a white lotus-shaped swelling; all over the head the small blood vessels expanded, forming patterns like the stylised lumps on the heads of Buddha statues. Like the horns of Moses and the Taoist mystics, two large, hard swellings periodically came and went. The arteries in his neck expanded and rose, blue and snake-like, into this head.

These images and descriptions are to be found in various religions and cultures. This suggests that, over the centuries, in different parts of the world, people recognized as sages, saints or evolved souls must have undergone a similar physical transformation.

A week after the 'explosion', UG experienced what seemed like death and rebirth. He felt his feet, his hands, his whole body go cold. The energy seemed to be ebbing out of him. There was no consciousness in him. Forty-eight minutes later, as he recalled, somebody called out his name. It was his landlady calling to say somebody was on the phone.[15]

UG went downstairs and spoke to his friend Douglas Rosestone. UG asked him to come over to his place. As the trains were not running and Valentine had told him that UG was dying, Rosestone ran the distance of 3 kilometres to UG's place. When he entered UG's room, he found UG in an arched position, what is known in yoga as the posture of the bow. When he asked UG what it was all about, UG told him simply, 'It's the final death.'

The separative thought structure—the sense of 'I'—had dissolved. The whole of the past had been wiped out. The body had undergone a radical mutation and started functioning very differently from the way it had functioned earlier. This did not correspond to anything like 'enlightenment', moksha or liberation, as is widely supposed. It was not a blissful or ecstatic state of being. For this reason, UG took to calling his transformation a 'calamity'. It was his way of debunking popular notions about the state he was in. The transformation he had undergone had to do with the body, not the mind, and it had been sheer torture for the body.

For a year after he underwent these experiences, UG did not say anything about them. He shunned public talks, did not start any ashram, wrote no books, disavowed any intention to uplift mankind or save humanity. When he started talking about himself, it was with small groups of people. For some forty years after his transformation, he kept travelling around the world, staying with friends and having long question-and-answer sessions that seemed like conversations. He also gave the occasional interview on radio or television.

UG made it clear that he had no message to offer mankind. He often joked that he entertained visitors only because it was rude to turn away people or call in the police. Nevertheless, it's hard to resist the feeling that he did feel an obligation to communicate a few basic messages. At the very least, he wanted to disabuse people of notions they may have picked up in the spirituality bazaar.

One author discerns three phases in his life after the 'calamity'.[16] In the first phase from 1967 to the late 1970s, he was soft and obliging in his interactions with people. He would refer to other sages and their teachings and certain religious texts approvingly.

He would explain the functioning of the body and the mind, his understanding of the 'natural' state, etc.

In the next phase, the 1980s and the late 1990s, he became what he is best recognized as—something of a raging sage. He debunked everything and everybody. He became famous for his subversive one-liners: love is war; mind is a myth; thought is your enemy; there is nothing inside you but fear; and so on. By negating and rejecting all our ideas and ideals, he wanted us to get a sense of the true nature of things.

In the final phase, which was the last ten years until his death in 2007, he became playful and steered clear of any serious conversation. He would invite friends to sing, dance and share jokes. Everybody would join in mocking and laughing at everything, including UG himself. It is well to bear in mind the phases he went through because one can often get the impression that he was saying different things at different times and contradicting himself. On JK, for instance, he sounds respectful at one point and scathing at another.

What we have by way of his 'teachings' is an enormous collection of recordings of his writings, audio tapes and videos. The themes are often repetitive but UG is always engaging. There is a refreshing lack of pretence to his statements. There is no evolved soul preaching to lesser mortals. Just somebody who's telling it like it is—without any ulterior motive and certainly without trying to gain anything for himself. In what follows, I propose to cover UG's views on a range of matters. I have thought it best to use quotes as often as possible instead of trying to paraphrase what he says. No paraphrasing can capture the intensity and boldness of UG's pronouncements.

* * *

UG's most significant contribution is the understanding that what is characterized as 'enlightenment' is a physico-chemical transformation of the body. He insisted that it is the body that undergoes a change, not the mind. As mentioned earlier, he preferred to call his experience a 'calamity'—it was his way of mocking those who think of 'enlightenment' as a spiritually elevated state. UG says:[17]

> There is absolutely no religious content to it and no mystical overtones or undertones to the functioning of the body. But unfortunately for centuries they have interpreted the whole thing in religious terms and that has created misery for us all.

UG has given us a vivid description not only of the process of transformation of the body but of the way the body functions once the transformation is over. Several things seem to happen to people who enter this state—the likes of the Buddha, Jesus Christ, Ramana Maharshi and UG himself.[18] In what follows, I will highlight important characteristics of the 'natural' state as described by UG. These are collated from various sources.

Thought, the entity that gives one a sense of individuality, seems to burn itself up. Thought is matter and when it burns up, the body gets heated and is covered with ash. All that is part of one's consciousness—the collective memories handed down through the genes and embedded in oneself—is flushed out.

Among many Brahmins, there is the practice of applying ash to the forehead, hands and the torso. UG believes that the yogis' practice of smearing ash on themselves was done in imitation of what they saw on the bodies of those who had got into the 'natural' state. Ordinary people may have followed suit.

When a person enters the state that UG talks about, the body automatically assumes poses that correspond to a number of classic poses taught in yoga. This is the energy in the body expressing itself spontaneously. Those who have watched people in that state may have been led to believe that if they assumed those poses, they too could get into the 'natural' state! That's how the practice of yoga may have started. Cause and effect seem to have got mixed up in the minds of ordinary people. The yogic pose follows the 'natural' state, not the other way around. Whatever the health benefits of yoga—and UG had misgivings about these as well—it cannot lead to the fundamental transformation implied by the 'natural' state.

As UG describes it, when one is going through the process of transformation, one's consciousness takes the shape of all those who have been in a similar state before—Buddha, Jesus, Mahavira, Muhammed, Socrates and hundreds of others. All these people are part of one's consciousness and now they begin to leave. This process goes on and on until only the uncontaminated, primordial consciousness is left. UG has dramatically described this process of expulsion as 'the saints go marching out'.

Thought, which directs and dominates one's activities, is relegated to the background. It surfaces only when required. Otherwise, there is only awareness. As UG puts it, thought changes from being a master to being a slave. In the initial days after coming into the 'natural' state, UG had serious problems. He could not put a name to various objects. He would point at a flower and ask,' What is that?' Valentine would say, 'That is a flower.' He would look at a cow and ask, 'What is that?' The knowledge was in the background; it never came to the forefront.

UG got used to this becoming a permanent part of being. When he looked at something, he didn't know what he was looking at. Those familiar with JK's teachings would know JK's question, 'Can you look at a flower without naming it?' There is only awareness of the flower—the word 'flower' does not pop into the mind. After listening to UG, we can infer that JK was describing his own state which was, perhaps, close to the 'natural' state. Somebody who is not in that state can never quite comprehend what JK is talking about.

Several glands become active or more active than before. The thymus gland is active in children and becomes dormant when one attains puberty. Thanks to this gland, children have extraordinary feelings. In a person who enters the 'natural' state, this gland becomes active again. This gives rise to an extraordinary sensitivity. UG interpreted 'affection' to mean, not an emotional feeling for something, but simply the body being affected by everything around it.

A couple of incidents in UG's life illustrate this point. UG was once staying at a coffee plantation in India. A lady happened to beat her child badly. UG watched but did not interfere. When somebody asked him about his seeming indifference, UG told him that the marks of the beating were to be found on his back as well. When consciousness is not divided, what happens out there happens within oneself—one is not separated from what is happening out there. The question of sitting in judgement on the lady beating up the child does not arise because there is no sense of 'I' and 'she'. In the 'natural' state, the separative consciousness that underlies all value judgement is missing. ('I am right, that person is wrong.')

A similar thing happened when UG, on a trip to Goa, was sitting near a hillock and Valentine climbed up to join him. She slipped and fell and injured her knee. UG hitched up his trousers to reveal that there were scratch marks on his knee as well.

There is an intense awareness of all that is happening within oneself and outside. UG said he could feel his pulse without an external aid—and at sixty-four different points in his body. He could listen to his heartbeat without a stethoscope. He could sense that his body was an electromagnetic field.[19] When he ate food, he could sense the blood rushing to his stomach. This rush of food produced an extraordinary enjoyment, a 'peace that passes understanding'.[20] Most people can't sense this because they are thinking of something or the other while having food. The interference of thought mars the enjoyment of food and it also interferes with digestion. UG conjectures that, perhaps, this is the reason that one is advised not to talk while eating.

The linking up of various sensations through thought is not there. The continuity that is provided by the sense of 'I' is broken.

The coordinating function is taken up by the pineal gland, which gives the necessary instructions to the body. This gland is called the *ajna* (command) chakra in Indian spiritual literature. In the absence of thought as coordinator, the sensations stay as 'pure and simple' sensations. The effect is best described by UG himself:[21]

> I may look at you as you are talking. The eyes will focus on your mouth because that is what is moving, and the ears will receive the sound vibrations. There is nothing inside which links up the two and says that it is you talking. I may be looking at a spring bubbling out of the earth and hear the water, but there is nothing to say that the noise being heard is the sound of water, or that that sound is in any way connected with what I am seeing. I may be looking at my foot, but nothing says that this is my foot. When I am walking, I see my feet moving—it is such a funny thing: 'What is that which is moving?'
>
> What functions is a primordial consciousness, untouched by thought.

The absence of thought meant that UG would be aware of somebody only when he was looking at that person. The moment the head was turned away, UG would not be aware of him. Out of sight was truly out of mind! JK often made statements—'dying to one's yesterdays', 'looking at one's wife without past images'—that people found mystifying. Spiritual leaders exhort us to 'live in the present' or 'live from moment to moment'.

We can now relate these statements to the state that UG talks about. In the 'natural' state there is no past, hence no yesterdays. One is effortlessly living in the present. There is no memory that intrudes into one's consciousness. So when one looks at one's wife, one is not influenced by all that has happened earlier. There is only the awareness of whatever is before oneself. Whenever UG encountered something of beauty—say, a beautiful piece of scenery—his body would respond by taking deep breaths. The word 'breathtaking' took on a new meaning for him. There was no thought intervening to call the scenery 'beautiful', only the natural response of the body.

These are not attitudes of mind or states of being that one can will. Quite the contrary. It is the very absence of mind or will that makes these experiences possible. For a person who has come into this state to exhort others to do any of the things mentioned above is absurd. One begins to understand what UG means when he says that no meaningful communication is possible between somebody who is in the 'natural' state and somebody who is not. The two individuals are functioning in very different ways. In one, thought is absent; in the other, thought is dominant.

In the 'natural' state, since one is living only in the present, untroubled by the past or the future, there are no anxieties or worries, no regrets or sorrows. Since the 'I' has disappeared, there is no greed or the desire to accumulate, to plan for the morrow. Pleasure and pain, which are constructions of thought, cease to be. Since there is no 'I' that needs to be gratified, the ego is dead. The egoless existence that sages preach to others is not something that one needs to strive for at all; it is what obtains in the natural course. It follows that if one is not in the 'natural' state, attempts to shed one's ego or forgo greed and desire are futile. Sermons to this effect are wasted. The whole quest for spiritual betterment, which is something of a thriving industry today, is doomed to failure.

The 'natural' state is not attained through austerities, self-mortification, intense meditation or any other effort prescribed over the centuries. UG emphasizes that what happened to him is utterly acausal. He did not get into that state through any particular effort of his. If anything, his reading of the scriptures, his doing meditation or yoga, his interactions with JK—everything that he did in the quest for 'enlightenment'—only retarded his efforts. Any effort that one makes reinforces the mechanism of thought, whereas the 'natural' state is all about the annihilation of thought. The quest for 'enlightenment' is the very antithesis of 'enlightenment'.

When one abandons the quest for 'enlightenment', when one grasps the fact that nothing that is born of thought can ever lead to 'enlightenment', then—perhaps, then—something may happen that triggers the 'natural' state. Even then, we have no assurances. It may well be that a few people are genetically programmed to come into that state. They are the chosen ones, so to speak. UG puts it very well:[22]

> What makes one person come into his natural state, and not another person, I don't know. Perhaps it's written in the cells. It is acausal. It is not an act of volition on your part; you can't bring it about. There is absolutely nothing you can do. You can distrust any man who tells you how he got into this state. One thing you can be sure of is that he cannot possibly know himself, and cannot possibly communicate it to you. There is a built-in triggering mechanism in the body. If the experiencing structure of thought happens to let go, the other thing will take over in its own way. The functioning of the body will be a totally different functioning, without the interference of thought except when it is necessary to communicate with somebody. To put it in the boxing-ring phrase, you have to 'throw in the towel', be totally helpless. No one can help you, and you cannot help yourself.

There is no way that one can come into the 'natural' state by seeking answers from others, by reading religious or philosophical texts, by invoking the blessings of godmen. What is required is a burning hunger for the question or questions one has and a rejection of all the answers one has received:[23]

> The search ends with the realization that there is no such thing as enlightenment. By searching, you want to be free from the

self, but whatever you are doing to free yourself from the self is the self. How can I make you understand this simple thing? There is no 'how'. If I tell you that, it will only add more momentum to that [search], strengthen that momentum. That is the question of all questions: 'How, how, how?'.

. . . And the answer must be found without any process. Any process takes you away from the question, waters down the question. The question becomes more and more intense in its own way. You don't want anything except the answer to that question. Nothing else. Nothing interests you any more except the answer for that question. Day in and day out, all the rest of your life, that is the only question for you—'How?'

That 'how?' is related to the answers given by others, so you have to reject all those answers. The question has to burn itself out, and the question cannot burn itself out so long as you are waiting for an answer either from within or from without. When the question burns itself out, what is there begins to express itself. It is your answer, not anybody else's answer. You don't even have to find the answer, because the answer is already there and will somehow express itself. You don't have to be a scholar, you don't have to read books, you don't have to do anything; what is there begins to express itself.

A few people seem to stumble into the 'natural' state every now and then. These are the ones venerated as religious leaders or sages over the years. As UG puts it, those who get into this state represent the end product of evolution. All consciousness is one. So the transformation that comes about in these individuals, the change in their consciousness, seems to affect all mankind.

UG speculates that this could be the reason that there is some sort of quest in most people, a certain restlessness. Because some individuals have, over the ages, broken out of the stranglehold of thought, there is a sense in the human consciousness that a better state is possible. Life pushes us all in the direction of freedom.

Alas, few of us make it. The 'natural' state eludes all but a chosen few.

At this point, the reader may well wonder what proof we have of UG's being in the 'natural' state. How can we be sure that these are not the concoctions of a clever mind or a con man? Well, it is open to the reader to go through the vast collection of UG's utterances to judge for himself whether these sound plausible at all. Besides, we do have the accounts of various people who were witness to UG's physical transformation. We also have anecdotes narrated by people who came into contact with him. These testify to a remarkable personality. I will mention a few from Mahesh Bhatt's biography.

Bhatt once spent time with UG at the hill station of Kodaikanal in Tamil Nadu. Bhatt had gone there with his friend, the Bollywood film star Parveen Babi, who was suffering from mental illness. Bhatt had heard stories about UG taking walks with cobras. When he asked UG about it, UG merely said, 'We will see.' Later that evening, when Bhatt and Babi went for a stroll with UG, all of a sudden, UG said, 'Stop', and holding Bhatt and Babi back, said, 'look and see for yourselves.' Bhatt spotted a king cobra with its whole family. Bhatt and Babi fled in terror.[24]

On another occasion, Bhatt was in Rome, looking for a black panther to cast in one of his films. By some coincidence, UG happened to be in Rome at the same time. Bhatt found a black panther in a private zoo owned by a trainer on the outskirts of Rome. The trainer took Bhatt and UG into the zoo and showed them the black panther. Soon, the panther began growling. UG gestured to the panther and said, 'Quiet, sit down.' The animal obeyed. This happened several times when Bhatt and UG were talking to the trainer. The trainer was surprised and wanted to know whether UG himself was a trainer![25]

Bhatt also talks about a remarkable encounter UG had with a *nadi* astrologer (somebody who tells your future by looking at sets of ancient palm leaves on which people's destinies are said to be written). From the account, it appears that Bhatt himself was present along with other friends.

The astrologer held out one end of a string and offered it to UG. The other end was attached to a bundle of palm leaves. The astrologer asked UG to part the stack of leaves at random by passing his end through the stack. The astrologer opened the leaf at which UG had divided the stack and began reading it:[26]

> What is there to say about this recluse who lives totally unattached like a droplet on a lotus leaf? This man lives like Bharata in the epic Ramayana, completely disinterested in the midst of all royal comforts and pleasures . . . This man will rise to prominence in his Ravidasa [the phase of the Sun] like the rising Sun . . . The light of his teaching keeps spreading everywhere. But he thoroughly disappoints those who come to him hoping to get somewhere . . . This man, whether he is eating, drinking, walking, sleeping, or doing anything, he always remains in Sahaja Samadhi [the 'Natural' state of Union] . . .

Bhatt speaks of the 'peace, security, comfort, intimacy and communion' that people derived from merely sitting in UG's presence. He has written of the current of energy that he himself experienced during his contacts with UG. Many others have written in a similar vein about their experiences with UG.

* * *

In the years following his transformation, UG expressed himself on a wide range of subjects. He refuted any suggestion that these were ideas he was producing. He insisted that whatever answers he was providing to questions came out of him without the interference of thought—somebody was throwing a ball and the ball was just bouncing back:[27]

You ask a question, so something comes out of it. How it is operating, I don't know. It is not a product of any thinking. Whatever comes out of me is not manufactured by thought— but something is coming out. You are throwing a ball and the ball is bouncing and you are calling that the 'answer'. Actually, what I am doing is only restructuring the question and throwing it back at you.

His views are provocative, outrageous, unsettling and even anarchic. They are a repudiation of everything that may be said to be mainstream or conventional.

For instance, UG didn't think India's vaunted spiritual heritage was of much use to the world. He did not deny that the heritage was considerable. India had produced many saints and saviours over the ages. But that heritage was not today helping India put its house in order. So, how could it be of any use to the world?[28]

First of all you must have economic stability—everybody must be fed, clothed and given shelter. There is no excuse for the poverty in this country—for thirty years we have been a free country. Why do these things still continue in this country?—that is my basic question . . . The heritage doesn't seem to be able to come to the aid of the people, unfortunately . . . because of the falseness, because it is false, because it doesn't operate in the lives of the people—that is why it cannot help to solve the economic problems of this country. We have talked for centuries about the oneness of life, the unity of life. How can you justify the existence of these slums? How can you justify the existence of ten crores of Harijans [i.e. one hundred million untouchables] in this country? Please, I don't have any answers; I am just pointing out the absurdity of our claims that our heritage is something extraordinary.

One of UG's most striking statements is that thoughts do not come from within a person, as all of us suppose. We believe that each of us has a mind or a brain that generates thoughts. Not so, says UG. There is no individual mind. There is only a World Mind or universal consciousness. Or, as he puts it, there is a thought sphere in which all of us operate.

All of us have our antennae that pick particular thoughts from out of this thought sphere. We are not separate from the universal consciousness. The brain is not a producer of thoughts but a reactor that processes these. All attempts on the part of brain physiologists and psychologists to locate the seat of human consciousness in the brain are, therefore, doomed to failure.[29]

> Thoughts are not really spontaneous. They are not self-generated. They always come from outside. Another important thing for us to realise and understand is that the brain is not a creator. It is singularly incapable of creating anything. But we have taken for granted that it is something extraordinary, creating all kinds of things that we are so proud of. It is just a reactor and a container. It plays a very minor role in this living organism.

Once we understand this, we also understand that the entire range of thoughts and emotions—anger, jealousy, hatred, lust, kindness, compassion, contempt, etc.—will be experienced by all. There cannot be morally superior individuals who don't experience any of these. There may be some who don't allow these feelings to get the better of them but it's not that they don't experience these feelings in the first place.

It makes no sense to ascribe negative or inferior thoughts to others—that chap is full of envy, that other guy is greedy, and so on. What is out there is also in here. The envy and greed that one sees in others is very much part of one's own make-up. To recognize this is to shed one's assumptions of moral superiority and to pause and reflect before condemning others. It is to be humbled into a recognition of our common heritage.

The fact that the individual mind is just part of the World Mind has implications for what we might do to bring about change in the world. Most ideologies and attempts to reform societies focus on what is outside oneself, in the world at large. UG makes it clear that these ideologies have no chance of success. They are all born of thought. And thought is fundamentally divisive; it separates the thinker or the 'I' from the rest of the world. Thought can only, therefore, breed more conflict. The mess that we see in the world is only a reflection of the mess within each one of us.

It follows that the only change one can bring about in the world is to change oneself. (To use the now hackneyed expression, 'Be the change you wish to see.') Any improvement in oneself constitutes an improvement in the world. The world is most dramatically impacted when an individual moves into the 'natural' state. All of human consciousness is affected when that happens. Such an individual is like a flower that radiates fragrance. The vibrations that he gives off seem to leave an impact on all of human consciousness. At some places, UG even suggests that the effects of such an individual linger in the universal consciousness long after the individual has passed away.[30]

> When the explosion takes place the whole structure of thought collapses and affects the whole human consciousness. This seems to be the only way we can affect the world by bringing about a structural change within oneself. This is the only way. All other reforms, all other intellectual pursuits, teachings, philosophies, they are all thinking about thinking itself, which is a pure and simple dialectical thinking. It is not going to lead us anywhere.

UG debunked the commonly held idea of a soul that survives death. It is the body that is immortal, not the soul:[31]

> This body disintegrates into its constituent elements, so nothing is lost. If you burn it, the ashes enrich the soil and aid

germination. If you bury it, the worms live on it. If you throw it into the river, it becomes food for the fishes. One form of life lives on another form of life, and so gives continuity to life. So life is immortal.

So much for the idea of a soul or atman that lives on forever after the body is extinguished, an idea that finds expression in the *Bhagvad Gita* and also in other religions. UG says bluntly that ideas such as soul, an afterlife and God are all born of fear, the fear of death. The individual or 'I' knows that death is inevitable and doesn't want to accept the fact. So, he creates the comforting idea of a soul that is permanent or indestructible.

* * *

UG was often compared—and sometimes confused—with his more famous namesake, JK, often hailed as one of the great teachers and philosophers of the last century. A brief word about JK would be in order.

As a small child, JK was identified by the theosophists as a person with the potential to become a great spiritual teacher. He was later educated and groomed by the theosophists for the role of World Teacher. In 1911, the Theosophical Society established the Order of the Star in the East and named JK as its head. In that capacity, he travelled widely delivering lectures and meeting people. When JK's younger brother, Nitya, was diagnosed with tuberculosis, JK and Nitya travelled to California in 1922 as it was felt that the climate there would help him to recuperate.

In the Ojai valley of California, JK underwent what was described as profound transformational experiences. These experiences involved physical pain. JK never spoke about these experiences at any length. Nitya died in California. This was a great shock to JK, especially because the theosophists had led him to believe that Nitya was intended to be with him in his life mission.

In 1929, at a meeting of the order in the Netherlands, JK dissolved the order, declaring, 'I maintain that Truth is a pathless land, and you cannot approach it by any path whatsoever, by any religion, by any sect.'[32] He dissociated himself from the theosophists and thereafter delivered talks on his own. Eventually, he was to found his own organizations, including the Krishnamurti Foundation, which became the principal vehicle for dissemination of his teachings. He died in California in 1986, aged ninety.

The lives of UG and JK seemed bound together in strange ways. They both had a long association with the Theosophical Society. The first contact between the two happened when UG was seven years old. UG was taken to the golden jubilee celebration of the society at Adyar. UG saw JK on stage and heard him speak. The next evening UG was wading in the waters of a nearby beach when JK happened to be taking a walk with some admirers. On seeing UG, JK broke away from his circle and joined UG in collecting shells.[33] Did the older man sense some potential in the child?

Between 1947 and 1953, UG listened to talks that JK gave at Adyar in Madras (now Chennai). There was no personal interaction with JK during that period. In 1953, during the course of a talk, UG sent him the following question:[34]

> Sir, what kick exactly do you get out of these talks and discussions? Obviously you would not go on for more than twenty years if you did not enjoy them. Or is it only by force of habit?

JK gave a long-winded reply, in effect saying that if anybody was speaking out of habit, he was exploiting people. If, however, there was an attempt to find the truth from moment to moment, it could not be characterized as habit as all continuity had come to an end.

A few days later, when JK talked about subconscious and unconscious states of mind, UG said that he could not see any mind in himself, let alone a subconscious and unconscious mind. JK responded by saying that he was using such terms for the benefit of the others, not for the likes of UG. Thereafter, UG stopped participating in the discussions.

A common friend arranged a meeting. Several meetings followed during the rest of JK's stay in Madras. As mentioned earlier, UG had a polio-stricken son. JK offered to try to heal him. He massaged the boy's legs for several days. It didn't work. During their meetings, UG would confront JK with highly provocative questions. Had JK arrived at his state through the method he was preaching to others? Why did JK continue to teach after disavowing the World Teacher role the theosophists had assigned him? Why had he started schools for children with a special approach to teaching when he did not believe in conditioning minds?

One day UG asked JK bluntly: Was there anything behind the abstractions JK was throwing at people? JK said vehemently, 'You have no way of knowing it.'

UG retorted, 'If I have no way of knowing it and you have no way of communicating it, what the hell have we been doing!' UG soon left for the US. JK continued to keep in touch with him through friends.

UG's next meeting with JK was in London in 1961, a time when, as we have seen, UG was adrift. When JK got to know that UG was in town, he sent word asking to see UG. When they met, JK tried to persuade UG to return to India and get reunited with his family. UG was in no mood to oblige. At JK's instance, UG attended JK's talks for three days at Wimbledon. Their next meeting was in the mid-sixties in Saanen where UG was staying with Valentine. JK and UG bumped into each other a couple of times.

The last encounters happened in August 1967 in the days leading up to UG's 'calamity'. UG attended JK's talks in Saanen. UG heard JK say, ' . . . in that silence, there is no mind; there is action . . .' It struck UG that he was precisely in that state! He walked out of the tent, never to meet JK again.

In the initial years after he got into the 'natural' state, we find UG discussing JK's teachings somewhat favourably. He makes laudatory references to the way JK develops an argument—looking at a problem from different angles before leading up to the main point and getting people to examine their premises and preconceptions about a topic. In his later years, we find him savaging JK and his teachings.

UG's basic criticism is that JK never quite discarded the role of World Teacher although he moved away from the theosophists who had wanted to cast him in that role. He merely substituted the Order of the Star with his own Krishnamurti Foundation. JK said there could be no teacher and taught that all authority must be shunned and yet produced seventy-two books totalling 4 million pages in twenty-two languages, around 2500 audio cassettes and 1200 video cassettes.[35]

UG remarks scathingly:[36]

> To me, Krishnamurti is playing the same game as all those ugly saints in the market whom we have in the world today. Krishnamurti's teaching is phoney baloney. There is nothing to his teaching at all, and he cannot produce anything at all. A person may listen to him for sixty, seventy or a hundred years, but nothing will ever happen to that man, because the whole thing is phoney. If the number of followers is the criterion of a successful spiritual teacher, JK is a pygmy. He is a mere wordsmith. He has created a new trap.

UG was also critical of the fact that JK had created a spiritual goal—'mutation of the mind'—that could be attained through particular techniques, such as 'choiceless awareness'. By this is meant being aware of one's thoughts and reactions without passing judgement on these. UG argued that 'choiceless awareness' was a meaningless concept because there was nobody inside oneself who was aware of anything.

There was no question of 'mutation of the mind' because there was no mind. Self-realization was an absurdity because there was no self to be realized. The only transformation that was possible was a complete change in the functioning of the body of the sort UG had himself undergone. And there was nothing one could do to bring about that.

It is not clear, though, whether UG's harsh criticism of JK should be taken at face value. Going through UG's comments on JK at various times, one does get the feeling that some of the remarks are intended for effect. They are meant to disabuse JK's followers of blind reliance on authority. His intention seems to be to dissuade them from seeking some magic pill for their problems in the form of JK's teachings.

For all his criticism of JK, UG acknowledged that JK had been an important influence on him. He seemed to have a certain regard for JK. When Mahesh Bhatt asked UG who was the most remarkable man he had met, he promptly said, 'Jiddu Krishnamurti'. When Bhatt pointed out that only that morning, he had treated the subject of JK with derision, UG simply said, 'I never say anything I don't mean.'[37]

The most dramatic proof that the lives of the two men were strangely intertwined came when JK passed away. On the night that it happened, sitting in a house in California 400 miles away from Ojai valley, UG seemed to sense that JK was dying. He called some of his friends and asked them if they could come over to his place right away. When they entered his room, they found UG sitting cross-legged in bed in his pyjamas. UG said to them, 'I don't think I am going to survive; the energy is so strong, the body can't take it.' His friends could see ripples moving down from his head to his face. His whole body seemed to be shaking. This went on for a while. UG kept his eyes closed in a yoga posture. He survived.[38]

* * *

Society conditions us to set morally lofty goals for ourselves: achieving peace of mind, becoming a good human being, leaving the world a better place. UG emphasized that these very goals were stumbling blocks to our being in harmony with the world around us.

We are all the time trying to be something other than ourselves, reaching out for some goal that society has conned us into seeking. We are thus in conflict with ourselves. Once the quest for something better ceases, the conflict within ceases. We are no longer in conflict with the world. Take, for instance, the ideal of being selfless. Trying to be selfless is a self-centred activity. When you stop wanting to be selfless, self-centredness ceases:[39]

> It (the body) is not interested in your virtues or vices. As long as you practice virtues, so long you will remain a man of vice. They go together. If you are lucky enough to be free from this pursuit of virtue, as a goal, along with it the vice also goes out of your system. You will not remain a man of vice. You will remain a man of violence as long as you follow some idea of becoming a non-violent, kind, soft, gentle person. A kind man, a man who is practicing kindness, a man who is practicing virtues is really a menace. Not the [so-called] violent man.

UG was also severe on people seeking answers to timeless questions such as the meaning and purpose of life, what happens after death, whether there is an afterlife, etc. He insisted that a living person would never ask such questions; he would just live. Only people who were not truly alive would pose such questions. These questions also arose from the relentless pursuit of pleasure. When one pleasure after another was satisfied, boredom set in. Then, people would begin to ask: Is there something more or beyond all this?

In the spiritual marketplace, there is no dearth of persons ready to cater to such needs:[40]

You are assuming that you are hungering for spiritual attainments and you are reaching out for your goals. Naturally, there are so many people in the marketplace—all these saints, selling all kinds of shoddy goods. For whatever reason they are doing it, it's not our concern, but they are doing it. They say it is for the welfare of mankind and that they do it out of compassion for mankind and all that kind of thing. All that is bullshit anyway. What I am trying to say is that you are satisfied with the crumbs they throw at you. And they promise that one day they are going to deliver to you a full loaf of bread. That is just a promise. They cannot deliver the goods at all. They just don't have it.

And the reason that spiritual leaders or godmen cannot provide moksha, salvation or enlightenment is because, as mentioned earlier, the transformation that needs to happen is utterly acausal. It's like being hit by a bolt of lightning, an accident that happens to one in a billion. Not only does it not come out of any determined pursuit, it's the very pursuit that must come to an end for the transformation to happen:[41]

> That is something which cannot be made to happen through your effort or through the grace of anybody, through the help of even a god walking on the face of this earth claiming that he has specially descended from wherever (from whatever heavens) for your sake and for the sake of mankind—that is just absolute gibberish. Nobody can help you. Help you to achieve what? That is the question, you see.

UG had interesting and outrageous things to say even about mundane matters such as diet and nutrition.[42] He rejected the view that health had anything to do with diet and exercise. He was vehement in his denunciation of nutritionists. He ate very little and yet was full of energy and vitality. A reporter once told UG that he was incredibly good-looking and youthful. UG replied,

'That's because I don't eat health food, I don't take vitamins, and I don't exercise!'

He believed that the body needed a little basic food and it could turn that into the energy it needed to survive. He put forward the radical view that the stomach had the capacity to digest almost anything. The idea of 'right food' was a concept created by the human mind. This concept had destroyed the natural capacity of the body to process whatever was given to it—and reject whatever was not right. In a radio interview in the US, he once claimed that during the siege of Leningrad in World War II, people had survived on mud. A lady from the former Soviet Union, who had survived the siege, later called him to say he was right!

> The body has intelligence of its own. Give it a chance. The human intellect we have cultivated over millions of years is no match for the intelligence of the body. It will take care of itself. So you can't eat wrong food.[43]

UG was equally severe on things like yoga and meditation and the notion that these could help achieve something called 'peace of mind'. He argued that the yogic poses and meditation brought a temporary sense of well-being. They could not, however, lead one on to the 'natural' state. The chant 'Om', repeated several times, changes the breathing pattern. In chanting it hundreds of times, one hopes that the pattern will change sufficiently to fall in line with that of the 'natural' state. This does not happen at all.[44]

Meditation brings a certain peace. So, people keep meditating in order to recapture that experience. However, if one abandons the notion of some mythical 'peace of mind', one accepts thoughts as they come and go. In the process one becomes peaceful.[45]

Let UG speak for himself:[46]

> Meditation is a self-centred activity. It is strengthening the very self you want to be free from. What are you meditating on? You

want to be free from something . . . There is a continuous flow of thoughts, and you are linking up all these thoughts all the time, and this is the noise you can't stand . . . So by repeating mantras, you create a louder noise, and you submerge the noise of thought, and then you are at peace with yourself. You think something marvellous is happening to you. But all meditation is a self-centred activity.

. . . Meditation is warfare. You sit for meditation while there is a battle raging within you. The result is violent, evil thoughts welling up inside you. Next, you try to control or direct these brutal thoughts, making more effort and violence for yourself in the process.

UG had little patience with talk of creativity, the great works of poetry, music and the arts. He believed that there was little that was original to so-called works of creativity. Almost everything that people did was an imitation of something else. Artists, writers and the rest were mere craftsmen:[47]

Artists pick something here and something there, put it together and think they have created something marvellous. They are all imitating something that is already there. Imitation and style are the only 'creativity' we have. Each of us has our own style according to the school we attended, the language we were taught, the books we have read, the examinations we have taken. And within that framework again we have our own style. Perfecting style and technique is all that operates there. You will be surprised that one of these days computers will paint and create music much better than all the painters and musicians that the world has produced so far. It may not happen in our lifetime but it will happen.

Even the taste for art, painting and music, he pointed out, was a cultivated taste. One was taught to appreciate these things.

Only when one did not use anything as a model could something creative emerge. Nature alone was capable of such creativity—no two faces, no two leaves were identical. Many pride themselves on their works of creation. Others are given to admiration of these. UG's dismissal of so-called creativity is chastening.

UG often expressed himself in extreme or frivolous terms. For instance, he exhorted people around him to simply focus on making money. He wrote the Money Maxims which one of his admirers has composed into a song that can be found on YouTube. There are 108 of these maxims. The number is intentional. As many readers would know, 108 is a number that is considered sacred in Hindu religion. Prayer beads typically come as a string of 108 beads. Choosing 108 maxims to extol the virtues of money was UG's way of mocking religion and spirituality.

The Maxims run as follows:[48]

1. Money matters most in life.
2. Be not shy about money-making.
3. Trust not anyone with money.
4. Nothing is free in this world, not even love.
5. One who worships the money god will be amply rewarded. One who worships the other God will be stripped naked and left in the streets.
6. Make money by hook or by crook.
7. Make money by any means.
8. Money talks; wealth whispers.
9. Miss not a chance to make money.
10. Quench not the thirst for money.
11. Money is the only thing that works.
12. Yes is for money and no is for everything else.
13. Money is the only visible support for life.
14. Money is the be all and end all of our existence.
15. Money is the only thing that will put you into the life of luxury.
16. Money is the word of the day.

17. One who does not exploit his assets to make money must be a damn fool.
18. Money should be the highest on your agenda.

There is more in this vein. UG's own life was the exact opposite of these maxims. At the end of each year, UG distributed whatever surplus was left in his bank account and started the year on a fresh note. (He kept getting gifts from admirers.) In prescribing these maxims, UG was trying to describe how the vast majority of people actually behave behind a veil of spirituality or goodness. He meant to convey that obsession with money is one of the realities of the world.

UG also composed his Ten Commandments. These can be said to be the very antithesis of the official version:[49]

1. Just fuck—don't talk of love
2. Steal but don't get caught
3. Yield to temptations—all and every kind
4. Kill thy neighbour, save thyself
5. Better to be a dog than a holy mackerel
6. Hate your mother—beat your bitch
7. Shoot all the doctors on sight and at sight
8. Better masturbate than meditate
9. Eat like a pig, a hog and swine all rolled into one
10. Get lost and stay lost

Again, UG is taking aim at the pretence and hypocrisy, the fears and phoney beliefs that characterize our lives. The devastating cynicism in his commandments is intended to get people to face up to the squalid reality of their thoughts and feelings. UG is telling people, 'This is what you are; none of the holy gospels to which you subscribe operates in your life.'

It's hard to encounter UG's writings without being changed in some way, however modest. His brutal honesty about our lives can be unsettling. He can be scary because he takes away all our crutches, demolishes our cherished illusions. However, after the initial shock of being stripped of whatever one is carrying, one begins to feel a little lighter. It is possible that a quality of courage enters one's life.

* * *

UG had a fall in the bathroom in 2004. He recovered from it. Three of his long-standing friends built an apartment for him in their villa in Vallecrosia on the Italian Riviera. In the years that followed, UG travelled indefatigably from one place to another, sometimes spending no more than a few days in one place. Most of these travels were in Italy, France and Switzerland.

UG had another fall in the bathroom in February 2007. His head hit the sink and started bleeding. UG passed out. When he regained consciousness, he heard knocking on the door of his apartment. UG managed to crawl his way to the door and open it. He had injured his leg and was helped on to a couch.

UG decided he did not want to carry on in a way that would make him even more dependent on his friends. He refused all medical help. As his health deteriorated, he decided it was 'time to go' and let the body take its own natural course. He remained confined to bed. His consumption of food and water decreased and stopped altogether. He defended his decision vigorously:[50]

> Don't call it suicide. You had no choice about your birth, but you have some control over your death. If I am sure of anything it is that I will fall again and I don't want to suffer like this. Don't tell me about your sacredness of life! What about all your own soldiers you are killing in Iraq and Afghanistan? There is no meaning and significance to suffering, sir! Don't tell me all that rubbish. Some ideas for you to preach in the church!

As word spread of UG's decision not to continue living, his friends from different parts of the world gathered in Vallecrosia. Some of them came after getting summons from UG. They sat around him, posing questions and getting responses as they had been for years. There are video recordings to be found on the Internet of UG's final weeks on the planet almost up to the last days. Although weak in body, UG remains his fiery self, mocking those with beatific thoughts and lashing out at pretenders in the spiritual market.

Some of his friends recalled that when UG had had a similar fall a few years earlier, he had told them he could see things happening in places as far as away as Australia. He even said he was out on the stars and he could see things on other planets.[51]

We have vivid accounts of UG's last moments from many people. Narayana Moorty, a close friend of UG's, is one of them.[52] UG called Moorty in California to say that he would like Moorty to visit him. 'I have to see you before I die. If I don't see you, I'll have to die in great pain!'

Moorty flew to France and was driven across to Italy. As he entered the room in which UG was lying and approached UG, he could 'feel myself entering into a vast field of energy in which I was then enveloped'. Moorty notes that despite the fact that UG's end was drawing near, there was a festive atmosphere in the place. People chatted away busily, videos and photos were taken, there were readings from UG's materials. Chocolate was passed around.

UG ate little—a small amount of rice sticks, idli or upma and a sip of orange juice or hot water—and he kept throwing up. He collapsed once on the toilet seat and thereafter did not walk at all. It was obvious that he was in pain although he showed it very rarely. Indeed, he seemed supremely unconcerned about his health; there was not even a trace of fear.

Ten days before he passed away, UG conveyed through Mahesh Bhatt that he wanted everybody to leave except for Bhatt and two others. His instructions were faithfully carried out.

UG died on 22 March 2007 at around 3 p.m. He had been in a coma for about four days prior to his death. There was no funeral and no ceremony. His body was taken to the crematorium where it waited in line for a week.[53]

UG had left instructions for the disposal of his funds. Much of it was to be given to deserving young girls of Indian origin who were studying abroad. His apartment in Gstaad had been rented until August. UG had told his friends that they were free to stay there and enjoy themselves.

Nothing better expresses the spirit of this irreverent, anti-guru than the following lines from what he called his 'Swan Song':[54]

> The demand for permanence—permanent relationships, permanent happiness, and permanent bliss—in any field is the cause of human misery. There is nothing to permanence. So don't be a damned fool! Go and make money.

7

John Pilger: The Journalist as Crusader

As the documentary opens, the camera focuses on an American general addressing a press conference. He is confident about America's ability to deal with all manner of threats. He smirks, 'All countries respect the power of the United States . . . and they respect how dominant we are in this region.'

This is followed by news clips from American TV channels that report on Chinese expansionism and how it threatens the world. The presenter of the documentary then pitches in. 'The threat of China is becoming big news . . . the world is being primed to regard China as a new enemy.'

The Coming War on China is John Pilger's sixtieth documentary. Like most of his documentaries, it has been broadcast in several countries. It's about how America seeks to contain the Chinese threat to its global dominance. One part of America's response has been to move two-thirds of its naval forces to Asia and the Pacific—or what President Obama called in 2011 the 'pivot to Asia'. Pilger notes that America had already surrounded China with 400 military bases 'in an arc that extends from Australia north through the Pacific to Japan, Korea and across Eurasia to Afghanistan and India'.[1]

The documentary ranges well beyond the rise of China and America's response. Its broad theme: America's policies towards China in recent years are merely an aspect of its central objective, which is to dominate the world. In pursuing this objective, America can be ruthless. In 1945, the US took over the Marshall Islands in the Pacific as a UN 'trust territory'. It committed itself to protecting the islanders' well-being. Instead, the islands became a site for testing America's nuclear weapons. From 1946 to 1948, America exploded the equivalent of one Hiroshima bomb every day in the islands. This led to severe contamination of the islands and its people. The story of the Marshall Islands takes up more than a third of the documentary. Pilger doesn't approve of America's policies towards the world—and he makes no attempt to hide the fact.

At one point in the video, the camera zooms in on declassified American government documents. These reveal a secret programme that started out with testing the effects of nuclear radiation on mice and ended up using the islanders as guinea pigs. The locals were resettled on islands that were known to have been contaminated. Many died. Others suffered deformities. There are moving images of some of them. Some of the islanders appear on camera to tell their tale of suffering. The experiments went on for twenty-eight years until the islanders were moved out by the NGO, Greenpeace. Thanks to widespread contamination, the islands, which were rich in fish, fruit and vegetables, now have to procure these from outside. Today, the largest of the islands hosts an American missile base aimed at China.

Cut to the rise of China. At the very outset of this section, Pilger makes clear that American hostility to China goes back a long way and, indeed, seems ingrained in American culture. The author of a book on China, James Bradley, makes the astonishing disclosure that way back in 1883, the US passed a Chinese Exclusion Act which kept the Chinese out of the US for nearly a century! The Chinese came to be viewed in the US as the Yellow

Peril. They were portrayed in American culture as 'uncouth and infantile'.

The demonization of China concealed an unsavoury truth about America's dealings with China: the enormous fortunes made by Americans out of the opium trade with that country. Bradley reveals a startling fact, one that has come to be widely accepted in recent years: much of the East Coast, including the celebrated universities of Harvard, Princeton and Columbia, was built out of the opium trade with China. The grandfather of one of America's most illustrious presidents, Franklin Roosevelt, was an important figure in the drug trade. Western powers, including the US, colonized and occupied China in order to be able to reap the benefits of the opium trade. The people of China were condemned to a long period of poverty and misery even as the West flourished at their expense.

The communist revolution of 1949 put an end to Western exploitation of China. It also gave rise, Pilger says, to 'paranoia' about China. We see Edward Teller, the father of the hydrogen bomb, warning way back in the 1950s that the US must be prepared for the possibility of a Chinese missile attack on the US.

When Pilger visited China after the Cultural Revolution, the nation seemed exhausted. Visiting China more than a generation later, Pilger was struck by the transformation that had come about. Millions had been lifted out of poverty; others had been lifted into the middle class. Shanghai was a modern international city bustling with commerce and industry. China, it seemed to Pilger, had beaten the US at its own game of capitalism—in 2015, China could boast of more dollar billionaires than the US. This was 'unforgivable'.

The Chinese were for long seen in the US as implacable foes. The truth, which was hidden from the public, was that the Chinese leader Mao Zedong had reached out to the US both before and after the communist revolution. He declared that China did not want any confrontation with the US. On every occasion, he was rebuffed. Pilger contends that, contrary to what most people believe, Mao was not against capitalism either. As is well known, Deng Xiaoping, who became China's Supreme Leader in the 1970s, made it clear that communism was not about 'shared poverty'. One of his famous quotes: 'To be rich is glorious'. In Deng's time, China embraced the market economy albeit under the state's close watch.

Pilger gets us to think about the stereotypes that characterize China; for instance, it is portrayed as a 'communist dictatorship'. The public in the West is told that because China is a one-party state, not much change can happen. Not true, says a Chinese businessman whom Pilger interviews. In the US, he says, you can change parties but you can't change policies; in China, you can't change parties but you *can* change policies. Over the past sixty years or so, China has seen phenomenal political reforms, perhaps more than in any other modern country. China, he adds, is a market economy but it's not a capitalist economy, meaning the owners of capital can't control the politburo in China the way they can control policies in the US.

Pilger does not gloss over the seamy side of China (at the time he visited the country). Large numbers of workers lived in miserable conditions, often with three families crammed into a tiny apartment. There's no escape from the Tiananmen Square massacre of protesters in 1989. It's also true that the famous dissenter and Nobel Peace Prize winner, Liu Xiaobo, languished in jail for thirteen years before succumbing to cancer. Nevertheless, Pilger contends, there *is* dissent and protest in China today, such as farmers' protests over their land being grabbed by the state or workers demanding better wages. Western media portrayals of a people repressed by a totalitarian state are not entirely accurate.

In the third part of the documentary, Pilger switches to the Japanese island of Okinawa. The island hosts an important American military base, one that Pilger sees as forming the front line for a coming war on China. In the past, it has been used for attacks on Vietnam, Afghanistan and Iraq, amongst others. Many in Japan resent the presence of the base and would like to see it closed. In 2014, the people of Okinawa elected a government on the single plank of closing down the American base there.

Pilger narrates how, during the Cold War, the US installed nuclear missiles at Okinawa. Most were aimed at China. On one occasion, the missiles were almost launched until a second order came that rescinded the one to launch them. The major who had given the order to launch was court-martialled and dismissed. 'We could have exterminated the whole planet,' says an officer of that time.

The camera moves to Jeju, a South Korean island which is a World Heritage Site and declared an 'Island of Peace' by the South Korean government. Less than 400 miles from Shanghai, the island hosts an American military base. Jeju is one of many choke points through which China's massive imports of raw materials pass. America's intention, says Pilger, is to be able to choke the flow of supplies to China in the event that things get out of hand. Jeju island, like Okinawa, has seen protests from locals who are outraged that the island could be caught up in a future conflict with China. The protests have been put down with a heavy hand.

America has a network of 700 bases around the world through which it projects its power globally. America does not rule over the countries that have these bases, including powerful countries such as Japan and Germany. The countries have their own governments. However, the presence of American bases and troops means they have no independent foreign policy.

American spokesmen, who appear in the documentary, justify these bases as intended to contain provocative behaviour on the part of China. Pilger sees them as increasing the risk of confrontation: a single Chinese warhead, Pilger quotes an expert as saying, would set on fire about 600 square miles of a major American city.

Pilger underplays China's violent past under communist rule and its provocative behaviour in recent years. He does not think it necessary to highlight the fact that China has laid claim to all of the South China Sea. The claim terrifies China's neighbours and they welcome an active American presence in the region. China's economic rise has been accompanied by an undisguised attempt on China's part to expand its influence over the rest of the world. As the world's dominant power, the US is bound to respond. Pilger would almost have us believe that the US is an ogre threatening an innocent China.

Nevertheless, his documentary is useful because it shows a side to the China story other than the one that is common in the Western media. It provides a historical perspective to China's rise and its equation with the US. The West sees China as a threat without ever acknowledging that the West itself has threatened and menaced China for long.

* * *

John Pilger is a celebrated journalist. He has won numerous awards for journalism (including Britain's Journalist of the Year award) and for documentaries (including an Emmy, America's equivalent in television of the Academy Award for movies).

Yet, unless you belong to the generation of the seventies or the eighties, you are unlikely to have heard of him or read him in print. His articles rarely appear in the mainstream media. They are to be found mostly at his own website or in relatively obscure journals or websites. Nor is he seen in the mainstream media. He appears most frequently on Russia Today, the increasingly popular Russian private channel that is something of a hate object today for the Western establishment. You can see dozens of Pilger's documentaries on YouTube but you will seldom see him on the BBC or CNN.

Pilger is not alone in facing isolation. He recounts how two great names in American journalism, Seymour Hersh and Robert Parry, have met the same fate. Hersh is, perhaps, best known for his exposé of the My Lai massacre in Vietnam, an episode in which American soldiers gunned down dozens of unarmed Vietnamese civilians. Parry brought to light the Iran-Contra affair, a White House-directed operation involving the arming of rebels in Nicaragua using funds generated by arms sales to Iran.

In 2016, Hersh and Parry both produced evidence that President Bashir al-Assad of Syria had not used chemical weapons. The charge of using chemical weapons had almost invited a massive US bombing campaign against Syria. Thereafter, both the journalists were banished from the mainstream.[2]

Pilger believes that journalism has deteriorated since the time he joined in the 1960s. The mainstream media in the West can no longer be trusted. More than at any time before, it sees its role as one of supporting and protecting the establishment:

> Although journalism was always a loose extension of establishment power, something has changed in recent years. Dissent tolerated when I joined a national newspaper in Britain in the 1960s has regressed to a metaphoric underground as liberal capitalism moves towards a form of corporate dictatorship. This is a seismic shift, with journalists policing the new 'groupthink', as Parry called it, dispensing its myths and distractions, pursuing its enemies.
>
> . . . Journalism students should study this to understand that the source of 'fake news' is not only trollism, or the likes of Fox news, or Donald Trump, but a journalism self-anointed with a false respectability: a liberal journalism that claims to challenge corrupt state power but, in reality, courts and protects it, and colludes with it.

Pilger says that there is no room for independent journalists in the mainstream media. True journalism is kept alive by websites such as wikileaks.org, consortiumnews.com, Zcomm. org, wsws.org, truthdig.com, globalresearch.org, counterpunch. org and informationclearinghouse.com. One might add Pilger's own website, which hosts his writings and documentaries. On YouTube, many of his documentaries, including *The Coming War on China,* are freely available.

To read Pilger and to watch his documentaries is not only to see another side to the issues of our time. It is also to get to know about issues, some of which hardly figure in the mainstream media. The plight of Aborigines in Australia; Israel's oppression of Palestinians (which is increasingly being blacked out by the mainstream media); the failure of the black regime in South Africa to bring about radical change in the country—Pilger has documented all this and more.

John Pilger was born in Sydney, Australia.[3] His first foray into journalism was a newspaper he launched as a schoolboy. Later, he trained for four years at Australian Consolidated Press. He left for Europe in the early 1960s with two colleagues. They set up an agency in Italy that quickly went broke. Pilger then moved to London. After a stint as a freelance journalist, he joined Reuters and, later, the London *Daily Mirror,* at the time Britain's largest-selling newspaper. He rose to become chief foreign correspondent at the *Mirror,* travelling all over the world, and covered numerous wars, including the Vietnam War. While still in his twenties, Pilger received Britain's Journalist of the Year award. He was the first journalist to win the award twice.

Pilger has reported from the United States in the 1960s and 1970s. His dispatches from Cambodia played a role in bringing home to the world the horrors inflicted by the Pol Pot regime. In 2009, he was awarded Australia's human rights prize, the Sydney Peace Prize. He has received honorary doctorates from universities in the UK and abroad.

Pilger embodies the journalism of a lost era. It was an era in which newspapers were more willing to invest in field reporting, commercial considerations had not come to dominate the editorial side, and journalists had not quite become mouthpieces of the establishment.

* * *

As the film commences, there's a snapshot of Palestinian men and children lined up before an Israeli battle tank. Several Israelis appear on the screen. One calls the occupation of Palestine a 'cancer'. Another says that he's ashamed of calling himself an Israeli. A third deplores the fact that every criticism of the Israeli establishment is construed as anti-Semitism.

These are scenes from Pilger's award-winning documentary, *Palestine Is Still the Issue*.[4] Much of the text is part of a larger essay on the Palestinian problem titled 'The Last Taboo'.[5] The documentary and the essay highlight the injustice done to the Palestinians and the enormous suffering they are still going through. These are things one rarely sees in the Western media these days. Palestinians are more commonly portrayed as compulsive terrorists.

The Palestinian issue is among the great unresolved issues of our time. It has festered for decades now, fuelling rage not only amongst Palestinians but across the Muslim world. Much of Islamic militancy and Islamic terrorism today draw their sustenance from the injustice meted out to the Palestinians.

In 1917, the British promised a home in Palestine for the long-persecuted Jews of the world. The promise was contained in the Balfour Declaration, named after Arthur Balfour, the then British foreign secretary. As Pilger notes, there was a certain cold calculation underlying the seeming act of generosity: the British needed a client state in the region, one that would watch over the Suez Canal and Britain's trade routes to India. Consequent to the declaration, large numbers of Jews from Europe and elsewhere moved to Palestine.

In 1947, the United Nations mandated the creation of separate states for Jews and Arabs in Palestine. In 1948, the state of Israel came into being. This was followed by a war between the newly created state of Israel and its Arab neighbours. The war ended badly for the Palestinians: they lost 78 per cent of their original land to Israel. Ever since, their fight has been for the remaining 22 per cent.

A bigger disaster befell the Palestinians after the Six-Day War in 1967 in which Israel routed its Arab neighbours. The Palestinians had been living in the Gaza Strip which was part of Egypt and the West Bank, which was part of Jordan. In the Six-Day War, Israel annexed both these territories, which have since come to be known as the Occupied Territories.

In the years since, hopes of a Palestinian state have steadily receded. Today, it's something of a distant dream or even a fantasy. Even if an independent state of Palestine is created, the Palestinians will be lucky if they get even 10 per cent of their original land. The more probable outcome now appears to be the complete expropriation of Palestinian lands and even the expulsion of Palestinians from where they are today.

Pilger's documentary, released in 2002, is a sequel to a documentary he produced in 1974 with the same title. In the first documentary, Pilger described how the creation of Israel in 1948 and the Six-Day War in 1967 had reduced Palestinians to refugees in their own land. 'What has changed,' Pilger says in his 2002 documentary, 'is that the Palestinians have fought back. Stateless and humiliated for so long, they have risen up against Israel's huge military regime, although they themselves have no army, no tanks, no American planes and gunships or missiles.'

Palestine, Pilger says in his introduction to the documentary, is today an open prison, one where every aspect of the lives of the Palestinians is controlled by Israel. Every now and then, Israeli tanks roll into one or the other of the towns in the West Bank or the Gaza Strip. These attacks are termed 'incursions' intended to combat 'terrorism'.

One such attack was Operation Defensive Shield, launched in March and April 2002 under Prime Minister Ariel Sharon. The Israeli army attacked a refugee camp with fighter bombers, tanks, bulldozers and helicopter gunships. The camp was defended by a few dozen men with rifles and booby traps. They killed twenty-three Israeli soldiers. Enraged by these losses, Sharon ordered the demolition of thousands of homes, some with people inside. Thousands of Palestinians were rounded up and effectively kidnapped. By an overwhelming majority, the UN Commission for Human Rights condemned Israel. Pilger notes that Israel had at that point defied 246 UN Security Council resolutions and twice the number of UN General Assembly resolutions.

During such attacks, the Israelis target Palestinian schools, offices, theatres, radio stations and the like. The intention is to degrade civilian life in the Palestinian territories. In one raid that Pilger documents, the ministry of culture was destroyed. 'The soldiers had urinated and defecated on the floors, on desks, on embroideries and works of art. They had smeared faeces on children's paintings and written—in shit—"Born to kill".'[6]

Earlier, in 1987, the Palestinians had risen in what was called the *intifada* (which means 'tremor'). They fought the Israelis with slingshots and stones. The Israelis used tanks and airplanes to suppress the revolt. Pilger's documentary has a stomach-churning scene of Israeli soldiers using stones to break the bones of a captured Palestinian youth. There was a second intifada in 2000. Between 2000 and early 2006, an estimated 3300 Palestinians had been killed by the Israelis, more than half of them unlawfully. Some 650 were children.[7]

Gaza resembles a concentration camp. Israel determines what can go in—food, medicines, etc. It also maintains a network of check posts through which Palestinians have to pass. Often, the wait at the check posts can last hours, if not days. In one sequence in the documentary, a Palestinian woman describes how she was stopped and turned back at a check post when she was on her way to hospital to give birth to her child. She and her husband made another attempt but to no avail. The child was born and it died before it could be taken to hospital.

Incidents such as these created the first Palestinian female suicide bomber in 2002. This was an ambulance volunteer who had seen Palestinians getting killed or treated brutally. She was herself shot in the leg twice by plastic-covered bullets. She decided she had to avenge her people. She picked up 10 kg of explosives, strapped it on her back and detonated the bomb in the midst of a lunchtime crowd in Jaffa.

Pilger visits a Jewish settlement in Gaza. (An estimated 42 per cent of Gaza at the time was occupied by Jewish settlements, condemned by the UN as illegal.) These are massive fortresses protected by giant walls and electrified wire. The settlers suggest these are needed for their protection. One settler says he is there because the land belongs to him—according to the Bible. Israel seizes land periodically and demolishes Palestinian houses in order to make room for settlers.

And yet it's always the Palestinians who are portrayed as terrorists. At least three Israeli prime ministers, Pilger notes dryly, were involved in acts of terrorism early in their lives. An Israeli historian, Ilan Pappé, says that suicide bombers are portrayed to the Israelis as the insane work of an insane people. There's no attempt to understand the broader context in which people are driven to such expressions of despair.

There are a few exceptions, though. In one moving interview in the documentary, an Israeli who lost his daughter in a suicide bomb attack says the suicide bomber was as much a victim as his daughter. The father is now one of a few brave dissidents in Israel. These are people who refuse to buy the official narrative about Palestinians and, in some cases, even refuse to serve in the Occupied Territories.

Pappé has challenged the Zionist view that the 1948 war with the Arabs, which led to the formation of Israel, was intended to prevent another Holocaust. He is part of a school of revisionist historians in Israel that argues that the Jews in Palestine followed a policy of destruction of Palestinian villages and deliberate expulsion of Palestinians in order to rid a future state of as many Arabs as possible. The Arab attack on Israel was a sequel to these acts of the Israelis. It's not that the Israelis reacted to another attempted Holocaust.

Pappé has also debunked the view that Israeli Prime Minister Ehud Barak made a generous offer of land to Palestinian leader Yasser Arafat—of 90 per cent of the Occupied Territories—and that Arafat perversely turned it down. What was offered was a token withdrawal from no more than 12 per cent of the Occupied Territories.

Pappé tells Pilger, 'By the summer of 2000, the Palestinians were left with an offer of 10 per cent of what used to be Palestine: what I would call a stateless state with no genuine sovereignty, with no independent foreign economic or political policies, with no proper capital and at the mercy of the Israeli security services. In return for this, Arafat was asked to declare the end of the conflict, that there would be no more demands for independence.'[8] Pappé has faced persecution and ostracism in Israel for his views. He has refused to back off.

Barak's non-offer is trumpeted as the famous 'peace' offer brokered by President Bill Clinton. It was presented at a famous ceremony on the White House lawns at which Clinton, Barak and Arafat were present. The story in the mainstream media is that the Palestinians have only themselves to blame for turning down a great offer. The oppressors are the heroes, the oppressed are the villains.

In August and September 2005, Israel announced with much fanfare its 'disengagement' from Gaza. The television channels were filled with images of Israeli settlers being forcibly removed from Gaza. What was not reported was that 5500 more settlers had been moved into the West Bank than had been removed from Gaza.[9] In 2006, the situation in Gaza worsened. An estimated 1.4 million people were reduced to virtually living in a cage, with no reliable electricity or water, ravaged by hunger and disease and subject to continuous attacks on civilians by the Israeli armed forces.[10]

Israeli impunity has to do with assured support from the United States. 'The struggle in Palestine is an American war, waged from America's most heavily armed foreign military base, Israel . . . without F-16s and Apaches and billions of American taxpayers' dollars, Israel would have made peace with the Palestinians long ago.'[11] Pilger quotes the South African leader Nelson Mandela as saying, 'Apartheid is a crime against humanity. Israel has deprived millions of Palestinians of their liberty and property [and] perpetuated a system of gross discrimination.'[12]

Towards the end of his documentary, Pilger asks a smooth-talking Israeli official whether Israel is willing to accept an independent state of Palestine. The official hums and haws and talks about a Palestinian 'self-governing entity'. Pilger can't help erupting. 'What right do you have to create somebody else's homeland?'

Pilger's film was broadcast by the Independent Television Network (ITV) in Britain and in other countries. It was broadcast at the untimely hour of 11 p.m. Yet a million and a half people watched it. It generated a torrent of mail. Some of it was abusive. Pilger was described as a 'demonic psychopath, an anti-Semite of the most dangerous kind'.

Pilger also received death threats. The chairman of the very company that had produced his film denounced him. The outcry prompted the Independent Television Commission, a regulatory body, to investigate the film. It rejected all complaints and praised the film's 'journalistic integrity' and the 'care and thoroughness with which [the film] was researched'.[13]

* * *

The plight of Palestinians is often compared with that of South Africans in the time of apartheid. Apartheid and white rule in South Africa officially ended in May 1994 when a government formed by the African National Congress (ANC) assumed office. In 1998, Pilger wrote and presented a documentary, *Apartheid Did Not Die*.[14] There's a companion essay on the subject with the same title.[15]

Pilger contends that not much has changed with the handover to black rule. He goes so far as to suggest that, in order to acquire power, Nelson Mandela and his associates had compromised the interests of the black population that constituted the majority in Africa.

The documentary and the essay begin by recounting the horrors of apartheid. Pilger visits Robben Island, off the city of Cape Town, where Mandela and his close associates were jailed. Mandela spent twenty-seven long years there in harsh conditions. Pilger is given a tour of the place by one of Mandela's former associates, Ahmed Kathrada (Kathy), who was himself imprisoned there for twenty-five years.

Kathy was confined to his cell for twenty-three hours of the day with the light always on. Even prison regulations discriminated on the basis of race. Since Kathy was coloured, he was treated a little differently from the Blacks. He was given better clothes and slightly better food. Pilger is astonished at Kathy's lack of bitterness, something that Kathy ascribes to the influence of Gandhi. In a letter from prison, Kathy had written, 'Unfortunately, my nature will not allow me to harbour hatred for anybody, no matter how deeply he may have wounded my feelings.'

Mandela managed to write his autobiography even while doing hard labour on the island. A fellow prisoner reduced it to fewer pages using smaller handwriting so that the manuscript could be more easily hidden from the jailers. The originals, written in instalments, were buried in a garden. When the authorities decided to construct a wall on the garden, the prisoners made frantic efforts to retrieve the originals. They were caught. As punishment, their books were taken away and they were denied studies for four years.

The apartheid regime ruled with brutality. Pilger tells of District Six in the centre of Cape Town. Home to some 55,000 Blacks, Coloureds and Whites, it was a model of plurality and tolerance. Outsiders saw it as a slum, marked by dirty streets and drug trafficking. Like many slums, however, it was full of life and had its own unique identity. In 1966, the apartheid regime declared District Six a 'Whites only' area. Soon, bulldozers arrived and all the structures in the district were reduced to rubble. The people living there were forcibly removed and dumped in a faraway place.

Pilger notes that an estimated 3.5 million South Africans were evicted from their homes and their land in the period 1960–82. Large numbers were banished to ten 'Bantustans' or 'tribal homelands' located in the most wretched and infertile parts of the country. Their South African citizenship was cancelled. The people there were declared 'migrant workers' for whom the employers, the white industrialists, did not have to provide pensions or even basic medical care.[16]

In 1990, the apartheid regime lifted the ban on the ANC. Nelson Mandela was released soon after. In 1994, the first-ever democratic elections were held and the ANC was voted to power. Pilger returned to South Africa after nearly thirty years, in late 1997. (He had been barred from entering after his last visit.)

He was shocked to find that there had been little improvement in the condition of the Blacks: the numbers of the poor had increased and half the population lived in poverty. Those who had been forcibly removed from their homes and relocated elsewhere continued to live in abject conditions, with little water and sanitation.

The ANC had promised to restore land taken away from the Blacks, who ended up owning just 7 per cent of all agricultural land. In the first decade of the ANC in power, less than 4 per cent of white-owned agricultural land was given back.[17] The new regime did not want to disturb white ownership as that might mean disruption of agricultural output.

Whites continued to throw landless labourers out of their farmlands. In the last decade of apartheid, 737,000 persons were evicted from white-owned farmland; in the first decade of the ANC, the number jumped to 942,000.[18] The Mandela government had passed a law to give landless labourers security of tenure. It was of little use as 99 per cent of the cases never reached the courts. Pilger notes dryly that Robert Mugabe, the much-reviled dictator of Zimbabwe, had done better for the Blacks of his country. When he visited South Africa, the black crowd gave him a standing ovation.[19]

In the 1970s, the ANC had declared that its objective was not just political democracy but the dismantling of the existing economic structure dominated by Whites. After assuming power, however, the ANC leaders acted differently. They allowed themselves to be co-opted into the existing economic structure. White businessmen were happy to give a stake in their businesses to a few luminaries from the ANC so that they could carry on as they did earlier. Cyril Ramaphosa, former secretary general of the National Union of Mineworkers and current President of South Africa, became one of the richest men in the country by getting into ventures with white businessmen.

Pilger's observations about Nelson Mandela are, perhaps, the most striking part of his essay. Mandela has been elevated to almost sainthood status in the international community. His standing is, perhaps, only a little removed from that of the Mahatma himself.

Pilger suggests that Mandela let his community down rather badly while deriving benefits for the ANC and his own charities.

Pilger writes:[20]

> In the early years of democracy, much of the inspiration for the new cronyism came from Mandela himself, who formed close personal relations with powerful white businessmen, regardless of whether they had profited from the apartheid years. The South African writer Mark Gevisser chronicled this, often drily, describing how Mandela fostered and clearly enjoyed the company of the 'captains of industry' . . .

The ANC leaders, once denounced as communists, were quick to embrace the market economy after coming to power. They adopted the standard prescriptions of the World Bank and the IMF. These included such elements as reduced government expenditure, privatization, greater foreign direct investment, free movements of capital and lower tariffs. Thabo Mbeki, who succeeded Mandela as President, called himself a 'Thatcherite'.[21]

Pilger suggests that, in adopting the economic model that they did, Mandela and his colleagues had struck a deal with the apartheid regime and with international capital: the status quo would not be disturbed too much. 'The unspoken deal was that whites would retain economic control in exchange for black majority rule . . .'[22]

How valid is Pilger's criticism of Mandela and the ANC? Let us grant that the black regime abandoned its communist principles. Let us also grant that many in the leadership enriched themselves after assuming power. But are their economic policies to be faulted for those reasons?

It may well be that the ANC leadership was being pragmatic. Once saddled with the responsibility that goes with power, the ANC may well have concluded that only market-oriented reforms could bring prosperity to South Africa. Similarly, in letting Whites continue to dominate the economy, the ANC may only have acknowledged the lack of entrepreneurial capability within the black majority. To have divested the Whites of the enterprises they were running may have meant that vital economic assets would go to waste.

Pilger is, perhaps, on firmer ground when he says that, in pushing through radical economic reform, the ANC might have consulted with a variety of constituencies within the country. It did not do so. The national executive of the ANC, Parliament, the unions, the public—none of these were consulted.

Pilger also has a point when he says that South African companies, which were alleged to have engaged in massive human rights abuses under apartheid, were not brought to account. In the 2000s, some of the victims sued the companies in American courts under a law that allows foreigners to bring human rights violations to American courts. The ANC government backed the companies, not the victims. It asked the court to drop the case saying that it would deter badly needed foreign investment in South Africa.[23] This may well have been a case of the government bending over backwards to appease the owners of capital.

An even more controversial part of the deal between the ANC and the apartheid regime was that the atrocities perpetrated during the apartheid regime would be largely overlooked. The ANC set up the Truth and Reconciliation Commission (TRC). Victims could appear before the TRC and provide testimonies of what they had been through. Those who had committed excesses could also appear and seek amnesty after making a full confession. The lofty ideal underlying the TRC was that a spirit of forgiveness would generally prevail.

It's not clear whether the victims or their families thought that justice had been done. One lady, whose husband was tortured and killed by the police, tells Pilger bitterly:[24]

One has the feeling that if Mandela's son had been killed in the way our children were killed . . . they [the ANC leadership] wouldn't be talking like that. They have every right to forgive their own torturers and jailers, but they have no right to forgive and protect Sizwe's killers [her husband] and deny his family justice . . . Justice is bringing the murderers to court, trying them, convicting them, punishing them.

The TRC chose to focus on those who took orders instead of those who gave them. In the process, the people primarily responsible for the horrors of apartheid were let off.

Pilger meets Mandela at the very mansion at which he had met a prime minister in the erstwhile apartheid regime. It's as if the guards had not changed—Afrikaner guards check his ID. One of them is carrying a copy of Mandela's memoirs. Mandela is unwilling to brook any criticism. He reels off the achievements of his government—the newly created constitution, the supply of water, improved healthcare, etc. (Elsewhere in his essay, Pilger does not contest many of these points.)

Pilger asks Mandela pointedly whether economic apartheid had not remained the same. Mandela tells him that it's important to bring about transformation without creating serious dislocation. There's no point, he says, in scaring away big businesses. He insists that more and more Blacks are sharing the wealth of the nation. He rejects the suggestion that Blacks continue to be evicted from their lands. Pilger is not convinced but the reader may see some merit in Mandela's contentions.

Pilger faults Mandela's foreign policy record as President. He says Mandela supported governments in Latin America that were guilty of serious human rights abuses. He invited General Suharto of Indonesia (notorious for his human rights abuses) to South Africa and conferred on him the nation's highest honour because Suharto had contributed to the ANC in exile. He recognized the government of Burma as legitimate despite its placing Aung San Suu Kyi, the leader of the democracy movement there, under arrest. Pilger believes that Mandela was more forthright on international affairs after he stepped down as President—for instance, he was extremely critical of the government of the junior George Bush.

Overall, Pilger's essay on South Africa is clinical and unforgiving. He cites facts and figures to show that the coming to power of the ANC has not brought about material change in the lives of the people. He believes the ANC could have opted for a very different set of economic policies. It could have reclaimed land and handed it to the dispossessed for them to run small-scale farms as cooperatives. It might have provided generous credit to the small-scale sector. And so on.

Pilger's criticism of the ANC regime would apply to many other former colonies, including India. Almost everywhere, the colonial elite was replaced by a new elite. The members of new governments everywhere moved into the palatial houses of the old rulers and adopted the same lifestyles. The institutions of the state—the army, the police, the judiciary—continued as before. Economic improvement has been slow in coming in most places.

However, it's not clear that an alternative route to development would have been preferable. The overthrow of the earlier structures—such as in the former Soviet Union, China or Cambodia—would have entailed an enormous cost in human suffering, perhaps greater than the suffering that has arisen from the slow pace of economic improvement.

Mandela seems to have taken the view that if the Whites were ousted from their dominance of agriculture and industry, serious economic disruption would follow. That would explain why he chose not to prosecute large numbers of those associated with the previous regime. It would also explain why he retained economic structures that were conducive to growth and opted for gradual empowerment and inclusion of Blacks.

Pilger is right in highlighting the corruption and venality of the ANC leadership. However, his criticism of the ANC's economic policies is more a critique of the capitalist mode of development than it is of the ANC in particular. The reader is left feeling that Pilger's criticism of the injustice of South Africa's economic structures is the wail of the leftists of old.

* * *

There are historically oppressed minorities in many countries. In this book, we have talked about the Dalits in India and non-Whites in South Africa. There are the American Indians and the Blacks of the United States. Australia has its Aborigines, the original inhabitants of that vast country. Pilger, an Australian himself, has chronicled the plight of the Aborigines in four documentaries spread over several decades. His last one, released in 2013, was *Utopia*, a place in the Northern Territory of Australia.[25] There cannot be a more complete misnomer. Utopia is a region where the indigenous people of Australia live in appalling conditions.

Australia is a rich country. Yet, at the time the documentary was released, large numbers of Aborigines lived in conditions of near destitution in makeshift homes with no electricity, poor sanitation and lacking other basic amenities. In one sequence, the camera moves from the tin shed of an Aborigine to the elegant house of a government official nearby that boasts of eighteen air conditioners!

The first prime minister of Australia, Edmund Barton, made it clear that the concept of equality of man did not apply to those who were not British and not white-skinned. Pilger's point in the film is plain enough: it's blatant racism that explains the condition of the natives of Australia.

Pilger visits Utopia, home to the earliest inhabitants and now regarded as the most disadvantaged place in Australia. The conditions of the people in Utopia are no different from those of Aborigines whom Pilger had filmed twenty-five years earlier. Resources are clearly not the issue. Utopia had around 1400 people. The whole of the Northern Territory had 50,000. Providing basic conditions for such a small number is hardly a problem. The problem is the attitude of the Whites. Australians are used to thinking of the Aborigines as inhuman, lazy, decadent and so on. Given that these perceptions are widespread, it is politically risky for any party to attempt to alleviate the lot of the Aborigines.

Pilger interviews the minister for indigenous health in the Australian government, somebody who has represented the Northern Territory in Parliament for a quarter of a century. The minister talks proudly of the investment his government has made in primary healthcare in the past three years. When asked to explain the neglect of decades and the fact that his government's investment in health is not making a difference on the ground, the minister loses his cool.

The National Museum in Canberra makes no mention of the native inhabitants of Australia. There are Australian scholars who claim that there was no invasion and no genocide in the history of Australia. The arriving British, they contend, had actually been welcomed by the natives! The erasing of the past and the reconstruction of history, like the demonization of the Aborigines, are intended to deny the Aborigines any place in the Australia of today.

Pilger runs into revellers during Australia's National Day celebrations, a day that celebrates the coming into being of the nation. The revellers don't want to be reminded of the past either. Nor do they show any contrition over the fact that the original inhabitants live in miserable conditions. It's their fault, one lady seems to suggest. Another lady notes cynically that history is all about somebody grabbing somebody else's land.

Pilger takes a trip to Rottnest Island near Perth. The island was a notorious concentration camp before it was converted into a luxurious resort. Thousands of young Aborigines were incarcerated, tortured and killed there. The tourist brochure on the island makes no mention of its dark past. Pilger visits a room in a hotel at the resort. The room costs A$240 per night. Pilger's escort mentions a chilling fact: in the same space were three cells, in each one of which seventeen people died at one point in time. Next to the hotel is a mass grave in which 300 Aborigines are buried.

The brutality, as we have seen earlier, is not in the past. In 2008, an Aboriginal man died while being driven 300 miles in a prison van in blazing heat. The temperature inside the van reached 56 degrees Celsius, so that man was virtually cooked alive. The director of prosecutions decided not to take action. Eventually, the concerned personnel, including the drivers, were fined for breach of health and safety regulations. A minister tells an incredulous Pilger that she decided to increase 'cultural sensitivity training' after the incident.

Australia has no qualms about jailing Aborigines in large numbers. Pilger is informed that one more prison is being built in Western Australia. It will be exclusively for Aborigines who form just 3 per cent of the population and are already the most imprisoned community on the planet.

The Aborigines of Australia have faced other forms of persecution. Prime Minister John Howard declared a state of emergency in the Northern Territory applicable only to black Australians. The reason he gave for the crackdown was the prevalence of child abuse among the Aborigines. He announced an 'intervention' that meant that the federal government would occupy vast portions of the Northern Territory, ostensibly to weed out paedophile rings. Howard's contention has since been hotly contested. A journalist and broadcaster tells Pilger that the claim about paedophile rings among the Aborigines was one big and cynical lie intended to smear the entire community. Australian troops swept through the Northern Territory spreading terror among the hapless Aborigines.

The unstated intention seems to have been the grabbing of land belonging to the Aborigines. Pilger notes that those who refused to hand over their lands on lease were denied basic services such as housing and sanitation. The ground for the onslaught on the Aborigines had been laid by a well-known TV programme which claimed that sex slavery was common among Aborigines. The programme ascribed the information to a source who was said to be a youth worker. His face was blanked out on the programme. An investigative journalist revealed that the source was, in fact, a senior government official.

Pilger says that several independent commissions found that the allegations were unfounded. One report that examined 11,000 Aboriginal children found that only one child had a condition that was not otherwise known—and it was not a case of sexual assault. An Aboriginal lady interviewed by Pilger suggests that the 'intervention' was aimed at laying hands on the huge deposits of uranium and other minerals in the lands occupied by the Aborigines. The story is not very different from the spread of the mining mafia into land occupied by tribals in India.

The supreme irony is that the predators were not so much amongst the Aborigines as amongst white Australians. Pilger narrates how young children in their thousands were stolen from their parents over the years and became cheap domestic help for the Whites. Many became victims of sexual abuse. Pilger calls the sexual exploitation of black women and children Australia's 'darkest secret'. The government, Pilger says, spent A$80 million in one year on surveillance and removing children in the Northern Territory but only A$500,000 on supporting the impoverished families. The scale of atrocities was large enough for one prime minister, Kevin Rudd, to tender a belated public apology.

Indigenous peoples everywhere have suffered injustice but Australia, Pilger suggests, is unique in the scale of the injustice it has inflicted on its indigenous people. In many places, there's been some attempt at justice and reconciliation. Land treaties have been signed recognizing the rights of the indigenous people. But not in Australia. The story of colonization and usurpation of land, which began two centuries ago, continues.

* * *

If Latin America is in the news, it is, for the most part, for the wrong reasons. An army coup. A financial crisis. A war of words, if not worse, with the United States. The US is known to treat Latin America as its own backyard, overthrowing and installing governments at will. The human cost of American intervention has been huge even if Latin American living standards are still better than those in Africa or South Asia. At the time of writing, Venezuela is passing through a mighty upheaval, thanks to a thinly disguised attempt on the part of the US to topple the popular government there.

In his documentary, *The War on Democracy*, Pilger turns his lens on a troubled continent.[26] The film is not among his better ones. Pilger tries to cover too much ground and ends up with a rather superficial treatment of the subject. The film takes in its stride Venezuela, Chile, Nicaragua, Guatemala and Bolivia in the space of just ninety minutes. Its theme is that the US will not tolerate left-leaning, popular governments there. It will not hesitate to prop up dictatorships that it perceives as friendlier towards America and American business interests.

Pilger documents how this theme played out in Venezuela. Hugo Chavez, who was President of Venezuela between 1999 and 2013, was seen as an 'extreme threat' (to quote a US official who's shown in Pilger's film). His crime, according to Pilger, was that he had wide acceptability among the poor and that his government took steps that favoured the poor and not the corporate and foreign interests in Venezuela.

Soon after assuming power, Chavez introduced a new constitution that was hugely popular among the people of Venezuela. The film has shots of supermarkets opened in the slums in the early days of Chavez's tenure. These supermarkets sold products at lower prices than elsewhere and the various items sold had the rights of the people written at the back of the packets. Chavez also introduced universal and free healthcare. Similarly, schooling became free for all and children had access to at least one hot meal at school. Adult literacy improved.

Pilger contends that Chavez's socialist policies angered the US and its cronies in Venezuela, and the two conspired to overthrow Chavez. In 2002, about a million protesters marched to Chavez's presidential palace. They were met there by a large number of Chavez's supporters. In the confrontation, there was a shoot-out and people on both sides were killed. This provided the trigger for an army coup. Chavez was removed from his palace and a businessman was sworn in as President. This led to widespread protest. Hundreds of thousands of ordinary people surrounded the palace. The organizers of the coup then threw in the towel. In less than forty-eight hours, the coup had failed and Chavez was restored to his presidency.

All of this is true. But it's not the whole truth. There's room for a more nuanced appreciation of the reality in Venezuela.[27] Chavez's policies, while well intentioned, led to a serious economic crisis in Venezuela, one from which it's yet to recover. After coming to power, Chavez used the boom in oil prices to spend on welfare measures and expand educational opportunities. However, when oil prices fell thereafter, the Venezuelan economy had to face the reckoning that follows any spending binge.

One consequence of the welfare spending was the failure to diversify the economy away from oil. Chavez's nationalization of industries across the board crippled entrepreneurship and killed many of them. Corruption and cronyism were rife in Chavez's ruling party and this was an important factor in the nation's economic decline.

Chavez died of cancer in 2013. Towards the end of his tenure, there was widespread discontent and disenchantment with his policies. According to one report, 10 per cent of the population has fled the country and 90 per cent of the remaining population is mired in poverty. In 2017, the inflation rate touched 860 per cent and the economy shrank by nearly 16 per cent. The nation's healthcare and transport systems have crumbled. Venezuela is today racked by civil strife that threatens to tear the country apart.[28] Not all of this can be said to be propaganda by the Western media.

Pilger's film was produced in 2007 when the follies of Chavez's rule and his bequest may not have been fully evident. However, the early signs were there and Pilger should have picked up on them. Even in 2007, his portrayal of Chavez as a man of the masses who was paying for standing up to the evil American empire was simplistic, to put it mildly. Like many other leftist intellectuals, Pilger seems to have fallen prey to a reflexive anti-American orientation. Pilger's dissent on a range of matters is valuable but dissent is effective only where there is a high degree of objectivity. Dissent that ignores the facts on the ground soon loses credence.

Pilger documents other instances of American meddling in Latin America. In Guatemala, the democratically elected President Jacobo Arbenz was overthrown in the 1950s because the Americans thought he was a communist. Philip Agee, a disillusioned CIA officer who spent much of his life exposing the CIA while being based in Cuba, tells Pilger that democracy has never meant a thing for the CIA. Cuba was ostracized and sanctioned for decades because it dared to have a different form of government and would not succumb to America's corporations while located just 90 miles from the USA.

The story of Chile runs along similar lines. The US government helped overthrow another Marxist government, that of Salvador Allende. The presidential palace was bombed by the Chilean armed forces. Allende refused safe passage and stayed put until he shot himself. In his place, the US installed General Augusto Pinochet. Thousands of Allende supporters were imprisoned and tortured.

The US government denied any role in the coup. Pilger cites secret CIA documents that indicate otherwise. A former CIA official based in Chile, whom Pilger interviews, denies that there was torture on any large scale. He insists that Chile exists as a nation today because of Pinochet. (The nation was facing popular unrest and a civil war at the time Pinochet took over. How much of this was spontaneous and how much was instigated from outside remains a matter of debate.) Most importantly, the ex-CIA official concedes that Allende was overthrown because large 'national security interests' (of the US) were at stake. He says nonchalantly, 'Sometimes . . . things have to be changed in a rather ugly way.'

The US set up a School of the Americas in Georgia for the security forces of Latin American countries. The security forces were trained in methods of interrogation, torture and even assassination. Pilger talks of death squads in El Salvador that killed thousands of people over a decade or so. His figure is hotly contested by the CIA official referred to above—the official suggests that the number of deaths could not have been more than 200. Pilger visits one village where alone, he claims, over 200 people were killed by a special battalion of the El Salvadorian army trained by the US.

In Nicaragua, during Ronald Reagan's term as President, the US provided support to a group called the Contras in their bid to overthrow the Nicaraguan government. America reserves for itself the right to intervene in Latin America (and, increasingly, almost anywhere in the world). Pilger asks the ex-CIA official what gives America the right to overthrow governments. 'National security interests', the official declares blandly. He adds, 'If you don't like it, lump it.' He couldn't have been more candid.

Pilger tells a similar tale about Bolivia. An unpopular President owing loyalty to the US. A mass uprising and a massacre. The flight of the President and the election of the first representative of the indigenous population, Evo Morales. Morales is still in power, a rare voice of the Left in Latin America today.

Pilger's accounts of Bolivia and other countries are sketchy and lacking in context. One gets the point about Washington wanting its puppets everywhere. However, one would like more detail on what policies were followed, how the economies fared and why it is that leftist movements flare up from time to time and often die down after a while.

The film concludes with Chavez claiming that the socialist idea has caught the imagination of Latin America. Chavez is no more, the Right is back in power in many parts of the continent, and Venezuela itself is plunged into turmoil. Pilger's film does little to dispel the notion that many left-wing writers allow virulent anti-Americanism to colour their narrative.

* * *

America's invasion of Afghanistan in October 2001 in the aftermath of 9/11 has been one of the defining moments in American foreign policy in the present century. The US had demanded that the Taliban regime ruling Afghanistan hand over Osama bin Laden, the mastermind of the 9/11 attack, whom it was believed to be harbouring. The Taliban, it is said, refused. The US then decided to rid Afghanistan of the Taliban.

Pilger documents the havoc caused by the invasion and the long and tangled relationship between the US and the Taliban.[29] Pilger says that civilian deaths as a result of the invasion are estimated to be anywhere between 1300 and 8000.[30] As many as 20,000 Afghans may have lost their lives because of the indirect consequences of the invasion, such as the massive dislocation of people.

As is well known, the Taliban was pretty much the creation of the US. They were part of the mujahideen, the guerrilla forces formed by various tribal groups and created and nurtured by the CIA, MI6 (the UK's external intelligence agency) and the ISI (Pakistan's intelligence agency). The guerrilla forces were created in order to overthrow the pro-Soviet regime in power in Afghanistan in the late 1970s and to draw the Soviet Union into a quagmire in Afghanistan.

The US reckoned that Afghanistan would turn out to be the Soviet Union's Vietnam and would bleed the Soviet Union's defence forces as also its economy. The assessment was to prove correct. The Soviet Union's nearly decade-long involvement in Afghanistan is widely believed to have been an important factor in its collapse. The American objective was thus met but it came at a terrible cost: the rise of Islamic militancy in Afghanistan, Pakistan and the Middle East. This is a legacy that the region and the West at large is having to cope with even today.

Pilger quotes Zbigniew Brzezinski, the late American foreign policy expert and national security adviser to President Jimmy Carter, as saying that the perception that America lent support to the mujahideen after the Soviet invasion of Afghanistan in December 1979 is incorrect. The support had started nearly five months earlier in a bid to topple the pro-Soviet government and was intended precisely to provoke Soviet intervention in the first place.[31]

For nearly seventeen years, the US cultivated and fanned a form of Islamic extremism. The jihadi ideology was actively taught in CIA training schools. The US provided millions of dollars for producing textbooks in Afghanistan that promoted murder and fanaticism.[32] In 1986, the CIA approved a plan put forward by Pakistan's ISI to actively recruit and train people from all over the world to join the jihad. In camps run in Pakistan, the CIA and the MI6 provided training in bomb-making, among other things. Osama bin Laden was one of the CIA finds in this effort. Those recruited by bin Laden were sent to the US to be trained in terrorism by the CIA.

Extremist sects were supported in Afghanistan, Pakistan, Algeria, Yemen and other places in a bid to destabilize nationalist and communist movements that were seen to be hostile to the US. Pilger reveals that during the NATO assault on Serbia, then under the regime of Slobodan Milosevic, in 1999 (just two years before 9/11), fighters from bin Laden's group, the al-Qaeda, fought alongside local groups supported by NATO.

Pilger explains the significance of Afghanistan in the American scheme of things. The Caspian Sea in the south of the former

Soviet Union has long been viewed as a great prize because it's said to contain a third of the world's oil and gas. The break-up of the Soviet Union and the creation of new states bordering or close to the Caspian Sea—Turkmenistan, Uzbekistan, Tajikistan, Azerbaijan and others—has ensured that the Russia that emerged from the break-up of the Soviet Union does not have privileged access to the Caspian. The West has sought to ensure that the new republics of Central Asia are reliant on Western capital.

For the US and the West, the next problem to crack was transporting the oil and gas from Central Asia to deep-water ports through pipelines. There were three possibilities available for a pipeline to the West: Russia, Iran and Afghanistan. Russia and Iran were both ruled out as hostile to the West. That left Afghanistan as the obvious choice. When the Taliban took over in Kabul in 1996, the *Wall Street Journal* was jubilant. It made no bones about the fact that the success of the extremists would help ensure a route for the oil and gas resources of Central Asia.[33]

The US made light of the Taliban's fundamentalism, including its persecution of women, and its poor human rights record. After the mullahs seized power in 1996, the US State Department dropped Afghanistan from the list of countries that 'protect and promote terrorists' despite the Taliban's known links with bin Laden.[34] America's leading energy companies were actively involved in plans to build a pipeline to transport natural gas from Turkmenistan through Afghanistan to Pakistan. Taliban leaders were flown to the US and wined and dined by the American oil company, Unocal. Among the representatives of the oil companies involved in the project were Dick Cheney, then former defence secretary, and Condoleezza Rice, later US secretary of state.

Osama bin Laden, who had by now become hostile to the US, upset these cosy arrangements by bombing two American embassies in East Africa in 1998. Even then, the US did not act against Afghanistan which was harbouring bin Laden. President Clinton declared that al-Qaeda was 'not supported by any state'.[35]

Discussions with the Taliban over the Enron pipeline continued. Pilger claims that it's not true that 9/11 was instrumental in turning the US against the Taliban. The invasion of Afghanistan had been planned two months earlier. America's concern was not about the Taliban sheltering bin Laden. Its concern was that the Taliban was losing control of Afghanistan to various warlords and it was, therefore, no longer a dependable business partner![36]

After 9/11, the US began aligning itself with these warlords, in particular, with a group called Northern Alliance. They were paid enormous sums to drive the Taliban out of Kabul and into the mountains. In Kabul, the US installed a government headed by Hamid Karzai. The writ of the government did not run beyond the cities. In the countryside the warlords ruled. They are as brutal as the Taliban. The Taliban was credited with stopping banditry and rape. Now, both have become rife in the areas from which they were driven out. Many say that travel by road was safe when the Taliban were in power but this is no longer the case.

One little nugget in Pilger's account is that the Taliban had achieved an almost total ban on the production of opium. The American and British invasion brought the ban to an end. As a reward for supporting the puppet government in Kabul, the warlords of Afghanistan were allowed to restart the planting of opium. Eighty-seven per cent of the world's opium production originates in Afghanistan, most of it consumed by young people in the West. So much for America's vaunted war on drugs.[37]

Towards the end of his essay, Pilger gives an account of an interview he had with John Bolton, now national security adviser to President Donald Trump and then undersecretary in the government of President George Bush Jr. Bolton tells Pilger that the US doesn't attack decent, law-abiding countries and democracies. Pilger asks him what gives the US the right to decide which country to attack and who is decent and who is not. Bolton tells him flatly that the wars against Afghanistan and Iraq were good wars and he is proud that America fought those.

I mentioned earlier that I wasn't very satisfied with Pilger's accounts of South Africa under Mandela and of Latin America. His exposition of America's involvement in Afghanistan shows him at his best.

* * *

Pilger's repertoire is vast and some of the themes he covers are entirely novel. He has documented how, in the late 1960s and the early 1970s, the UK expelled the entire population of the Chagos Islands in the Indian Ocean in order to make way for an American military base at Diego Garcia, one of the islands. He has shone a light on the killings in East Timor in South-East Asia during the occupation of the country by the regime of General Suharto of Indonesia. He has witnessed and chronicled the genocide perpetrated in Cambodia by the Pol Pot government in the 1970s. He has made a film on a mutiny among American troops drafted for the Vietnam War and the killing of unpopular officers. In 1977, he ventured into Czechoslovakia to capture the voices of dissidents at the time of the Soviet occupation of the country. This is only an illustrative list of the themes Pilger has dealt with. When it comes to suffering and injustice, the world is truly Pilger's oyster.

Now seventy-nine, Pilger remains indefatigable in the pursuit of causes dear to him. In recent months, he has taken up the cause of Julian Assange, the Swedish founder of WikiLeaks, the website that has accessed and leaked confidential documents of various governments, notably those of the US. A little background on the Assange case would be useful.[38]

Following some leaks from WikiLeaks in 2010, the US government initiated a criminal investigation against Assange. In November 2010, Sweden issued an international arrest warrant against Assange in connection with allegations of sexual assault made against him. Assange, who was in the UK at the time, denounced the move as a pretext for Sweden to hand him over to the US. The British police arrested Assange and released him on bail. While on bail, Assange sought and was given asylum by the Government of Ecuador. He took refuge in Ecuador's embassy in London and stayed there for almost seven years.

In April 2019, following several disputes that Assange had with Ecuador (now under a pro-US government), his asylum was withdrawn and he was arrested by the British police. Assange was found guilty of jumping bail and sentenced to fifty weeks in prison. In May 2019, the US government was quick to charge Assange under the Espionage Act of 1917. The Swedish government reopened its investigation into the allegations of sexual assault against Assange. He is now lodged in a jail in the UK.

Pilger is clear that Assange is paying for the crime of exposing the high and mighty. 'Assange's crime is journalism: holding the rapacious to account, exposing their lies and empowering people all over the world with truth.'[39] Assange, Pilger asserts, is being punished for exposing 'the truth about the homicidal way America conducts its colonial wars, the lies of the British Foreign Office in its denial of rights to vulnerable people, such as the Chagos islanders, the exposure of Hillary Clinton as a backer and beneficiary of jihadism in the Middle East, the detailed description of American ambassadors of how the governments in Syria and Venezuela might be overthrown, and much more'.

Pilger warns that the extradition of Assange to the US could set a terrible precedent for journalists and publishers. In principle, the editors of the *Guardian*, who have published some of Assange's leaks, and the editors of other papers, such as the *New York Times* and the *Washington Post*, could invite prosecution for the same reasons for which Assange faces prosecution. Even if that does not happen, the prosecution of Assange itself would have a chilling effect on the publication of leaks and investigative journalism in general.

Governments and people having any sort of power want to limit information and cover up their failings and crimes. Pilger has pitted himself against authority. He stands squarely in favour of the weak, the dispossessed, the victims of the arbitrary exercise of power. He may have his ideological biases but it's hard to fault his motivation. The astonishing thing is that he remains a force to be reckoned with despite his being virtually ostracized by the mainstream media. Perhaps, it's sheer luck that he even remains free after having done so much to antagonize those in power in the Western world.

It's a tribute to the power of the Internet and media such as YouTube that Pilger is able to continue his crusade against injustice. The troubling question for us all is how long people like him will be able to do so. The mainstream media is the handmaiden of vested interests. Can the world of the Internet and social media stay for long beyond their reach? Will the world of journalism throw up any more Pilgers?

Notes

Chapter 1: Arundhati Roy: India's Irrepressible Gadfly

1. B.R. Ambedkar, *Annihilation of Caste*, Navayana, New Delhi, March 2014, downloadable version available online
2. Rajmohan Gandhi, 'Independence and Social Justice: The Ambedkar-Gandhi Debate', *Economic and Political Weekly*, Vol. 50, 11 April 2015.
3. http://www.independent.co.uk/arts-entertainment/books/features/arundhati-roy-s-book-on-caste-rejected-by-some-anti-caste-activists-9929233.html
4. https://indiankanoon.org/doc/505614
5. https://indianexpress.com/article/india/india-news-india/arundhati-roy-gets-contempt-notice-from-bombay-high-court/
6. https://www.livemint.com/Politics/bylmdtR4jqxnDhMAhAIsIL/SC-stays-contempt-proceedings-against-Arundhati-Roy-in-Bomba.html, https://www.sci.gov.in/supremecourt/2016/1000/1000_2016_Order_03-Jul-2017.pdf
7. http://timesofindia.indiatimes.com/home/sunday-times/Theres-something-about-Mary/articleshow/15871684.cms
8. https://en.wikipedia.org/wiki/Mary_Roy
9. Arundhati Roy, *The Shape of the Beast: Conversations with Arundhati Roy*, Penguin India, New Delhi, May 2008, p. 33.
10. Rajmohan Gandhi, 'Independence and Social Justice: The Ambedkar-Gandhi Debate', *Economic and Political Weekly*, Vol. 50, 11April 2015, p. 36.

11. Rajmohan Gandhi, Ibid., p. 39
12. Arundhati Roy in B.R. Ambedkar, *Annihilation of Caste*, Navayana, New Delhi, March 2014, p. 16.
13. Ibid., p. 23.
14. Ibid., p. 57.
15. Ibid., p. 58
16. Arundhati Roy, 'All the World's a Half-Built Dam', *Economic and Political Weekly*, 20 June 2015, Vol. L, No. 25, p. 167.
17. Ibid.
18. Arundhati Roy in B.R. Ambedkar, *Annihilation of Caste*, Navayana, New Delhi, March 2014, p. 65.
19. Ibid., p. 68.
20. Ibid., p. 68.
21. Ibid., p. 35.
22. Ibid., p. 36.
23. Ibid., p. 36.
24. Ibid., p. 36.
25. Ibid., p. 38.
26. Ibid., p. 46.
27. Ashwin Desai and Goolam Vahed, *The South African Gandhi: Stretcher-bearer of Empire*, Stanford University Press, October 2015, p. 298.
28. Rajmohan Gandhi, 'Independence and Social Justice: The Ambedkar-Gandhi Debate', *Economic and Political Weekly*, Vol. 50, 11 April 2015, p. 39.
29. Arundhati Roy in B.R. Ambedkar, *Annihilation of Caste*, p. 54.
30. Arundhati Roy, 'Azadi,' *Outlook*, 8 September 2008,http://www.outlookindia.com/magazine/story/azadi/238272.
31. https://www.theguardian.com/world/2010/oct/26/arundhati-roy-kashmir-india
32. Arundhati Roy, 'Azadi', *Outlook*, 15 July 2016, https://www.outlookindia.com/magazine/story/azadi/297536
33. https://en.wikipedia.org/wiki/Temples_of_modern_India
34. http://scholar.harvard.edu/files/rpande/files/large_dams_in_india.pdf
35. Arundhati Roy, 'The Greater Common Good', *Outlook*, 24 May 1999, http://www.outlookindia.com/magazine/story/the-greater-common-good/207509
36. Ibid.
37. https://www.internationalrivers.org/sites/default/files/attached-files/world_commission_on_dams_final_report.pdf

38. Arundhati Roy, 'The Greater Common Good', *Outlook*, 24 May 1999, http://www.outlookindia.com/magazine/story/the-greater-common-good/207509

39. B.G. Verghese, 'The Greater Common Good II', *Outlook*, 12 July 1999, http://www.outlookindia.com/magazine/story/the-greater-common-good-ii/207770

40. Arundhati Roy, 'The Greater Common Good', *Outlook*, 24 May 1999, http://www.outlookindia.com/magazine/story/the-greater-common-good/207509

41. Ramachandra Guha, 'The Arun Shourie of the Left', *The Hindu*, 26 November 2000, http://www.thehindu.com/2000/11/26/stories/13260411.htm

42. http://cgwb.gov.in/INTRA-CGWB/Circulars/Report_on_Restructuring_CWC_CGWB.pdf

43. Ibid., p. 43.

44. Uday Mahurkar, *Centrestage: Inside the Narendra Modi Model of Governance*, https://books.google.co.in/books?id=5MZfAwAAQBAJ&pg=PT50&lpg=PT50&dq=uday+mahurkar+and+Sardar+Sarovar+Project&source=bl&ots=wtFsZjGg_I&sig=ACfU3U3ei1RT-mn6RibvB6JDjU9lD46rl-Q&hl=en&sa=X&ved=2ahUKEwjV773KpuvkAhUm6nMBHQEQD-oQ6AEwCHoECAkQAQ#v=onepage&q=uday%20mahurkar%20and%20Sardar%20Sarovar%20Project&f=false

45. Swaminathan A. Aiyar, 'Members of the Same Tribe', *Economic Times*, 13 September 2017, https://swaminomics.org/category/articles/et-articles/

46. http://www.dnaindia.com/india/report-sc-clears-deck-for-compensation-to-oustees-of-narmada-project-2316511

47. Ramachandra Guha, 'Adivasis, Naxalites and Indian Democracy', EPW, 11 August 2007, Vol. 42, pp. 3305-3306.

48. Arundhati Roy, 'Walking with the Comrades', *Outlook*, 29 March 2010, http://www.outlookindia.com/magazine/story/walking-with-the-comrades/264738

49. Ibid.

50. Ibid.

51. Ibid.

52. *http://www.thehindu.com/opinion/lead/the-continuing-tragedy-of-the-adivasis/article4756954.ece*

53. Arundhati Roy, 'Walking with the Comrades', *Outlook*, 29 March 2010, http://www.outlookindia.com/magazine/story/walking-with-the-comrades/264738

54. Ibid.
55. https://www.theguardian.com/global-development/2013/feb/15/land-rights-activists-india-forest-act
56. Arundhati Roy, 'Capitalism: A Ghost Story', *Outlook*, 26 March 2012, https://www.outlookindia.com/magazine/story/capitalism-a-ghost-story/280234
57. Ibid.
58. Ibid.
59. https://www.outlookindia.com/website/story/confronting-empire/218738
60. https://www.theguardian.com/world/2002/sep/27/iraq.politicsphilosophyandsociety
61. Arundhati Roy, *Listening to Grasshoppers*, 'And His Life Should Become Extinct: The Very Strange Story of the Attack on the Indian Parliament', Hamish Hamilton, India, 2009, pp. 43-76.
62. Madeline Bunting, 'Dam Buster', *Guardian*, 28 July 2001, https://www.theguardian.com/books/2001/jul/28/fiction.arundhatiroy
63. https://www.vogue.com/article/arundhati-roy-ministry-of-utmost-hapiness-novel
64. https://www.theguardian.com/books/2001/jul/28/fiction.arundhatiroy
65. Ibid.
66. http://www.vogue.co.uk/article/arundhati-roy-interview

Chapter 2: Oliver Stone: The Moviemaker as Iconoclast

1. https://www.nytimes.com/2017/06/25/opinion/oliver-stone-putin-trump.html
2. https://newrepublic.com/article/143443/natural-born-buddies-shared-ideology-oliver-stone-vladimir-putin
3. https://www.thedailybeast.com/the-putin-interviews-oliver-stones-wildly-irresponsible-love-letter-to-vladimir-putin
4. *The Putin Interviews: Oliver Stone Interviews Vladimir Putin*, Amazon Digital Services LLC, June, 2017.
5. Ibid., loc no.: 3463-69, Kindle edition.
6. Ibid., loc 185.
7. Ibid., loc 250.
8. Ibid., loc 287.
9. Ibid., loc 361.
10. Ibid., loc 603.
11. Ibid., loc 703.

12. Ibid., loc 786.
13. Ibid., loc 1591.
14. Ibid., loc 1884.
15. Ibid., loc 1884-85.
16. Ibid., loc 1895.
17. Ibid., loc 1966.
18. Ibid., loc 2004–2009.
19. Ibid., loc 3514.
20. Ibid., loc 3573.
21. Ibid., loc 842.
22. https://www.youtube.com/watch?v=eiuplgzbCC4
23. https://www.theguardian.com/tv-and-radio/2017/jun/13/the-putin-interviews-review-first-oliver-stone-loses-then-the-gloves-come-off
24. http://www.nytimes.com/2012/11/25/magazine/oliver-stone-rewrites-history-again.html
25. Ibid.
26. Stephen Lavington, *Oliver Stone*, Virgin Books, Great Britain, 2004, p. 2.
27. https://www.hollywoodreporter.com/news/oliver-stone-drugs-savages-336691
28. Stephen Lavington, *Oliver Stone*, Virgin Books, Great Britain, 2004, p. 20.
29. Ibid., p. 84.
30. Matt Zoller Seitz, *The Oliver Stone Experience*, Abrams, 2016, p. 189.
31. Ibid., p. 189.
32. https://dealbook.nytimes.com/2011/10/17/oliver-stone-faces-down-wall-street/
33. https://www.archives.gov/research/jfk/warren-commission-report/intro
34. https://www.amazon.com/Trail-Assassins-Murder-President-Kennedy/dp/1620872994
35. https://www.theguardian.com/us-news/2017/oct/26/jfk-assassination-files-lee-harvey-oswald-national-archives
36. Stephen Lavington, *Oliver Stone*, Virgin Books, Great Britain, 2004, p. 165.
37. https://www.rogerebert.com/interviews/oliver-stone-finds-the-humanity-in-nixon
38. Ibid.
39. Stephen Lavington, *Oliver Stone*, Virgin Books, Great Britain, 2004, p. 216.

40. Matt Zoller Seitz, *The Oliver Stone Experience*, pp. 330-31.
41. https://www.theguardian.com/film/2008/oct/04/oliver.stone.george.bush
42. Ibid.
43. https://www.independent.co.uk/arts-entertainment/films/news/snowden-film-labelled-preposterous-by-former-nsa-deputy-director-a7333371.html
44. http://www.indiewire.com/2016/09/oliver-stone-snowden-interview-independent-1201724763
45. https://en.wikipedia.org/wiki/Snowden_(film)
46. Oliver Stone and Peter Kuznick, *The Untold Story of the United States*, Brilliance Audio, 2014, Kindle edition, loc 74-80.
47. Ibid., loc 150.
48. Ibid., loc 471-81.
49. Ibid., loc 5920-27.
50. Ibid., loc 5920.
51. Ibid., loc 6655.
52. Ibid., loc 7995.
53. Ibid., loc 8779.
54. Ibid., loc 9409.
55. Ibid., loc 9711.
56. Ibid., loc 10841.
57. Ibid., loc 10847.
58. Ibid., loc 12195.
59. Ibid., loc 12399.
60. https://www.thedailybeast.com/oliver-stone-defends-his-history.
61. http://variety.com/2000/more/reviews/oliver-stone-s-usa-film-history-and-controversy-1200463408

Chapter 3: Kancha Ilaiah: Challenger of the Hindu Order

1. Kancha Ilaiah, *Why I Am Not a Hindu*, Samya, Calcutta, February 1996, p. xi.
2. Ibid., p. viii.
3. Ibid., pp. 12-15.
4. Ibid., pp. 55-56.
5. Ibid., p. 1.
6. Ibid., pp. 71-102.
7. Ibid., p. 74.
8. Ibid., pp. 76-77.

9. Ibid., p. 82.
10. Meera Nanda, 'Ambedkar's Gita', *Economic and Political Weekly*, 3 December 2016, Vol. 51, No. 49, pp. 38-45.
11. Kancha Ilaiah, *Why I Am Not a Hindu*, Samya, Calcutta, February 1996, p. 71.
12. Ibid., p. 100.
13. Ibid., p. 101.
14. Ibid., p. 43.
15. Ibid., p. 53.
16. Ibid., p. 41.
17. Ibid., p. 117.
18. Ibid., p. 120.
19. Ibid., p. 130.
20. Ibid., p. 132.
21. Kancha Ilaiah, *Post-Hindu India: A Discourse on Dalit-Bahujan Socio-spiritual and Scientific Revolution*, Sage Publications India Pvt. Ltd, New Delhi, 2009.
22. https://www.indiatoday.in/magazine/up-front/story/20171030-india-caste-revenge-post-hindu-india-kancha-ilaiah-shephard-dalit-1067336-2017-10-20
23. https://indianexpress.com/article/india/hyderabad-chappals-thrown-at-dalit-writer-kancha-ilaiah-under-fire-from-vysya-community-for-his-book-4857851/
24. https://drive.google.com/file/d/0B1HsQbGlNpEfeTd4YjBSWk1sTTg/view
25. Kancha Ilaiah, *Post-Hindu India: A Discourse on Dalit-Bahujan Socio-spiritual and Scientific Revolution*, Sage Publications India Pvt. Ltd, New Delhi, 2009, p. 179.
26. http://www.dnaindia.com/india/report-institutes-like-iits-and-iims-should-be-closed-down-1023204
27. Kancha Ilaiah, *Why I Am Not a Hindu*, Samya, Calcutta, February 1996, p. 63.
28. Kancha Ilaiah, *Post-Hindu India: A Discourse on Dalit-Bahujan Socio-spiritual and Scientific Revolution*, Sage Publications India Pvt. Ltd, New Delhi, p. 164.
29. Ibid., p. 167.
30. Ibid., p. 170.
31. Ibid., p. 177.
32. Ibid., p. 276.
33. Ibid., p. 281.

34. Ibid., p. 287.

35. Ibid., p. 237.

36. Ibid., p. 238.

37. Ibid., p. 244.

38. Ibid., p. 264.

39. Ibid., p. 266.

40. Kancha Ilaiah, *God as Political Philosopher: Buddha's Challenge to Brahminism*, Samya, 2000, Calcutta.

41. Ibid., p. 119.

42. https://www.outlookindia.com/magazine/story/whose-ambedkar-is-he-anyway/296950

43. https://www.nationalheraldindia.com/opinion/ambedkar-has-become-an-icon-in-the-last-27-years-part-i

44. https://www.nationalheraldindia.com/opinion/had-bjp-been-in-power-in-1947-where-would-dr-ambedkar-bepart-ii

45. https://economictimes.indiatimes.com/news/politics-and-nation/sc/st-act-supreme-court-recalls-directions-of-mar-2018-verdict/articleshow/71391987.cms?from=mdr

46. http://www.truthaboutdalits.com/kancha_ilaiah_articles/gandhi_today_kancha_illaiah_article.htm

47. https://www.youtube.com/watch?v=0KF2tajhvSM0.

48. Kancha Ilaiah, *Buffalo Nationalism: A Critique of Spiritual Fascism*, Samya, Kolkata, July 2004, p. 42.

49. Ibid., p. xxv-xxviii.

50. Ibid., p. xxviii.

Chapter 4: David Irving: Maverick Historian

1. http://www.spiegel.de/international/holocaust-denier-released-from-prison-david-irving-free-after-13-months-in-jail-a-455726.html

2. https://www.independent.co.uk/news/uk/jews-attack-publisher-of-irving-book-protesters-to-demand-company-abandons-plan-to-print-goebbels-1531572.html

3. https://www.nytimes.com/1996/06/02/books/essay-in-the-shadow-of-goebbels.html

4. https://www.vanityfair.com/news/1996/06/hitlers-ghost-christopher-hitchens

5. Ibid.

6. http://www.nybooks.com/articles/1996/09/19/the-devil-in-the-details

7. http://www.fpp.co.uk/reviews/JG_Richard_Cohen.html

8. https://en.wikipedia.org/wiki/David_Irving#Libel_suit

9. Ibid.

10. https://www.newyorker.com/magazine/2001/04/16/blood-libel

11. http://www.kevinmacdonald.net/irving.htm

12. https://en.wikipedia.org/wiki/David_Irving

13. https://www.newyorker.com/magazine/2001/04/16/blood-libel

14. http://www.fpp.co.uk/Letters/Requests/Payne291001.html

15. https://en.wikipedia.org/wiki/David_Irving

16. *Apocalypse 1945: The Destruction of Dresden*, free download, http://www.fpp.co.uk/books/Dresden/Apocalypse_2007.pdf, p. 275.

17. Ibid., p. 243.

18. Ibid., Foreword.

19. https://www.theguardian.com/books/2004/feb/22/historybooks.features1

20. http://www.british-values.com/index-to-articles/bombing/dresden/irving.html

21. *Apocalypse 1945: The Destruction of Dresden*, free download, http://www.fpp.co.uk/books/Dresden/Apocalypse_2007.pdf, p. 267.

22. http://www.fpp.co.uk/reviews/Mares_Nest.html

23. *The Trail of the Fox*, 2005, free download, http://www.fpp.co.uk/books/Rommel/Rommel_2005_web.pdf, p. 4.

24. Ibid., p. 5.

25. Ibid., p. 7.

26. Ibid., p. 29.

27. Ibid., p. 55.

28. Ibid., pp. 56-57.

29. Ibid., p. 94.

30. Ibid., pp. 205-06.

31. Ibid., p. 230.

32. Ibid., p. 253.

33. Ibid., p. 314.

34. Ibid., pp. 338, 344-45.

35. Ibid., p. 453.

36. David Irving, *Hitler's War*, free download, http://www.fpp.co.uk/books/Hitler/2001/HW1.pdf, p. xxiv.

37. Ibid., p. ix.

38. Ibid., p. x.

39. Charles Sydnor Jr, 'The Selling of Adolf Hitler: David Irving's Hitler's War', *Central European History*, Vol. 12, No. 2 (June 1979), pp. 169-99, 182.

40. Alan Bullock, *New York Review of Books*, 26 May 1977.

41. David Irving, *Hitler's War*, p. xxviii.

42. Ibid., p. 454.

43. Charles Sydnor, Ibid., p. 183.

44. David Irving, *Hitler's War*, p. ix.

45. Patrick Buchanan, *Churchill, Hitler and the Unnecessary War: How Britain Lost Its Empire and the West Lost the World*, Crown Forum, July 2009.

46. David Irving, *Hitler's War*, p. 321.

47. Ibid., p. 332.

48. Ibid., p. 380.

49. Viktor Suvorov, *Icebreaker: Who Started the Second World War?*, London, 1990, Hamish Hamilton, London, cited in Teddy J. Uldricks, 'The Icebreaker Controversy: Did Stalin Plan to Attack Hitler?', *Slavic Review*, Vol. 58, No. 3, Fall 1999.

50. Teddy J. Uldricks, 'The Icebreaker Controversy: Did Stalin Plan to Attack Hitler?', *Slavic Review*, Vol. 58, No. 3, Fall 1999, p. 630.

51. Ibid., p. 640.

52. Ibid., p. 635.

53. Ibid., pp. 250-51.

54. Ibid., p. 274.

55. Ibid., p. 425.

56. Ibid., p. 429.

57. Ibid., pp. 473-74.

58. Ibid., p. 486.

59. https://en.wikipedia.org/wiki/Erich_von_Manstein#Battle_of_ Stalingrad

60. David Irving, *Hitler's War*, p. xii.

61. Ibid., p. xi.

62. Ibid., p. 296.

63. Ibid., p. 662.

64. Ibid., pp. 14-15.

65. Ibid., p. 296.

66. David Irving, *Nuremberg: The Last Battle*, free download, http://www. fpp.co.uk/books/Nuremberg/NUREMBERG.pdf, p. 116.

67. David Irving, *Hitler's War*, pp. 278-79.

68. Ibid., p. 509.

69. Ibid., pp. 170-71.

70. David Irving, *Nuremberg: The Last Battle*, free download, http://www. fpp.co.uk/books/Nuremberg/NUREMBERG.pdf

71. Ibid., p. 16.
72. Ibid., p. 39.
73. Ibid., p. 18.
74. Ibid., p. 47.
75. Ibid., p. 56.
76. Ibid., pp. 61-64.
77. Ibid., p. 75.
78. Ibid., p. 64.
79. Ibid., pp. 65-66.
80. Ibid., p. 109.
81. Ibid., p. 139.
82. Ibid., p. 167.
83. Ibid., pp. 168-69.
84. Ibid., p. 261.
85. Ibid., p. 194.
86. Ibid., p. 271.
87. Ibid., p. 311.
88. Ibid., p. 311.
89. Ibid., p. 361.
90. Ibid., p. 429.
91. https://www.dailymail.co.uk/news/article-3996138/Still-spouting-poison-Hollywood-makes-movie-views-Holocaust-denier-David-Irving-continues-pervert-history-make-money-s-it.html
92. https://www.theguardian.com/uk-news/2017/jan/15/david-irving-youtube-inspiring-holocaust-deniers

Chapter 5: Yanis Varoufakis: Economist as Iconoclast

1. Yanis Varoufakis, *Adults in the Room: My Battle with Europe's Deep Establishment*, The Bodley Head, London, 2017, p. 8.
2. Ibid., p. 15.
3. https://www.yanisvaroufakis.eu/beginnings-from-the-dictatorship-of-the-colonels-to-the-tyranny-of-economics
4. George A. Provopoulos: The Greek financial crisis—from Grexit to Grecovery. Speech by Mr George A. Provopoulos, Governor of the Bank of Greece, for the Golden Series lecture at the Official Monetary and Financial Institutions Forum (OMFIF), London, 7 February 2014.
5. Yanis Varoufakis, *Adults in the Room: My Battle with Europe's Deep Establishment*, The Bodley Head, London, 2017.
6. Ibid., pp. 23-24.

7. Ibid., pp. 25, 27.
8. Ibid., pp. 41, 46-47.
9. Ibid., p. 102.
10. Ibid., p. 104.
11. Ibid., pp. 113-14.
12. Ibid., p. 124.
13. Ibid., p. 147.
14. Ibid., p. 303.
15. https://www.reuters.com/article/us-eurozone-greece-varoufakis-germany/greeces-varoufakis-becomes-unlikely-heartthrob-in-germany-idUSKBN0LD1RI20150209?feedType=RSS&feedName=worldNews
16. Yanis Varoufakis, *Adults in the Room: My Battle with Europe's Deep Establishment*, The Bodley Head, London, 2017, p. 181.
17. Ibid., p. 356.
18. Ibid., p. 358.
19. Ibid., p. 387.
20. Ibid., pp. 387-88.
21. Ibid., p. 389.
22. Ibid., p. 415.
23. https://adamtooze.com/2017/07/01/reading-varoufakis-frustrated-strategist-greek-financial-deterrence
24. Yanis Varoufakis, *Adults in the Room: My Battle with Europe's Deep Establishment*, The Bodley Head, London, 2017, p. 381.
25. Yanis Varoufakis, *And the Weak Suffer What They Must?: Europe, Austerity and the Threat to Global Stability*, Vintage, UK, 2017.
26. Ibid., p. 19.
27. Ibid., p. 74.
28. Ibid., pp. 78-79.
29. Ibid., p. 113.
30. Ibid., p. 141.
31. Ibid., p. 93.
32. Yanis Varoufakis, *Talking to My Daughter About the Economy: A Brief History of Capitalism*, Farrar, Straus and Giroux, May 2018, Kindle edition.
33. Ibid., p. 46.
34. Ibid., p. 47.
35. Ibid., p. 58.
36. Ibid., p. 62.

37. Ibid., p. 84-85.
38. Ibid., p. 156.
39. Ibid., p. 162.
40. https://www.npr.org/transcripts/500126088?storyId=500126088?storyId=500126088
41. https://www.theguardian.com/news/2015/feb/18/yanis-varoufakis-how-i-became-an-erratic-marxist
42. https://www.yanisvaroufakis.eu/2019/04/05/ft-alphachat-28-mar-2019-on-democracy-europe-the-uk-and-greece/
43. https://www.yanisvaroufakis.eu/2019/03/07/our-plan-for-a-european-spring-diem25/

Chapter 6: U.G. Krishnamurti: The Anti-Guru

1. Mahesh Bhatt, *U.G. Krishnamurti: A Life*, Viking, New Delhi, 1992.
2. Ibid., pp. 149-50.
3. Ibid., pp. 178-79.
4. Ibid., pp. 179-80.
5. This biographical sketch draws on Mahesh Bhatt's book, cited above, Mukunda Rao, *The Other Side of Belief: Interpreting U.G. Krishnamurti*, Penguin Books India, 2005, and a biographical note written by Terry Newland in his introduction to a collection of UG recordings, *Mind Is a Myth*, available at http://www.ugkrishnamurti.net/
6. Mahesh Bhatt, *U.G. Krishnamurti, A Life*, Viking, New Delhi, 1992, pp. 21-22.
7. Ibid., p. 23.
8. Mukunda Rao, *The Other Side of Belief: Interpreting U.G. Krishnamurti*, Penguin Books India, 2005, p. 90.
9. Ibid., pp. 97-98.
10. Mukunda Rao, *The Biology of Enlightenment*, HarperCollins Publishers India, pp. 41-43.
11. Ibid., pp. 45-48.
12. Mahesh Bhatt, *U.G. Krishnamurti: A Life*, Viking, New Delhi, 1992, pp. 83-84.
13. Ibid., p. 87.
14. Mukunda Rao, *The Biology of Enlightenment*, HarperCollins Publishers India, p. 55.
15. Ibid., pp. 57-58.
16. Ibid., pp. 14-16.

17. U.G. Krishnamurti, The *Courage to Stand Alone*, http://www. ugkrishnamurti.net/ugkrishnamurti-net/courage.htm. (Note: the website does not have page numbers for the material it carries.)
18. Mukunda Rao, *The Biology of Enlightenment*, HarperCollins Publishers India, pp. 142-43 and pp. 12-13; Mahesh Bhatt, *U.G. Krishnamurti: A Life*, pp. 100-03; *Mind Is a Myth*, http://www.ugkrishnamurti.net/
19. Mukunda Rao, *The Biology of Enlightenment*, HarperCollins Publishers India, pp. 156-57.
20. Ibid., p. 162.
21. U.G. Krishnamurti, *The Mystique of Enlightenment*, http://www. ugkrishnamurti.net
22. Ibid., Part Two.
23. Ibid., Part Two.
24. Mahesh Bhatt, *U.G. Krishnamurti: A Life*, Viking, New Delhi, 1992, pp. 25-26.
25. Ibid., pp. 126-27.
26. Ibid., pp. 123-25.
27. U.G. Krishnamurti, *The Mystique of Enlightenment*, Part Four, 'Betwixt Bewilderment and Understanding', http://www.ugkrishnamurti.net.
28. Ibid., Part Three, 'No Power Outside of Man'.
29. Mukunda Rao, *The Other Side of Belief: Interpreting U.G. Krishnamurti*, Penguin Books India, 2005, p. 262.
30. Mukunda Rao, *The Biology of Enlightenment*, p. 11.
31. U.G. Krishnamurti, *The Mystique of Enlightenment*, http://www. ugkrishnamurti.net.
32. Mahesh Bhatt, *U.G. Krishnamurti: A Life*, Viking, New Delhi, 1992, p. 17.
33. Mukunda Rao, *The Other Side of Belief: Interpreting U.G. Krishnamurti*, Penguin Books India, 2005, p. 34.
34. Mahesh Bhatt, *U.G. Krishnamurti: A Life*, Viking, New Delhi, 1992, p. 46. The narrative that follows is based on pp. 47-54.
35. Mukunda Rao, *The Other Side of Belief: Interpreting U.G. Krishnamurti*, Penguin Books India, 2005, p. 34.
36. Ibid.
37. Mahesh Bhatt, *U.G. Krishnamurti: A Life*, Viking, New Delhi, 1992, p. 44.
38. Mukunda Rao, *The Other Side of Belief: Interpreting U.G. Krishnamurti*, Penguin Books India, 2005, pp. 242-43.
39. U.G. Krishnamurti, The *Courage to Stand Alone*, Part II: I cannot create the hunger in you http://www.ugkrishnamurti.net/ugkrishnamurti-net/ courage2.html

40. Ibid.
41. U.G. Krishnamurti, *The Courage to Stand Alone*, Part II; I cannot create the hunger in you http://www.ugkrishnamurti.net/ugkrishnamurti-net/courage2.html
42. http://www.travelswithug.com/resources/UGCookbook.pdf Ibid.
43. Mukunda Rao, *The Biology of Enlightenment*, HarperCollins Publishers India, p. 263.
44. Ibid., p. 266.
45. Ibid., p. 268.
46. Mukunda Rao, *The Other Side of Belief: Interpreting U.G. Krishnamurti*, Penguin Books India, 2005, p. 311.
47. Mahesh Bhatt, *U.G. Krishnamurti: A Life*, Viking, New Delhi, 1992, p. 134.
48. http://www.ugkrishnamurti.org/ug/money-maxims
49. Louis Brawley, *No More Questions: The Final Travels of U.G. Krishnamurti*, Penguin Books India Pvt. Ltd., New Delhi, 2012, pp. 88-89.
50. Ibid., p. 235.
51. Ibid., p. 348.
52. Narayana Moorty, 'My Last Visit with UG', http://www.ugkrishnamurti.net/
53. Louis Brawley, *No More Questions: The Final Travels of U.G. Krishnamurti*, Penguin Books India Pvt. Ltd, New Delhi, p. 371.
54. http://ugkrishnamurti.net/ugkrishnamurti-net/SWAN_SONG.htm

Chapter 7: John Pilger: The Journalist as Crusader

1. http://johnpilger.com/videos/the-coming-war-on-china-english-subtitles-
2. http://johnpilger.com/articles/hold-the-front-page-the-reporters-are-missing
3. http://johnpilger.com/biography
4. John Pilger, *Palestine Is Still the Issue*, https://vimeo.com/17401477
5. John Pilger, 'The Last Taboo', in *Freedom Next Time*, Black Swan, UK, 2007, pp. 91-220.
6. http://johnpilger.com/articles/palestine-is-still-the-issue
7. John Pilger, 'The Last Taboo', in *Freedom Next Time*, Black Swan, UK, 2007, p. 122.
8. Ibid., p. 152.
9. Ibid., p. 208.

10. Ibid., p. 211.
11. Ibid., p. 217.
12. Ibid., p. 218.
13. Ibid., pp. 188, 196.
14. https://www.youtube.com/watch?v=P_gggPRLeic
15. John Pilger, 'Apartheid Did Not Die', in *Freedom Next Time*, Black Swan, UK, 2007, pp. 239-350.
16. Ibid., p. 266.
17. Ibid., p. 271.
18. Ibid., p. 272.
19. Ibid., p. 274.
20. Ibid., p. 282.
21. Ibid., p. 285.
22. Ibid., p. 295.
23. Ibid., p. 321.
24. Ibid., p. 301.
25. http://johnpilger.com/videos/utopia-subtitled-version-
26. http://johnpilger.com/videos/the-war-on-democracy
27. https://quillette.com/2019/03/25/venezuela-and-the-half-truths-of-noam-chomsky/0
28. https://www.theguardian.com/world/2018/dec/06/on-the-road-venezuela-20-years-after-hugo-chavez-rise
29. John Pilger, 'Liberating Afghanistan', in *Freedom Next Time*, Black Swan, UK, 2007, pp. 351-414.
30. Ibid., pp. 352-53.
31. Ibid., pp. 365-66.
32. Ibid., pp. 366-67.
33. Ibid., p. 372.
34. Ibid., p. 372.
35. Ibid., p. 375.
36. Ibid., p. 376.
37. Ibid., p. 412.
38. https://en.wikipedia.org/wiki/Julian_Assange- ok
39. http://johnpilger.com/articles/the-assange-arrest-is-a-warning-from-history

Acknowledgements

I would like to acknowledge the help and support I have received from the following:

IIM Ahmedabad granted me leave to work on the book

Radhika Marwah, commissioning editor at Penguin Random House, was quick to respond to my book proposal and provide invaluable guidance throughout

Clare Stewart did a thorough a painstaking job of editing the manuscript in several versions

Shantanu Ray Chaudhuri and his team did a thorough job of proofreading and corrections in the final stages

Ishan Rangarajan helped draft one section of a chapter

Mukunda Rao shared his perspectives on U.G. Krishnamurti

My wife, Jayashree Rammohan, commented on portions of the manuscript

My mother, Padmini Vijayaraghavan, kept prodding me on by asking about the progress of the book

To all of them my deepest thanks.